2nd Dec 2022

THE OUTDOOR SWIMMERS' HANDBOOK

Collected Wisdom on the Art, Sport and Science of Outdoor Swimming

KATE REW

Founder of The Outdoor Swimming Society

By the same author:
Wild Swim

1

Rider, an imprint of Ebury Publishing,
20 Vauxhall Bridge Road,
London SW1V 2SA

Rider is part of the Penguin Random House group
of companies whose addresses can be found at
global.penguinrandomhouse.com

First published by Rider in 2022
www.penguin.co.uk

A CIP catalogue record for this book is available from the British Library

ISBN 978-1846047282

Printed and bound by Firmengruppe APPL, aprinta druck, Wemding,
Germany

Text illustrations by Lucy Rose Cartwright Illustration
Graph on p.160 redrawn from the *U.S. Coast Guard: Addendum to the
National Search and Rescue (SAR) Manual*, COMDTINST M16120.5 and
COMDTINST M16120.6. 1995. For full picture credits, see p.296 as an
extension of this copyright page.

CONTENTS

To Kari,
without whom none of this may have happened,
and to Tim,
who made much of it possible.

Introduction

JUST AS THERE WAS a time before triathlons, skateboarding, surfing, mountaineering or mountain biking, there was a time when mass-participation open-water swims were not commonplace. That time was 2006. In the fresh grip of a love for adventurous swimming and eager (messianic in fact) to get more people out of pools and into British rivers and lakes with me, I set up 'Breastrokes', a one-mile charity swim, and I chose the two best-known lakes I could think of (perhaps the only two lakes I could think of) in which to host it: the Serpentine in the middle of London, and Windermere in the Lake District.

The newly formed 'The Outdoor Swimming Society' (OSS) sold 300 tickets to each event. Finding 300 people with the same desire to swim In. A. Lake. drew gasps of surprise and column inches everywhere in Britain. In Windermere, swimmers docked at an island for hot chocolate halfway around, where people sloshed about in the shallows exclaiming how incredible it was, this outlandish, maverick thing they were doing. No one had trained in a lake for the swims; they got fit in a pool and came for the novelty.

The Great North Swim was established in 2008 and the rest is zeitgeist: swimming has gone from being a relatively niche activity to being popular again, with millions of people all over the world leaping in. If you say you're going swimming now, most people will picture you in a river or the sea, not a pool, even if it's midwinter. The sort of swim challenges once only dreamt about by locals who knew the waterways and the British Long Distance Swimming Association (established in 1956) have since entered the mainstream. Today, there are open-water lake and wild swim groups offering warm welcomes across the country, and swimmers across the world are looking to the UK to work out how to create a similar culture of free, nomadic swimming where they live. Swimming the length of Windermere remains the UK marathon crown, but today there are swimmers everywhere who are exploring their local seas and waterways for the sheer joy of it.

Yet people have always swum. The first book on the theory and techniques of swimming was presented to the world in 1587 by Cambridge don Everard Digby in his *De Arte Natandi* ('The Art of Swimming'). Some of the advice in his technique guide-come-safety manual is still valid today: avoid murky ponds in which animals have been washed and be careful about jumping in feet first. The book includes forty-three woodcuts of swimmers captured in a familiar visual frame: a river runs vertically down the centre of the page, banked by reeds and oak trees, with one person swimming, a second leaping naked into the water (sometimes backwards) and a third either preparing to swim or putting on his socks afterwards. The strokes may have altered (it seems swimmers were less constrained 400 years ago) but the playground and the human urge look much the same as they do today.

The earliest record of swimming, however, dates to much further back, and is depicted on the walls of a cave in the mountainous Gilf Kebir plateau in Egypt. There, three figures dive off the sandstone and are buoyed up by what appears to be the sluice and joy of a downstream Neolithic drift. The rock-art figures – whose creation is dated by the British Museum to about 6,000 to 9,000 years ago – carry with them all the happiness of a river float: arms up, bellies and spirits buoyant.

In 2006, the OSS, similarly uplifted by the swimming experience, set out a manifesto to help people escape chlorine captivity, leading with the pledge that we would 'celebrate and enlarge the beauty of every day by going for a nice, long swim' (a nod to the John Cheever story 'The Swimmer'). Our focus ever since has been to persuade people to follow suit. An ever-growing band of individuals got involved: someone created a website, someone took photos, someone else bought a hot tub and everyone went swimming. Our lawyer, Nathan Willmott, wrote a 'Swim Responsibility Statement' so we could come out in public and say 'Let's go swimming!' without fear of losing our homes. (This was a time when outdoor swimming was largely thought to be a dirty, dangerous and illegal activity, and there was fear of being sued.)

Artist and friend Kari (pronounced Car-ee) Furre viewed the whole thing as an exercise in giving people permission – permission that wasn't ours to give, she observed wryly as we bobbed about in Loch Ness at dusk, as there has never been much to stop people swimming. But at this point in history people needed to hear that it was 'allowed', so we went around 'sanctioning' swimming. We made swim friends everywhere, leading by example and sharing this wonderful, life-enriching thing we were doing at festivals, on TV, on the radio, in the press and on Facebook. No one had any kit; it was towel and trunks, or T-shirt and pants if the swim was spontaneous. A neopagan element punctured our urban existence, with full moon swims exposing us to the hooting of owls in the woods and to midsummer parties at Parliament Hill Lido where people wore flower crowns. The OSS logo was spotted with excitement on hoodies in pubs and bobbing on red hats like buoys in the sea.

The OSS 'Regional Rep' programme, whereby a few swimmers across the UK started social swim communities in their areas via Facebook, mushroomed into the hundreds of independent social wild swim groups that exist today. There was an infectious freewheeling energy to it all – even the bad times were good times. There were days when we cancelled or aborted swims for fear of sewage or blue-green algae, when in retrospect we were just unfamiliar with tree pollen, and the occasions when whimsical swim plans ('Let's swim down a tributary into the Thames!') had very gritty executions, leaving us cold and desperate in driving rain. No one understood how tides worked so on estuary swims we waded around in mud quite a lot. But you never regret a swim, so we kept going. There was a silent swim preceded by meditation, and a 'secret swim' at a festival. There was the time a fire engine filled our hot tub for us in about five seconds. I am proud that in 2010 we ran the first ten-kilometre swim aimed at the public, the Dart 10k, and a ten-mile swim followed soon after.

In 2015, I finally swam the Dart 10k myself (like a ship's captain, my job was to be at the helm, not head down and unreachable in the water), and the experience of swimming around Sharpham Bends flanked by an army of fit, capable swimmers, the sense of joint strength and capability, rose up like a rush. It was a high point for me, a marker of how far we had come as a community – all of us amateurs out there in this big(ish) river, capable of swimming for hours, in all weathers, engaged together in wordless communion with this thing that we love. It will stay with me, as will the finish party we organised for adventurer Ross Edgley after he swam around the coast of Britain in 2018.

For the 'Great British Swim' finish party, 300 of us arranged to meet Ross in the water on a November morning, swimming half a mile offshore to join him and flank his return. At this point he had averaged over twelve hours of swimming a day for 157 days without, as far as we knew, grumbling once. Witnessing the swim from his weekly vlogs had been inspiring and staggering. We trod water, looking out over the horizon, and then someone saw him in the distance and a huge guttural roar erupted among us. People were slapping the water, hollering and punching their fists into the air. Waves of noise rose up and receded. We were, apparently, beside ourselves: that this swim had happened, and that the man who had accomplished it was in our water. Then he looked up and stopped, and there was a stand-off of sorts: him looking at us, beaming, and us facing him, roaring. The noise was on a knife-edge between tremendous and terrifying. Then he gestured for us to come closer and everyone gathered around, slithering over each other like a mosh pit of seals to high-five him and hug him. I still get teary thinking about it. It was a community embrace for what he insisted on calling a community effort – for while all we did was cheer, for every swimmer out there charting new swims (and there are many, male and female) there is a support crew holding warm glucose drinks and being cheerful, making their dreams happen.

What drives all this? Passion. Almost by definition outdoor swimmers are both fiercely independent and free-spirited, so making a community out of ourselves is somewhat of a challenge. We are a society of people who don't follow, a tribe of non-joiners, but one thing many of us share alongside a love of water is the desire to share our finds, questions and experiences.

But against all the things I have done these last sixteen years, all the recces, all the planning, all the risk assessments, all the swims, all the learning, sharing and chat, there was one thing I didn't do. Right at the start, I remember sitting in a café in Soho, London, being introduced to executives from an ad agency, Fallon, who were taking on the pro bono work of creating The OSS logo. I was telling them how we (an ever-changing 'we') wanted to share the information and inspiration to get people swimming. A kaleidoscope of ideas and possibilities tumbled out. 'But don't you need to tell them how to do it safely?' someone asked, spotting what was not on the list. 'Doesn't that have to be part of the platform?'

Eugh. Health and safety. 'Danger Deep Water'. After years of not nailing down this safety aspect of The OSS, here it is: what swimmers talk about when they talk about swimming. In these pages, you will find the collected learnings of the swimming community since swimming's recent resurgence. Outdoor swimming today is largely based on an oral tradition, with knowledge passed around on the banks: this book is like an overheard catch-up. For as well as running some of the country's most iconic swims and working out for myself how not to get stuck on any swim I've attempted, I have been doing what writers do: playing secretary to the world, listening in, listening out and writing it all down. I thank everyone who has been a happy part of that journey: all the new friends, the volunteers and swimmers that have made the swimming world today the huge and expansive thing that it is.

I hope that this handbook is both poetic and practical. We start in nature's swimming pool in the chapter 'Understanding Lakes', covering phenomena such as fear of deep water, lake breezes, information (rather than misinformation) about quarries and how to decode a mountain map. Then we move on to 'Understanding Rivers', from their clear and bubbling upper reaches to downstream drifting swims, covering flow, waterfalls, eddies, debris and the most likely places to find a river pool. The section 'Freshwater Field Guides' presents a swimmer's view of some of the plant life and bird life you may encounter as you swim, as well as listing the three biomarker species that denote water purity. The chapter 'Understanding Seas' hurls us about between messy waves and rock formations, covering tides and swims beyond the beach, while the 'Understanding Estuaries' chapter tackles everything I have learnt by trial and error on swimming through these liminal spaces. Weather is a swimmer's contact sport, and the chapter 'Weather' shows how understanding weather forecasts, mountain environments, the effects of storms, prevailing winds and what it's like to swim in them are all part of the journey. The 'Marine Field Guides' section will introduce you to creatures such as jellyfish (and what they are like to swim with) and also includes entertaining side-lines, like how to press seaweed.

We have to understand our own minds and bodies as well as what's out there in order to swim, so in 'Understanding Cold' we cover how cold water feels, and how we physically and mentally respond to it, describing the effects of acclimatisation, afterdrop, cold shock, cold incapacitation, hypothermia and lesser-known phenomena such as the screaming barflies and cold water urticaria. While cold is a continuum, winter swimming is a different beast to swimming the rest of the year, so in the chapter 'Winter & Ice Swimming' we consider the violence of the low temperatures, and important things such as how to cut a channel in ice (otherwise, how will you get in?).

The chapter 'Night Swimming' looks at topics such as the difference between sunrise and nautical dawn, as well as ways to increase your chances of seeing a full moon. The next chapter, 'Planning a Swim', details issues of access, kit and people – always the most unpredictable element in a swim.

The best way to be a safer swimmer is to be a stronger swimmer (there is no such thing as a safe swim spot, there are only safe swimmers – if you can't swim, anywhere is a risk), but swimming isn't about not dying, it's about living; so in the chapter 'Swim Better', you will find springboard suggestions to help you develop your swimming as a sport and an art, including covering the four main strokes, sighting and weatherproofing your stroke, as well as other things that swimmers do: float, otter, porpoise, duck-dive, do side stroke and (when required) find ways to make their peace with pools.

As well as creating a movement these last few decades, swimmers have created a language, so the 'Outdoor Swimmer's Dictionary' appendix will help you become familiar with useful vernacular.

Modern life has made many of us feel tamed and now we want to turn to swimming for rewilding. When swimming, we are not passively consuming the landscape, we are pulled into it, breeze flattening the water surface beneath our faces, warmth draining from our bare feet like colour leaches out of the landscape in the cold autumn light. We are there, damp from the clag by a tarn, underneath the belly of a swan as it takes off. We are part of the planet and all the elements again, in a place where moons wane, storms swell and life ebbs and flows throughout the seasons.

It is never just about the swimming. It's about connection with nature, connection with self and connection with others. It's about adventure, joy, challenge, health, fitness, endurance and escape. People swim for all sorts of reasons: for the mental or spiritual uplift, or as a creative practice. They swim because it helps them think or stops them thinking. And because it's free (and so much easier on the joints than activities on land).

With huge thanks to everyone who's been a part of the journey so far, and the best of luck to you on the next stage of yours. May swimming help you celebrate and enlarge the beauty of many days ahead.

KATE REW

'Those who dwell among the beauties
and mysteries of the earth
are never alone or weary of life'

RACHEL CARSON,
The Sense of Wonder

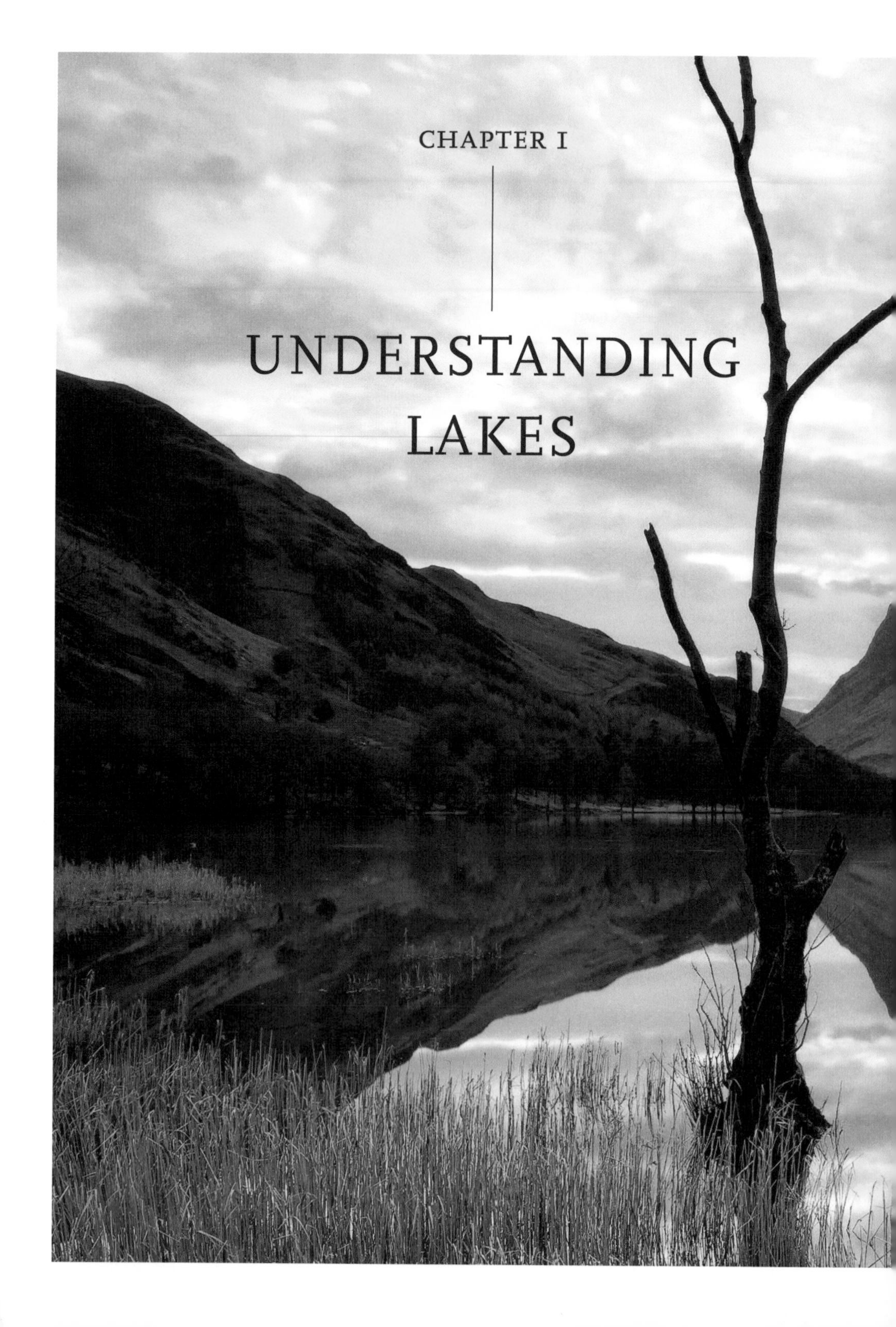

CHAPTER I

UNDERSTANDING LAKES

'Many, many people must have come there alone,
from time to time, from age to age,
dropping their thoughts into the water,
asking it some question, as one did oneself this
summer evening. Perhaps that was the reason
of its fascination – that it held in its waters
all kinds of fancies, complaints, confidences,
not printed or spoken aloud, but in a liquid state,
floating one on top of another,
almost disembodied'

VIRGINIA WOOLF,
'The Fascination of the Pool'

GETTING TO KNOW LAKES

STILL CLEAR DEPTHS, CRAGGY shorelines and tiny islands: lakes offer a potent mix of pleasures for the swimmer. I like the 'first in' feeling at dawn, when the still water appears to steam and smoke in the early rays of sunshine; and heading to small islands with solitary wind-bent trees. I like floating on my back looking for eagles or swallows or any other bird on the wing, and swimming around them staying close to the shore, following its lumps and bumps or the drop-off beneath. Even when the wind creates chop that is like headbutting cold walls of water over and over again, there's a satisfaction in progressing from one end to the other. I don't always like swimming over the dark deep middle of the lake on my own (what is down there?), but I continue to do it anyway as a character-building exercise.

There are 40,000 lakes and 570 reservoirs in the UK and many variations on the theme. With no current and shorelines all around: so far, so natural swimming pool. Here's what you need to know to transition to swimming in them.

TARNS, QUARRIES, RESERVOIRS, LOCHS AND OTHER TYPES OF LAKE

Maps create a flat Earth with water the lowest point, but the slopes of our hills and hummocks continue beneath water. When you put your head under the surface of a lake and start swimming out, that's human flying: out over the valleys we can't see and don't know about, the vast swathes of Earth that are less charted. Perhaps there would be less 'what is down there' fear if we grew up knowing: rocks. Water and rocks are down there, plus some plants, fish and lots of sediment.

The defining feature of a lake is that they have very little current. In the UK and much of Europe, most lakes are glacial, formed by large bodies of ice scouring out depressions in the rock that have since filled with water. But across the world there are many variants:

Cenote: Found in Yucatan, Mexico, cenotes are subterranean groundwater lakes. Often bright blue, clear, and spotlit by sunlight. They form where limestone has been dissolved, leaving huge airy bubbles in rock that fill with water: a secret magical-world kind of swimming. Called 'sinkholes' in Australia and the US.

Crater lake: Left behind after the top of a volcano has blown – deeply picturesque but not common.

Fjord: Similar to Scottish sea lochs, fjords are deep narrow valleys left behind by retreating glaciers and filled with sea-water. Often huge in scope, with giant cliffs and equally breath-taking temperatures. Fjord roughly translates as 'to travel across' or 'to reach the other side' – which (with boat cover) you may feel drawn to do.

Lake: A lake is a body of (fresh or salt-) water surrounded by land. There is no threshold for size, although I have heard that for a water body to be classed as a lake rather than a pond a swan needs to be able to take off on it.

Llyn: Welsh word for lake, pond or pool. *Ll* is pronounced as a 'thl' sound or (for English speakers) something closer to 'cl'. This makes Llanberis (heart of many a Snowdonia swimming tour) *Clan-berris*, and Llyn Padarn something more like Clin Padarn.

Loch: Lake or sea inlet. Irish, Scottish Gaelic and Scots word. A loch is a large body of water almost completely surrounded by land. Peaty lochs take on the shades of beer; saltwater lochs are like arms of the sea – they function more like lakes than open sea as a result, except with tidal influxes of sea creatures. Often cold and clear: dive down and see bubbles rise up through it. Sea lochs (the same thing as a fjord) can have the same characteristics in terms of weather and water conditions, but also have a tidal element.

Lough: Northern Irish term for lake.

Mere: Lake or pond, perhaps a wide lake that is shallow for its size. 'Lake Windermere' is a tautology: the most famous 10.5-mile (18 km) endurance swim in England is just 'Windermere'.

Oxbow lake: Formed as a river changes it course, and can be small and stagnant.

Pond: Small body of water. Can be man-made or natural.

Quarry lake: Depression in the earth caused by humans taking a chunk of something – granite, gravel, sand, slate, tin – out. Can be dramatic, with sheer rock walls and surreal blue-green turquoise water.

Reservoir: Large natural or man-made body of water used as a water supply. Can feel unnatural (side plantations of non-native conifers don't help) and need 'breaking in'. Contrary to urban myth, you are not going to pollute it by swimming in it, as water is filtered before it arrives at our taps.

Tarn: Small mountain lake created by glaciers. 'Tarn' is what they're called in the Lake District, but they are also known as corries in Scotland, cirques in the Alps and Pyrenees, and cwms in Wales. They look like bowls of water on a mountain scale, and are often smaller the higher up a mountain you go.

Water: Cumbrian word for lake, as in 'Rydal Water'.

SWIMMING AT ALTITUDE:
NOTES ON TARNS AND HIGH MOUNTAIN LAKES

Sitting in wild lonely places that free the spirit, high glacial lakes – tarns, cwms, corries, cirques – are sometimes called the eyes of the mountain. There are tarns that lie in valleys and those that lie on ridges, torrents of rain collected in their bowls.

In 2009 I moved to the Lake District for a few months, intent on swimming as many tarns as I could. I knew little about mountain environments but wanted to get up high into a land that felt wind-whipped and wild. I made a database of 139, with notes on which might be swimmable.

I found bathymetric maps and surveys conducted since 1947 by the Brathay Exploration Group, published as *Tarns of the Central Lake District.*[1] Bathymetry is the measurement of depth and from these maps I could see where the deeper water was and was not, and from their notes on sediment and vegetation I made guesses about shallow murky water and blanket bog.

I swam in good ones and bad ones, shallow ones and broody ones, broiling hot ones and ones that didn't get any sun, every one delivering a sense of surprise and discovery when I turned a corner and saw it. I was tagging along with local painter William Heaton Cooper in spirit, picking up on thoughts he'd had fifty or so years earlier through his book and *The Tarns of Lakeland,* and I got to know the mountains a little through him.[2] Soon I made a real friend, who I stopped as she ran dripping past me while I was out looking for one of the Angle Tarns. Together we explored the tarns, and she held my towel on days the rain made me wet faster than I could dry myself.

The key things to note about hunting down high swims is that you need to be as prepared as you would be going walking up a mountain. The weather changes fast, the terrain may be rough and the walk long, and it is colder the higher you go (air temperature decreases by 1 °C with every 100 metres higher you go). Water temperature varies with height, size, depth, source (rain, snowmelt) and exposure to sun. Glacial tarns are often north-facing.

MARATHON SWIMS IN LOWLAND LAKES: ENDING A SWIM NICELY BROKEN

The length-of-Windermere swim remains the UK marathon crown, but there are swimmers striking out with metaphorical flags everywhere trying to plant them in an opposite shore just for fun. There is something about a lake that invites you to make tracks: to see if you can cross it or make it to the end of it, to go out there and swim till you are nicely broken.

Many of my favourites are (unsurprisingly) in the Lake District. Buttermere, separated by a spit of land from Crummock (where a long swim can be continued), has a clear, distinctly green-blue colour caused by the hardness of the rock, and some trees to sight on. Wastwater is wonderfully wild. Derwent has enough islands to play swimmer's pinball.

If you are looking for a lake challenge, it is generally safer to hug the shore where the water is shallow and you can exit it at any time. The further you wander from this safe zone, the more important it is to be visible and have a support crew. A primary hazard of a long swim is stealth chilling, where you end up with cold incapacitation and are far from shore and safety. Lowland lakes are generally in the bottom of valleys, making them easier to access, path- and road-wise, when compared to mountain lakes.

DEEP WATER FEAR

Lakes have a way of screaming 'swim me' and 'what is DOWN there?' simultaneously.

Looking back on the three passions that governed his life, the analytic philosopher Bertrand Russell spoke of how he sought love to ease loneliness: 'that terrible loneliness in which one shivering consciousness looks over the rim of the world into the cold unfathomable lifeless abyss'. I can feel like that when I'm swimming in a deep lake: the abyss in my local lake is 40 metres deep. The lake and I are well acquainted now but in the early days I would feel vertiginous and think about sinking. Lakes have always been the primary roaming ground of deep-water fear. Our forefathers created a supernatural cast of lake monsters, shapeshifters, spirits and hybrid beasts to have fear-provoking parties with. Lagarfljót, a lake in Iceland, purportedly has a slug the size of a bus, which was first sighted in 1345.[3]

Some try to explain the fears away with theories: four otters swimming in a row might look like a serpentine monster such as Nessie. Floating logs might take on the form of the giant crocodilian monsters that tickle the feet of bathers. Gas bubbles might be mistaken for huge heath worms (the basis of the Lagarfljót monster).

Rationalising the story doesn't, however, dispel the fear; knowing it's illogical rarely loosens its grip. If you start to feel overwhelmed, roll onto your back and take some deep breaths. There are a few tactics for dealing with it, some of which you might have tried when you were young and had monsters under your bed:

One, take a friend. In swimming as in life, a friend will often protect you from staring into a cold unfathomable abyss.

Two, keep your head above water with breaststroke or turn on to your back to keep thoughts in daytime mode, away from nightmares of the dark. Tow floats might help here: something unwaveringly afloat above the dark and endless deep.

Three, do exactly the opposite of that and plunge your head in. This is the Feel the Fear and Do It Anyway school of management: you just decide you own the fear switch, and turn it off.

Four, replace the intrusive thoughts with something else you prefer, such as counting strokes. In life it is always true that if we let our thoughts run wild, without any control, they will control us. Swimming is one of many practice grounds where we can choose what we think: let the thoughts pass while you focus on the sensation of swimming, nudge them aside with a pleasant focus, such as your hands moving the water, water gliding down the sides of your body, the sound of your breath. Think about the weather, the landscape.

Whatever strategy you try the suggestion is that you do all of this gently, when you're ready, and don't force yourself into a situation that makes you uncomfortable. What does it matter if you always swim close to the shore?

For me the fear remains lightly managed but is not gone or vanquished for ever. I was swimming alone at twilight recently, in a local reservoir where nobody goes. One minute I was awash with the swans and the clarity, the cool ribbons of water on my skin, the dimpsy light. The next I was drenched in dread, in fear for my feet. On a GPS map my swim would have looked like a ball hitting a wall: she swam so far, then bolted for shore.

If it's someone else suffering from the fear, don't be overly pushy – a panicked swimmer in the water is not nice and can be dangerous. Should a swimmer lose their nerve then be authoritative – get them to lie on their back and take some deep breaths, calm them down, and start guiding them back to shore. Keep reassuring them as you go, rather than avoiding the situation, and tell them when you can feel the bottom again and when you are nearly there. Then get them out of the water and warm, and focus on the good bits of the swim and what they did achieve, rather than making too much of the situation.

According to phobia specialists we are never too old for treats, and rolling out positive rewards after a fearful swim (whether actual treats or positive self-talk about the overall experience) will help tip the scales towards an experience being life-affirming and pleasurable.

How deep is the water actually? The majority of UK lakes are between 5 and 20 metres. The sea is deeper but we generally swim at its shallow edges. Outliers for depth include Loch Morar, the deepest lake in the UK, at 310 m deep, Loch Ness at 240 m, and Wastwater, in the Lake District, at 76 m.

LAKE TURNOVER

In the early days of The Outdoor Swimming Society (OSS) one of the team bought a hot tub, strapped it to the roof of his car, and drove it around the country to festivals, full moon swims and newly emerging swim events. Rolling around Hammersmith roundabout at midnight, high on life and seeing the delight on people's faces as they clocked the tub on the roof, will be with me till I die. The hot tub was also how we learnt that hot water rises and sits on top of cold: at the Great East Swim bathers were greeted by water that was scalding on the surface, and 'freezing' beneath ('stir hot tub' is now listed on the volunteer briefings).

Water – in lakes, and in hot tubs – divides into layers, which is why you may find your feet dangling in much colder water in summer. Water has different densities at different temperatures and reaches its densest at 4 °C.

In summer, the surface layer warms and sits above cooler layers. At this point some swimmers drive down through the invisible line into the wall of cold water, looking forward to cool waters' return, while others try to make themselves as flat as possible to stay in the thin warm layer.

In winter, the stratification is re-established but the other way around: water below 4 °C rises (in the same way ice floats) and warmer water sits below it. When it occurs ice acts as an insulating blanket stopping the whole lake and all that lives in it freezing solid.

In between, the lakes turn over or overturn. It's a huge seasonal stir: millions of cubic gallons of water across the planet rising and falling as the planet takes a deep breath. In autumn, the top of the lake cools and sinks to the bottom, taking oxygen with it, while the water below starts to rise. Decomposed organic material can rise from the depths, making lakes murkier, bringing a whiff of sulphur. (After turnover fish may return to living at great depth where oxygen levels have risen).

In spring, any surface ice melts, the temperature of the top layer rises above 4 degrees and starts to sink. Strong winds and sun help the layers move and mix.

SUMMER

Warm water rises, so in summer lakes develop a warm top layer (epilimnion) and a colder bottom of lake (hypolimnion).

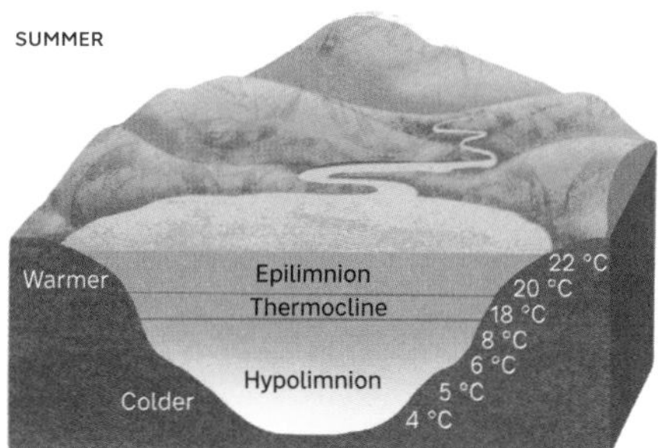

AUTUMN

In autumn, the top layer chills and sinks, and the (by now possibly oxygen-deficient) bottom layer is stirred up, helped by autumn winds. The planet takes a big seasonal sigh and temperate lakes turn over.

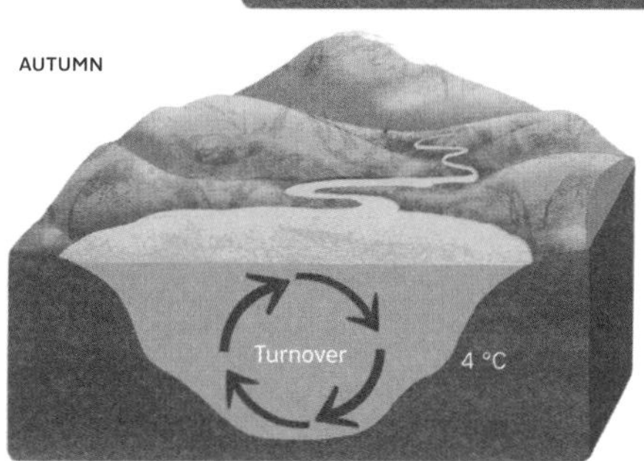

WINTER

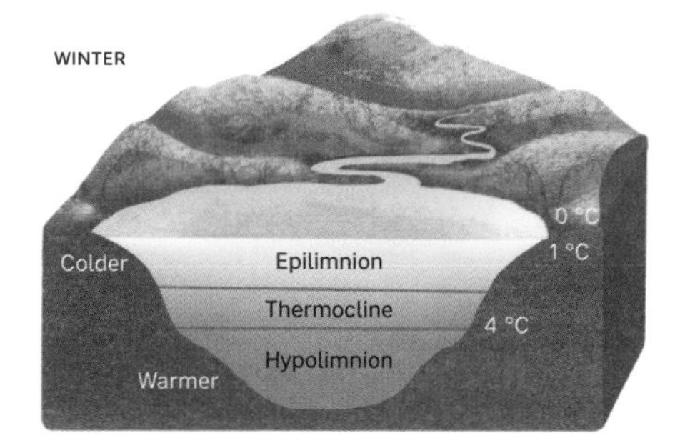

By winter, new layers have established: the coldest water (below 4 °C) is now found on the surface and may freeze, and the warmest water (4 °C) has sunk to the bottom.

SPRING

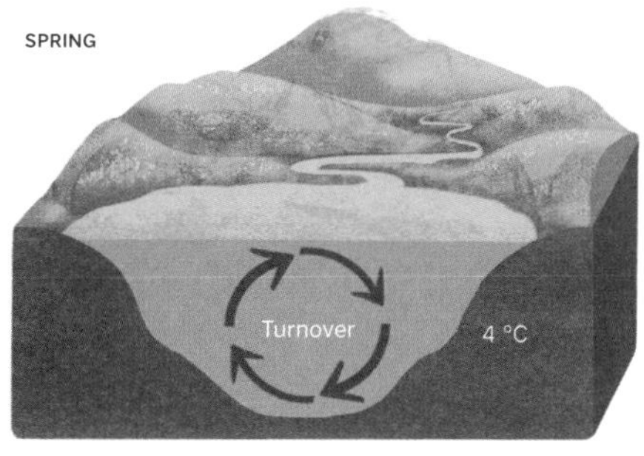

In spring, the planet takes another deep breath: lakes start to warm, the surface layer sinks, and spring storms help the stir.

SEASONAL LAKE TURNOVER

Shallow lakes rarely stratify; they mix throughout the year, as a result of wind. In larger lakes, once they are established the strata are quite stable: deprived of sunlight and warm air, the lower layer continues to get colder and denser, while the top layer (called the epilimnion) grows warmer and lighter, and the greater the density difference the more the layers persist and fail to mix. Cold nights, rain and wind will bring the surface temperature down a bit, while sunny still days will warm a lake up a bit, but the big layers remain.

Water may be warmer by the shore than it is at a lake's centre – be aware of this if you are planning to cross a body of water, and plan your kit for it.

The depth of epilimnion varies; you might find your feet in it or that you stir up cold pockets when you jump in.

LAKE WIND AND WAVES

Very little changes in a lake – there are fewer phenomena such as tides and currents to affect a swim – and that can be part of the appeal. But what lakes do have is wind. Sometimes strong wind, which makes it easy to swim out, but hard to swim back. Without the friction of grass, trees, houses and hills, wind can race across the flat open surface of a lake, picking up speed and slaptastic waves as the air travels. The shore furthest from the wind is often where the roughest water and sharpest exposure is. (See page 140 for more on fetch.)

THE COLOUR OF LAKES AND LOOKING FOR CLARITY

The colour of lakes shifts with the weather, season, time of day and time itself, with its upswings and downswings of sediment, algae, plant life and animal, vegetable, mineral companions.

There's a joy in clear black water: watching light loop on the surface as I hobble off a rocky shore, then seeing myself through it, limbs of an albino astronaut in space. The reflections on dark water can be sharp as a pin, so you see two landscapes, one in the air and its pair, mirrored upside down in the water.

There's an earth-soak feel to peaty lakes: I'm not in love with bog juice squeezing up between my toes as I hop between tufts of cotton grass, but it's later, when fully immersed in the orange-brown water, that you can feel its basic wealth. (Bog skincare is actually a thing, it turns out – peat has been used for centuries as an astringent, and for its anti-allergenic, antibacterial and anti-inflammatory properties, reducing itch in conditions like dermatitis and psoriasis.)[4]

Then there's the blues. Occasionally you may find clear light blues in lakes from silica sand bottoms. Dark-blue water gets it colours from being clear and deep. Calcium carbonate – from limestone and slate bedrock, for instance – can make water startling shades of bright blue. Who can resist water that is turquoise, or kingfisher-blue? Not I.

What makes a lake clear and a lake murky? Sediment particles, planktonic algae and dissolved organic matter. Spring-fed lakes sat in rocky mountains or volcanic craters have a high chance of clarity. Lower lakes will fill with sediment, brought in by rain, even if they started out as a rocky bowl in the first place. Deeper lakes have more chance to clear, so you can see into the water.

It's an uncommon joy to be in a clear lake of any colour, especially if it's shallow enough to see the bottom and you can swim over tree trunks, sand ridges, fallen rock, fish. My local reservoir has a bank of water lilies I like to swim along, finning along with my head on one side; elegant and sparse, the long stalks take on the fluid asymmetry of an art nouveau design as they rise to the surface.

That leaves the greens. Most algae is completely harmless, so you needn't worry about swimming in it. Led by some determined toddlers, I have swum in water thick and green as paint ('just don't put your head in!' 'Oh, you've jumped in and it's streaming out of your nose already...'). Algae-filled lakes (such as London's Serpentine some summers) will be filtered by your swimming costume, leaving streaks of green on you and it. Low levels of algae occur when the soils surrounding a lake are fast-draining and healthy. Algae blooms are encouraged by a variety of factors (see page 16 for more).

QUARRY LAKES

'I love being in the womb of what was once a tor; I think of how the heart was ripped from her, and how nature has mended her wounds with a skin of turf and moss... making a place for animals and birds to drink and wash, and for me and Honey to swim'

LYNNE ROPER,
Wild Woman Swimming

There can be a post-industrial drama to abandoned quarries, a sense things are a little off: steep cliffs in a flat area, say, water a strange and startling bright blue. Sometimes the almost subliminal oddness is their existence in places where there is no other water, or very few plants either side of the shore (they lack the 'marsh zone' of natural lakes). They are often small but very deep, with dramatic cliffs and surreal water (one in Wales is called 'Dali's Hole').

Quarry lakes are often very young, less than 100 years old, creating pioneer conditions for both species and swimmers. Depending on how long it's been since the aggregate equipment has been packed up and moved out, you may find flora just starting out.

The water purity and clarity can be good as the water is nutrient-poor – quarries are often dug into rock, so don't have the silt and nutrient present around natural lakes, and it takes time to accumulate the fertility of natural lakes. Their depth, a result of economic pressure to mine as much as possible from a limited surface area, means that the water stratifies, giving a lake clarity. Old clay pits are less likely to silt, creating clear blue clean water.

Quarry lakes have been excluded by legislation that places monitoring demands on other water bodies, but their prevalence means this is changing. In 2021, a group in the Netherlands released research on 154 quarry lakes left behind by sand and gravel mining in their area, in which they looked at what quarry lakes offer local ecosystems.[5] They found that hydrologically isolated from other water courses as they are, quarry lakes provide homes for different species than other nearby lakes; this makes an argument for greater inclusion in water management strategies.

Exhausted quarries are often reclaimed as nature reserves, public parks, ponds, watersports centres and holiday villages. But there can be years in between purposes where they are left in limbo, winking at swimmers and locals, with some of them being used unofficially. Many are close to towns (it makes sense to move building materials the shortest distances).

I have a few near me and am interested in how human overlays – rather than the water itself – make them either appealing or dangerous. One of my local quarries is a commercial centre for divers and swimmers, while another used to be advertised as having fatal qualities to keep people out, but is now being rebranded as 'a mineral lake' surrounded by chalets.

Here's what we all need to know about quarry lake pleasures and hazards:

- Quarry lakes are smaller and deeper than natural lakes, and edges may drop away sharply, leading a non-swimmer to paddle straight out of their depth. Even sand and gravel quarries that start with sandy beaches may plunge at some point.

- Slate, sand, gravel and limestone quarry lakes often have better visibility and chemical and biological quality compared with other lakes; but often isn't always: abandoned metal mines can be acidic and polluted with metal such as cadmium, lead, zinc, copper, nickel, arsenic and iron. Today there are laws against mines polluting groundwater and waterways – but they didn't come in till 1999, and many mines were abandoned before then.

- Quarry lakes can be colder than a river, lake or the sea at the same time of the year. This may happen where there are submerged inlets of water into the quarry lakes from underground mine shafts so the water has not been warmed by the sun. They do stratify, like other lakes, with warm water on the surface – but you may still touch the colder layer, or find it stirred up by jumping or wind.

• They may contain old equipment and jagged submerged edges, or have been used for dumping vehicles – but this may be far below swimmers (and similar vehicles have been sunk as scuba-diving attractions at some quarry lakes).

• They are popular places for tombstoning, which has risks of its own: the impact of jumping from a height can cause serious hurt and spinal injuries.

• Rescues can be complicated by their geography, and absent phone signal.

• Stone quarries have an increased risk of rock falls.

• Silica banks can collapse quite easily.

RESERVOIRS

Reservoirs are human-made but not always people-friendly. Perhaps it's the monoculture forests that sometimes flank their sides: tall dark walls of non-native firs, somehow audibly silent and palpably empty. Perhaps it's the long absence of people: water bodies are like houses to me, they feel different when deserted – the same unnerving sense you get from an abandoned building or deserted car park. Or perhaps it's simply the practice of landowners conferring a threat level on them to keep people out.

When they woke up on 24 January 2003, swimmers in Scotland found 800 reservoirs had become welcoming, as a result of the Land Reform Act granting them access overnight: the dangerous water with the sucky pipes had become part of their natural playground.[6] Since 2016 the wild swim group SOuP (Sheffield Outdoor Plungers) has been quietly subverting the standard practice of keeping swimmers out of reservoirs (while welcoming sailing, paddleboards, anglers, walkers, cyclists) by swimming in them, and calling their patch of England the 'Sheffield Lake District'. To them, their reservoirs now seem as warm and friendly as any natural lake, although access is still contested. (See 'Access: Is It Legal?' in Chapter 9.)

The key difference between a reservoir and a lake is the dam wall, which is where a river was blocked, causing water to back up behind it, and any machinery attached to it. In a lake there will be a natural bank on the downstream side, with an outlet river. In a reservoir there will be a dam wall. This is what spooks swimmers – reservoirs have controlled flow out of them, and no one likes the idea of going down a plughole when water is released.

Research any reservoir you want to swim in and observe exclusion zones around any infrastructure – I always give dam walls a wide berth by swimming at the other end of the reservoir. Taking part in a guided swim down the Salt River in Arizona (a chain of four reservoirs), I swam the width of the Theodore Roosevelt Dam. This cautious, high-speed crossing of a huge hydroelectric dam was conducted like a military operation, with us bunched together like a tag-team crocodile and told not to stop till we reached the other side. The 'safe' distance between a swimmer and dam is not easily calculable, so left to my own devices I just leave a ridiculously large space. Be wary of swimming downstream from reservoirs for similar reasons.

Swimming away from the outlet end of a reservoir has other advantages: the non-dam end is likely to have gently sloping access beaches, and it will keep you away from any fuss from bystanders (people often visit dam structures).

The outlet channels for water from a reservoir are visible from above – they are generally close to the dam and may be part of it (spillways) or separate outlet towers. What you can see, you can avoid swimming near. The other possible bit of machinery in some reservoirs is aerators, which function to mix thermal layers in summer. We understand they should be marked with buoys. (The danger in the vicinity of aerators is a sudden loss of buoyancy caused by the air bubbles in the water).

Hydropower reservoirs are the ones that release water with no notice, very quickly, at huge volume, as they need a huge amount of water to travel quickly through the dam/underground system to produce electricity from it. In the unlikely event of this happening when you are in it, get out quickly.

Other reservoir risks may be familiar from elsewhere: reservoirs can have steep sides where exit is difficult, so be conscious of whether you can get out before you get in. Striking out for the other side carries the risk of misjudging distance or ability and growing cold and weak on the way – they are big deep bodies of water generally, and the water in the centre can be colder than that on the shore sides. They can be windy places, so be aware of swimming offshore with the wind behind you and then struggling to get back. The warm layer may not be deep, so it's possible that you will suffer from cold-water shock jumping in. Also, there may be other water users, such as sailors or anglers.

ALGAE AND INSECTS

When thinking of other water users, it pays to be aware of the non-human variety too. These can include the likes of algae and insects.

ALGAE BLOOMS AND BLUE-GREEN ALGAE

Algae production is at its highest over summer. Many water bugs (in lakes, but also rivers and the sea) feed on algae and it is part of a healthy lake ecosystem, but sometimes a combination of factors such as still water, warm sunny weather and nutrients from, for example, sewage, fertiliser and manure can trigger a 'bloom'. A bloom is a rapid increase in algae, and it can have a negative impact on plants, insects, fish, wildlife and swimmers, both by deoxygenating the water and by releasing biotoxins.

Blue-green algae has a big reputation as something to be fearful of. It is toxic to dogs, but you don't need to be that spooked: globally, it occurs naturally in fresh water in small quantities and only poses issues when in a bloom – at which point it's reasonably likely the way it looks or smells will put you off swimming anyway. Part of the fear comes from confusion – some places have up permanent WARNING! TOXIC: BLUE-GREEN ALGAE signs, which is confusing when the water looks clear of algae.

Blue-green algae is not actually an algae, but a type of bacteria: cyanobacteria. Blooms are more common in shallow water. A lot of intensively farmed land and dense human activity around a lake make it more likely as that carries nitrogen and phosphorus into the water (from run-off, lawn food, garden fertiliser and septic tanks). In 2010 the Great North Swim in Windermere had to be postponed because of blue-green algae, and phosphates in washing products used in surrounding holiday accommodation were pointed at as a possible cause. A combination of voluntary manufacturer action and phosphate legislation has made many laundry detergents, washing-up liquids and dishwasher pods phosphate-free now, but it's well worth checking the details on all products thoroughly.

While generally a lake phenomenon, it can happen in rivers: in summer 2021 there was a bloom on the Wye, next to some chicken farms.

TESTING ALGAE BLOOMS

A bloom can look like paint has been spilled on the shore, or like pea soup – bright green and thick with colour. There are other things a bloom like this could be confused with: duckweed, which on closer inspection looks like small green lentils or tiny green granular quinoa. Tree pollen can also form shoreline surface scum, coating the surface of the water, but this will tend to be yellowy and dusty.

A lot of blooms will keep you out of the water instinctively because of bad smells, dead fish or general look, but if you are not sure, you could collect a sample in a large Mason or Kilner jar (a pint or more) and leave it to settle in the fridge overnight. Use gloves and collect a sample just below the surface of the water (avoid the top layer of scum). Fill the jar three-quarters full; algae gives off gases that may cause pressure build-up in the jar that could lead it to explode. Wipe the jar clean and leave undisturbed in the fridge overnight. If the algae settles on the bottom of the jar, it is likely normal algae. If it settles on the top, it may be blue-green algae. Two per cent of blue-green algae species don't float, so there is a margin for error.

Blooms can also clump together to look like mats of green algae. A stick test is useful here: find a long one so you can put it in the water without potentially getting the algae on your hands. Slowly lift part of the surface mat out of the water. If the stick comes out draped in stringy silky strands, the mats are probably filamentous green algae, which is not a health hazard. If it comes out looking like it's been dipped in paint, then it's more likely blue-green algae.

There is a type of blue-green algae that creates brown mats and foaming edges on the shore, which make water look stagnant and smell unpleasant and can stain the water purple and brown. This type would hold together in the stick test, but while I have swum in almost everything, I don't know anyone who would swim in that. If you do suspect blue-green algae on the shore, it is likely the bacteria concentration in the lake as a whole is higher, but if you're looking at an expanse of several miles of water a bloom along one shoreline doesn't mean the whole lake is out. Blooms can come and go over a space of days.

As to why you are avoiding it? It can cause itching. When high levels of toxic blue-green algae are touched, inhaled or swallowed it can cause rashes and irritate and inflame the skin, eyes and throat; cause diarrhoea, nausea or vomiting; and lead to allergic reactions or breathing difficulties (although health effects are not likely from water that is not noticeably suffering a bloom). If you suffer from any of these issues after a swim where there might have been algae, do tell your doctor.

To pose a health risk to people, there needs to be more than 8 ppb (parts per billion), ten times the concentration of algae than that which poses an issue to dogs (0.8 ppb).

DUCK FLEAS, SWIMMER'S ITCH AND WATERBORNE PARASITES

It's a beautiful summer's day. You wade in the shallows trailing your hands and chilling your heels, watching a duck nestle in the reeds. Then you get home and develop small red bites that itch for three days and are still visible weeks later.

Swimmer's itch (also called cercarial dermatitis) is an allergic reaction to small parasites that may be in warmer lake water. The parasites (known as duck fleas) may infect snails in the water, and from there try to make it to live in duck, geese or swans. When you start itching, it's from the parasites attempt to burrow their way into your skin as they look for an avian host. The attempt fails, but can cause an itchy allergic reaction. The itching is usually but not always immediate; small red pimples can appear within twelve hours, with blisters to follow. Children can suffer more as they spend more time in the shallows where infected snails may be.

Like all allergic reactions, there's a lot of individual variation in who is affected, even in the same water, and how badly. The more often you swim in affected water, the more intense and immediate symptoms are likely to become. Among those affected there is a lot of chat about what temperature water kills duck fleas but no community consensus: the reaction is so unpleasant that those who most want to know are the least likely to want to use themselves as crash dummies in tests.

Wetsuits may be protective. Showering immediately and/or drying off quickly with a towel will help . Once bitten, common remedies for itching and allergic reactions may help: antihistamines, Epsom salt baths and corticosteroid creams.

Duck fleas are not permanent residents in any body of water. So while it's best to avoid swimming in places where they are a known problem, they may not be a problem that persists.

CHAPTER 2

UNDERSTANDING RIVERS

'Will you look at us by the river!
The whole restless mob of us on spread
blankets in the dreamy briny sunshine
skylarking and chiacking about for one
day, one clear, clean, sweet day in a
good world in the midst of our living'

TIM WINTON,
Cloudstreet

At its simplest, a river or stream is a body of water that flows only in one direction, from source to mouth. A river develops as it journeys, much like us. It begins small and clear-skinned, bright-eyed and magical: a bundle of energy moving fast over rocky riverbeds and tumbling down waterfalls.

Gradually it grows in size and presence – there can be some tricky teenage years, caught between weirs and a city centre, between being shallow and deep – but in time a river can grow big and warm and stately, and start to encompass you as a swimmer, putting its arms around you and carrying you along. Find an old river meandering through water meadows and you'll find a river that knows where it is going and that there's no need to hurry.

A. A. Milnes's Christopher Robin thought that if he 'watched the river slipping slowly away beneath him, then he would suddenly know everything that there was to be known'. That's how it can feel to be in a mature river. Like all your messiness is taken away, leaving you meandering along with it, mind empty of all that doesn't matter and full of a wordless unarticulated sense of what does. Transcendent wisdom tends to evaporate like beads of water on skin when we exit, but if we're lucky we can still come home, smelling of river water and sunshine, relaxed and content.

As you may be able to tell, I have a deep love of mature rivers – quasi-spiritual, neopagan, till-I-die love. I love the softness – of air and fresh water. The sense of going somewhere without having to dream it or will it myself (what a gift). The gentle pull downstream and all that goes with it: floating along, feeling buoyant, going with the flow. I like being immersed in the landscape – sunk down and made part of it. I'm a lover of the lonely landscape, and the fact that man-made mess – houses, roads, pylons, cars – often disappears behind a foreground of reeds, bushy banks and trees, leaving just the things that are wild in view, is a win for me. I like that my nose is pressed into the roots of nature, Roger Deakin's 'frog's-eye' view of the world, without attracting stares because I am on my belly in mud. River swimming is about absorption on all levels: of us into nature and landscape, and nature into us.

SOURCE TO SEA: RIVERS AROUND THE WORLD

The first step to understanding river swimming anywhere in the world is to see them as a whole, on a source-to-sea journey. Understanding the basic characteristics of highland and lowland rivers allows broad but sound guesses at the kinds of swims you will find in a country when you travel.

On the scrunched-up island of the UK, highland and lowland swims are found in close proximity: waterfalls, jumping-in spots, and plunge pools giving way downstream to rope swings, lazy meanders and then estuaries, where the fresh water mixes with salt water and the tide helps or hinders your eventual arrival at the sea. The journey is a continuum – rivers will broaden, speed up, increase in volume and become less rocky and more meandering gradually. The middle sections of rivers are often semi-rural and may run through farmland and private estates, so access may be an issue. They will likely have weirs or mill races, and some whitewater, but on a much lesser level than the highlands.

Abroad, familiar features are amplified, the swimming stakes raised.

In New Zealand, highland terrain dominates; both the North and South Island are mountainous, with the spines of the Kaikōura Ranges in the South producing clear, cold water speeding over rocky riverbeds and sharp gradients. Knees get knocked; currents may make conditions unswimmable. In mountainous regions (for example, the Alps, Pyrenees, Iceland, Norway and North America), rivers may be fed by glaciers and snowmelt in summer, increasing river volume and flow. A glacially fed river is a milky bright blue-grey-green – a result of fine particles of pulverised rock scattering sunlight. Glacial rivers are very cold, even on the sunniest days.

In America, lowland rivers abound; as a result of it being one of the world's biggest land masses water has a long way to travel to the

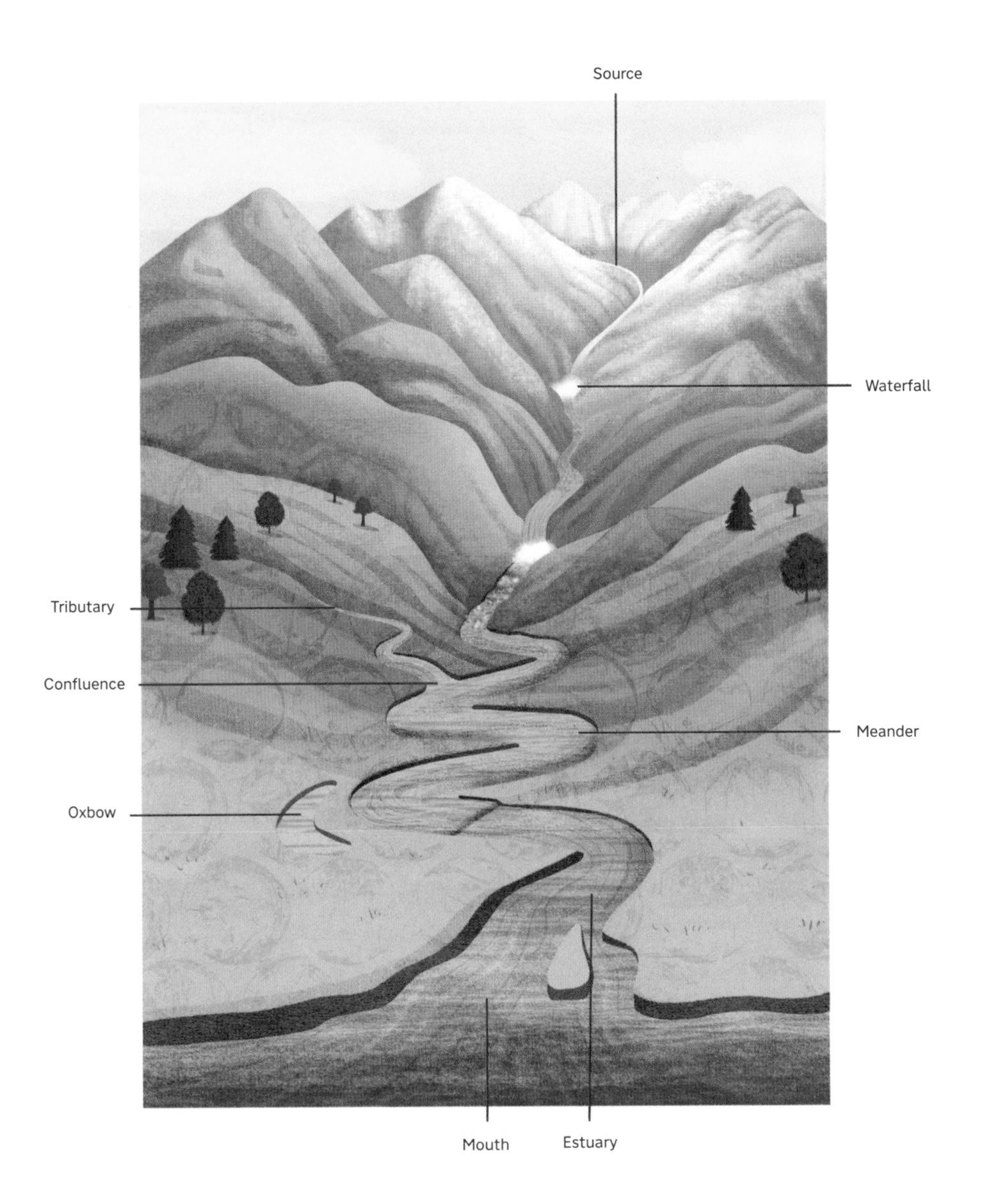

SOURCE TO SEA

ocean, producing some of the planet's longest and widest rivers. The Mississippi is 11 miles wide at one point. In 2002 one endurance swimmer, Martin Strel, took it on, swimming its entire length, 3,885 kilometres (2,414 miles) in 68 days (our longest river is a tenth of that, the Severn, at 220 miles).[1]

In Europe, as in the States, rivers cross big sweeping areas of flat land and have time to become huge, bigger in width, depth and volume of water than we are used to here. The Danube rises in the Black Forest in Germany and travels 2,850 kilometres through eight countries (Austria, Slovakia, Hungary, Croatia, Serbia, Bulgaria, Romania and the Republic of Moldova) before it finds its way to the Black Sea in Ukraine. It is largely untampered with and its middle section is a wildlife corridor, a European Amazon, with large flood-plain forests and wild wetlands, a haven for white-tailed eagles, black storks, beavers and otters.

And as for Australia? It may be just as you imagine: rivers the colour of chocolate milk, at least in the Northern Territory, where crocodile presence is measured in 'density per kilometre' (yikes! 15 per kilometre at some points). Crocs are also connected to another geographical feature; they are fond of billabongs, the ponds left behind when a river changes course (here in the UK, called an oxbow lake). (It may be some relief to know crocs only occur in northern parts of Australia; two-thirds of the continent is croc-free with a diverse range of swimming rivers, from clear tropical streams to alpine creeks and slow lowland rivers.)

Wherever in the world you plan to swim, picture a relief map of where you're going, and you can start to take educated guesses about the river swims you may find when you get there.

HIGHLAND RIVER SWIMMING

Mountain high, river deep: water is a slave to gravity, and having begun its journey from a spring, lake or snowmelt, a river will erode the bed of the stream downwards as well as travelling downhill. It creates gorges, gullies and ravines like lost worlds: damp, dark and heavy with moisture and moss.

Closer in, the rocks themselves may be sculpted by the currents that pass and waterfalls occur where soft rock erodes more quickly than hard, creating an overhang and a plunge pool beneath (named after the water that plunges into it, not the swimmers that follow). In highland areas, these deeper pools have often been found and colonised by climbers before swimmers came along; not that long ago, for example, Black Moss Pot in the Lake District was a secret passed between sweaty climbers coming down from the crags, a place to stop and cool off. But wherever you walk there will likely be dipping spots there for the finding and taking. Jacuzzis to sit in with cold cascades to pummel your shoulders, rock baths just big enough to take the heat and swell out of hiking legs, round basins formed by stones and pebbles have whirled around in the current.

It's often worth taking goggles and aqua shoes uphill even if you are packing light; visibility can be stunning, of both rocks and fish, and aqua shoes allow you to walk along a stream bed, or rock-hop looking for other pools. The general rule of thumb with jumping is 'if you can't see the bottom, don't jump, you don't know what's in there'. Mountain pools can provide an exception but even if you can see the bottom, get in and test the depth first; if light is glinting off it there may be blind spots and judging depth through water is hard. Many a swimmer has come out with a severely bruised coccyx, having not seen what lies beneath. Upland, weather changes fast. See page 148 for more information.

In the highlands water has travelled the least distance since falling as rain and it is at its highest elevation, so is at its coldest. Air temperature varies significantly with elevation. The higher you go, the more you can expect temperatures in the range of 'invigorating'. Upstream water is often clear (if peat-stained) and if you're upstream of where people live or camp, and the upper reaches have not claimed the lives of any sheep, it is often clean enough to drink.

Plant and animal life is scarce at the top of a mountain both in and out of the water, and species diversity increases as streams travels downhill. At greater altitude you will find scree slopes, lichens, buzzards, mounds of pinky-purple moss campion and few plant and animal species in the water. But as water drops, diversity increases. Below 1000 metres, trees like birch, rowan and hawthorn appear, joined by ospreys, butterflies, and wet heath, bog and grassland plants – bracken, heather, lemon-scented fern, carnivorous sundew and bog asphodel. In the water, aquatic life increases in a river continuum.

UNDERSTANDING WATERFALLS AND PLUNGE POOLS

Plunge pools beneath waterfalls can be fantastic to swim in – they are at their deepest directly beneath waterfalls and generally have relatively slow flow. The bigger the drop, the deeper the plunge it may have created. There may be a shallow lip on the lower side of the pool, which is easy to walk in and out from. If there is a deep pool, with a current to swim against, it may work as a natural endless pool, but be aware of high water flow (see page 42, on sieves and syphons).

In a waterfall you are placing yourself under a weight of water, which will be felt on a spectrum from nicely massaging, to more forceful than any shower you ever took, to feeling like being at the bottom of a pile-up on an escalator.

BUBBLES MEAN LOST BUOYANCY

Where there is whitewater, foaming water, or water disturbed by rocks or falls, you will be more likely to sink. Bubbles mean lost buoyancy:

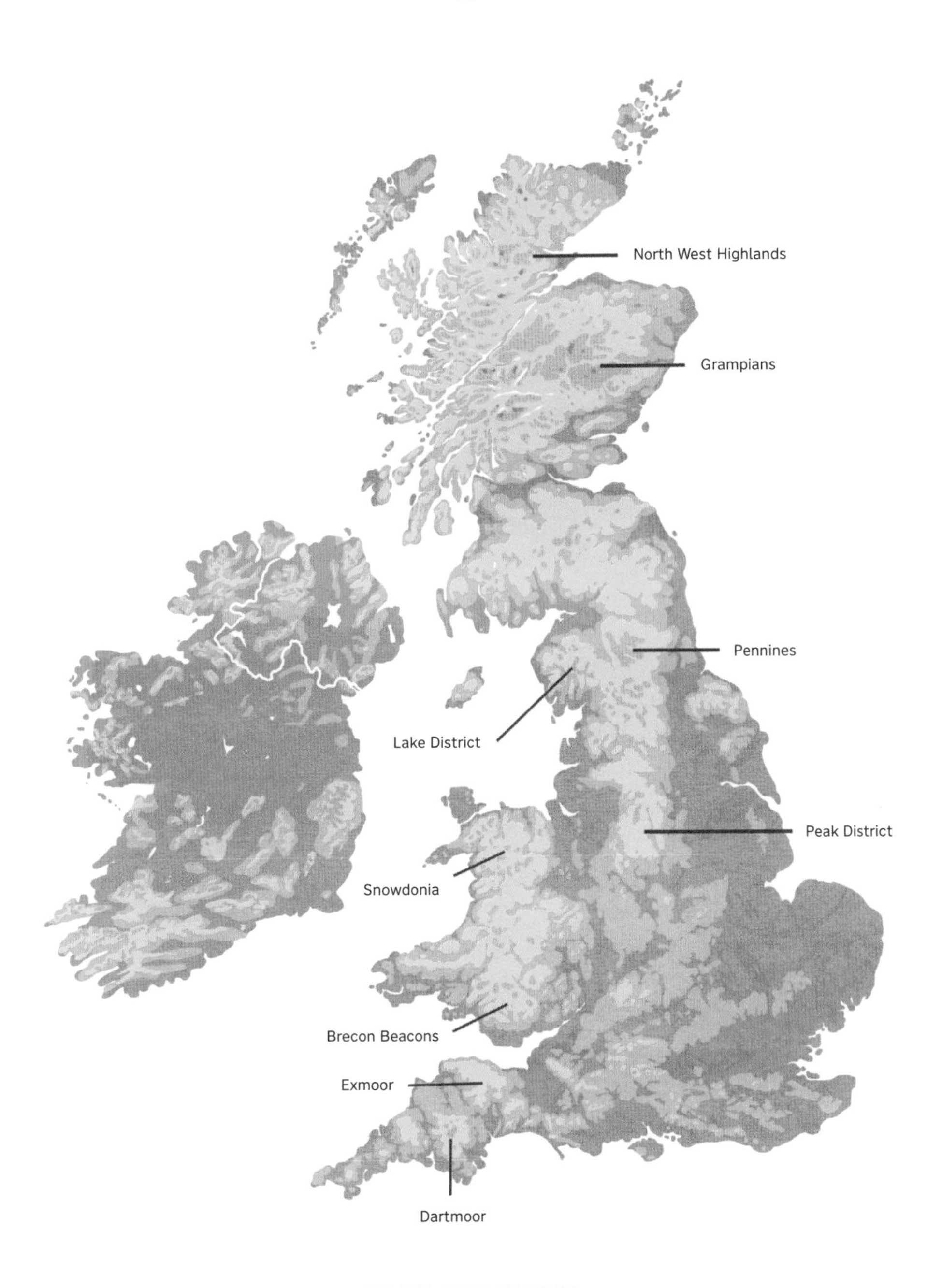

UPLAND AREAS IN THE UK

air bubbles have lower density than water, so where there is white-water (which is water mixed with air) you will be less buoyant. This can be problematic for less able swimmers.

Waterfalls vary hugely with rainfall and flow rate, so always assess them on the day, before you get in. Hazards include slippery rocks and insufficient water to cushion a jump when water levels are low. Logs and rocks can come down in waterfalls – in countries with bigger waterfalls this is a more regular hazard than here in the UK.

Hazards increase with scale and force: it is possible for circular currents to be formed under a waterfall with water hitting the bottom of a plunge pool, bouncing back up, and then joining the downward stream at the surface, creating a circular current or stopper. (See page 41.)

FOAM

Foam in rivers is a natural event, caused by tumbling water and natural surfactants. Surfactants are compounds that (among other things) cause bubbles – they occur naturally as the organic matter in streams and rivers breaks down, releasing fatty acids. You will also see foam during storms at the sea. Natural foam is often tan or brown, as it collects organic matter and occurs more often in tannin-rich rivers. It often arises in tandem with other natural events – rain and wind in autumn, or rising water temperature and accelerated decay in summer. Downstream you may find foam that is caused by pollution and man-made surfactants from detergents and fertilisers.

HOW TO DECODE A MOUNTAIN MAP

Rock River, Milk River, Alligator River, Wild Cattle Creek: new world names often say a lot about a place, but ancient names can be just as descriptive if you know how to decipher them. If you're scouring a map to find a swim in Great Britain, knowing some of these old words may help you choose the right spot. Nordic, Old English and Gaelic influences on toponymy have travelled with people, so the divisions presented in the following table are not absolute.[2]

FEATURE	CUMBRIA	WALES	SCOTLAND
Stream, brook	Beck	Nant (brook, or small valley)	Gil Burn (large stream or small river) Allt (fed by streamlets) Sruth (current, stream)
River	Calder (rocky, fast-flowing river)	Afon	Abhainn Uisge (literally 'water')
Waterfall	Force/ Foss	Pistyll Rhaeadr	Eas Steall (torrent)
Mountain	Fell (used across North of England)	Mynydd	Beinn (mountain) Bràigh (upland country) Brae (hillside)
Valley	Dale (used across North of England)	Cwm Glyn (deep valley)	Gleann/ Glinn/ Glen (narrow valley) Srath/ Strath (wide or broad valley)
Ravine, gorge or canyon (deep valley)	Gill/ Ghyll (used across North of England)	Hafn	Linn (also used for waterfall)
Pool in a river	Pot Dub	Pwll	Poll Sloc Lin (also used for pond or lake)
Rock or crag	Craig	Craig	Creag/ Craig
Confluence, river mouth	Aber	Aber	Inbhir/ Inver

DECODING A MOUNTAIN MAP

LOWLAND RIVER SWIMMING

As a river progresses to the sea more rivers join it: the River Severn, the UK's longest and most voluminous river, has twenty-one tributaries join it before it exits into the Bristol Channel.

In the lowlands, rocky banks are replaced by water meadows and cornfields. Birdsong is joined by the acoustics of passing trains, tractors and cars. The landscape becomes flatter, more fertile, and more sediment-rich – the banks thick and full with plants and trees, the river home to an increasing diversity of fish and insects. The stream itself is no longer clear; now it clogs up brown or green.

Lowland rivers are closer to sea level and start to wind through the landscape rather than dashing straight downhill. The water has also been in the river longer and exposed to solar energy, so is warmer. Even if a river is moving in a stately way the volume of water has force and will lift you up and carry you (as well as sediment) downstream on A to B swims.

Lowland rivers are more likely to experience human interference such as levees, weirs, mills and flood defences, and to flow through urban areas and contain sewage outflows, both of which can lower water quality.

An unexpected feature of a lowland river is how hard it is to know where you are; the river you swim is never the river you imagined or observed from the banks. Landmarks disappear along with houses, and from the water the main channel can be indistinguishable from inlets and tributaries. One summer a friend planned a 10-kilometre swim for us, down a tributary of a river and then into it. On the map it was so easy: after two or three kilometres we'd literally flow into the river and swim back to our cars. How could we go wrong? Except, except, somehow, we never saw the confluence, and spent most of the swim not sure we were in the right river...

WORKING OUT WHERE TO GET OUT BEFORE YOU GET IN

If the current is sufficiently strong that you can't swim upstream against it, then you will not be able to get out where you get in, so be sure to identify exit points before entry.

Use tall or uniquely identifiable objects as markers so you can 'sight' them from the water, including features on the bank opposite. I used to swim a stretch on the Oxfordshire Thames where exit points were miles apart. From land the get-out point was clear as day: where a footpath bent down to a small beach, just before a new field. Except that from the water we couldn't see the footpath or fields; in the water we were on a slow motorway with high banks of reeds and foliage. Chat too much, have your head down too long, and you'd swim right past the exit spot.

Be aware of getting in from banks that overhang deeper water, but are eroded beneath them – for example, where tree roots and grass have clung on to bank on the surface. While the getting in is fine as you can lower yourself into deep water, you need upper body strength to haul yourself out if there is nothing to put your feet on.

FINDING RIVER POOLS

Looking for a pool where it's deep enough to swim within a small or shallow river? Look by bends, especially bends below river cliffs, where currents have led to the erosion of deeper pools. Also look by bridges, small waterfalls, small weirs and rocky spits – all things that hold up the water or lead to erosion.

BRIDGES

There's an excitement about swimming under bridges, from small brick ones that make quiet dark echo chambers and slightly speedy river tunnels, to huge ones worthy of architectural admiration from below. My swims have taken me under audacious bridges, from the skewed brick arches of Moulsford Railway Bridge over the Thames (how did the engineer do that, bend brick?) to the Dundas Aqueduct in Somerset (the water above as well as below). Then there are the ancient ones, like the clapper bridges of upland areas, bridges of huge flat slabs of rocks like balancing stepping stones.

So, lots to enjoy bridge-wise. The majority of bridges cause no issues – there can be some constriction of flow as the river goes between the bridge supports, which will cause the river flow speed to increase, and water can also swirl around the supports and cause small eddies and whirlpools downstream. If you are swimming under a bridge, line yourself up early on the path you want to take between the supports and adopt a defensive feet first position if the water becomes shallow. Be aware that they can be fatal, with the chief hazard being the possibility of being pinned to a pillar by a wall of water.

Jumping off bridges is a popular pursuit that gives me the shivers – partly my fear of heights, and partly because of the risk of low water levels and obstructions below causing life-changing injuries. The higher the bridge, the harder the impact when you hit the water's surface, and the greater the depth required to jump safely. Always check a location before jumping by getting in and locating the deep area of the river first, wait till the last person is clear and, if in doubt, stay out, or find something smaller to hurl yourself from.

ROPE SWINGS

Rope swings often adorn the river banks for all to use: it's worth checking there are no rocks or branches underneath. Prepare yourself for three things: how cold and gaspy the water may feel (I always have my children get in and catch their breath before the jumping starts), how heavy you might be when you jump (adult problem), and being ready to let go at the apex of the swing.

MUD UNDERFOOT

For some, the silky silty experience of a riverbed underfoot is like sinking your feet into a pillow, a soft cloud mattress of sediment (proper name: cowbelly). For others, it's the reason they don't river swim at all – I have one friend who only swims in lakes with stone beds. If soft river mud is not your thing, these are options: reframe the sensation, block the sensation (with neoprene socks or aqua shoes) or avoid it.

WEIRS

Weirs are a man-made barrier in the river channel, placed to change the speed of the river flow. Originally formed for millstreams, flood relief or to make rivers navigable for boats, weirs tended to be placed in lowland rivers; however, as hydro schemes increase they are appearing in highland areas more and more.

A canoeist or kayaker will tell you there is no such thing as a safe weir, yet weirs often make popular bathing spots as deep, slow-flowing pools gather upstream of them. Some weirs are unsafe for swimmers in all conditions, others vary between safe and unsafe with water level. As a rule, the steeper the weir, the more dangerous it is.

If the upstream pool is big and used by swimmers the weir edge is likely to be the main hazard. At low flow it will contain the river like a pool edge and the hazard is slipping if you walk on it. After rain and in higher flow, you may see a sheet of water, like molten glass, pouring over the top of it. This will have force, and you want to stay away from it; get pulled over the top and you may be caught in a stopper at the bottom (see page 41). Water will speed up close to the weir structure – the distance at which this pull occurs will increase the higher the river level.

As water cascades down a weir wall, it can create a mossy stone water slide with a waterfall at the end that looks fun to play in, but I never swim downstream of any them – my fear is that by establishing a precedent of going in downstream of a weir my children might do it on a different day or at a different weir where it isn't safe, and be sucked into and trapped by a stopper. Also, water doesn't hurt, but concrete and metal do, and in the UK there is a policy of not repairing weirs at the moment to enable rivers to start reverting to their normal state, so if they break they are just left there, and bits of concrete and metal reinforcing rods may be sticking up or out. The broken bits will all tend to be downstream.

HIGHLAND SWIMS AND TERRAIN	LOWLAND SWIMS AND TERRAIN
Hilly, mountainous surroundings	Wide open landscapes
Rocky riverbeds	Meanders, floodplains and water meadows
Clear water	Warmer water – has soaked up solar energy
Colder water – owing to elevation	A to B swims may be possible (go with the flow)
Purer water – close to source	May be urban
Plunge pools	More suspended sediment, reduced water visibility, reduced water purity
Waterfalls with white water, Jacuzzis and natural endless pools	There may be river cliffs, river beaches (made by naturally deposited pebbles, gravel and sand), shallow sections, white water and river pools – deeper sections that run to shallow
Rock-hopping, jumping and sunbathing rocks	May encounter artificial features – mills, 'levees' (artificially created or natural long embankments to protect against flooding) and weirs (can be dangerous, but can create swimming spots just upstream of themselves)
Canyons and narrow, steep-sided river channels	Navigable rivers are shared with other water users
Snorkelling – good visibility, submerged rocks, fish	May run through private land

HIGHLAND AND LOWLAND SWIMS AND TYPICAL TERRAIN

FLOW –
WHERE THE FAST WATER IS

Flow is one of the attractions of rivers, but there are things to learn: where to find it, what to do if it's going in the opposite direction to expected (an eddy), and the hazards it creates.

On a straight river the fastest flow is generally found in the middle of the channel, the thalweg, where the water is deepest and further from the friction of the riverbed and banks slowing it down.

Where there is a bend, the thalweg is found on the outside of the bend, and the slower shallower water on the inside of a bend. On a long river swim it may seem like cutting a corner will get you home fastest, but if it puts you in shallow (and sometimes silty) slow water, then taking the 'long way around' and swimming around the outside of the bend might be the quickest option. If you are racing, finding the thalweg matters. Overheard at one OSS event: 'Tom took three minutes off me on that bend specifically because I went up the middle. Schoolboy error.'

Bends in rivers amplify over time – the faster water on the outside of the bend is erosive, creating a deeper channel, while the slower water on the inside of a bend deposits whatever it holds – sand, silt, pebbles – making the water slower and shallower still and sometimes creating a beach. Where there are big looping meanders, a short walk on land can give a long swim home. Eventually the water may cut through the remaining bank, leaving an oxbow lake.

If you had the whole river to yourself then you might choose your swim path purely on flow, but your position in the river will often be influenced by other water users – staying away from the riverbanks if there are anglers, or tucking in to the riverbank (as you would a pedestrian to a hedge) if there is boat traffic.

When getting in, if the flow is already strong at the edges then it is worth considering whether the middle might be too fast to be comfortable. Manoeuvring yourself is more difficult the faster a river gets. Where the current is really strong, you need to act early (often much earlier than you think) if you want to get somewhere and may need to swim aggressively at an acute angle to cross a current.

The whole river will speed up wherever it is pinched, either sideways, because of a narrow constriction in the banks or a bridge or obstruction, or upwards, because the riverbed becomes shallow. Water has more force when it's moving fast, so as well as creating possible riffle and 'swoosh' sections (see below) you may be exposed to more hazards, and need to be particularly cautious when what is downstream is unknown.

Flat water is the smooth water travelling downstream and is generally a good place to be – smooth surface water generally means no obstructions in the river channel, or that any obstructions are deep enough to not need to worry about. Any patches of whitewater indicate something hidden below the surface. Big waves and whitewater suggest deeper features; bubbly white turbulence suggest shallower features.

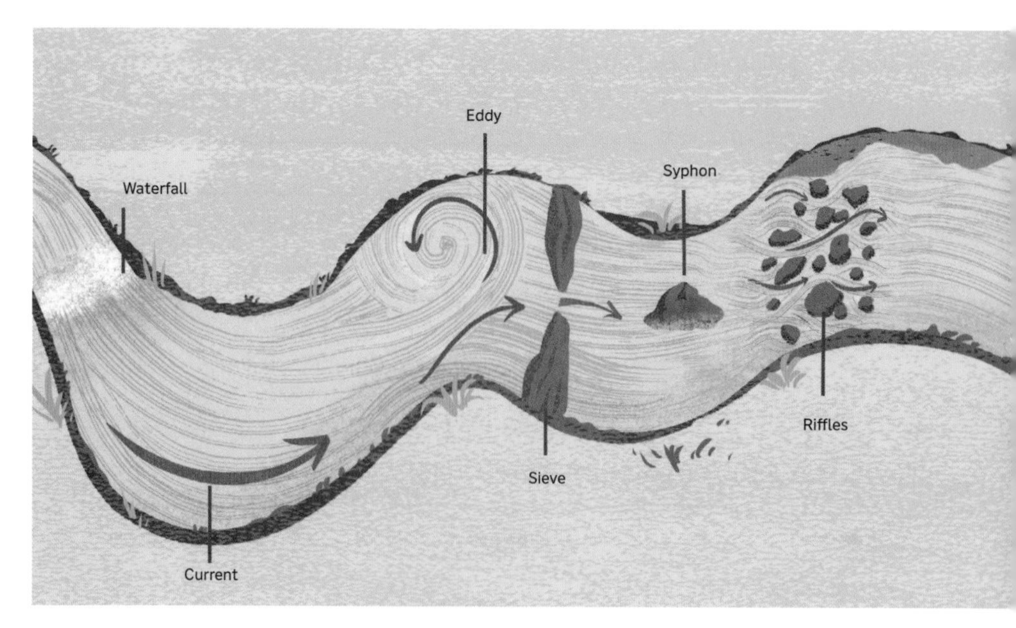

RIVER FEATURES

RIFFLES

Riffles are the shallow parts of a river where the surface of the water is agitated by rocks underneath. You will be able to spot these sections by their bumpy broken surface, often with pebbles and rocks above the surface of the water. What you won't know till you go through them is whether you will run aground. The river will speed up when it hits the shallows, so get prepared early – either get up and walk, or lie on your back, feet facing downstream, keeping your bum lifted, and scull your way down.

Riffles can be fun – enjoy the bumps and the scenery – but they can lead to the odd grazed knee or elbow, and if you get dragged along by the river or hit a big rock they can be quite uncomfortable.

Aqua shoes are handy in shallow rivers – walking on sharp stones and pebbles in a current is hard even if you do have what my friend calls 'summer feet'. (These are aspirational in my house: the result of so much barefoot time your hardened soles can cope with virtually anything).

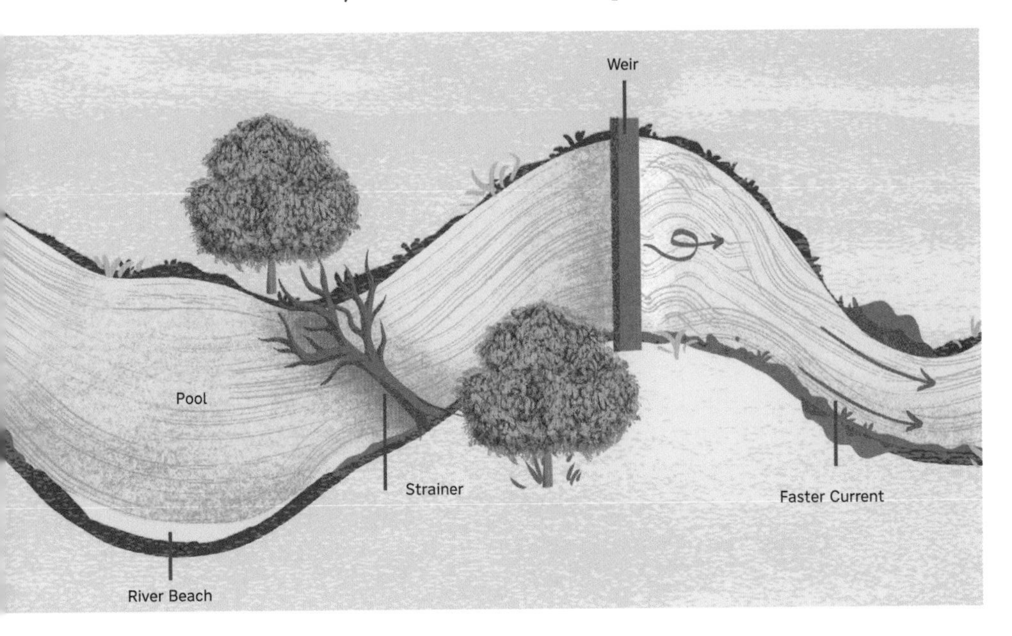

RAPIDS

Rapids are not good places for swimmers. I once spent three months as a trainee whitewater raft guide on the Zambezi, a Grade 5 river (river grades go from 1 to 6, with grade 6 being unsafe to run). There is one rapid, called Gulliver's Travels, where if someone falls off the raft at the top, near 'Indicator Rock', they have 700 metres of Grade 5 whitewater ahead of them. It's a horrible swim: 90 long seconds of being churned around where you may not get to take a breath, as the force of water keeps pulling you under. At the moment clients fell in (which was rare) they were day-trippers still, full of sunshine and fun, but by the time I could haul them back into the raft at the other end of the run they were desperate and scared, and would look at me with the wild shocked eyes of those who feel they've almost died. Wherever there are rapids there is some version of Indicator Rock: a point in the river where it stops running smoothly and conditions change. This is the point where you need to get your wits about you and change gear fast. It's always all right until it's not.

Respect a river's force, recce it, research it, and if you see disturbed water ahead or things start speeding up, act fast and decisively, move to safety, and then work it out.

SWOOSHING

Swooshing is the name given by swimmers to the sensation of swimming in fast flow. The inaugural Swoosh is at Bantham in Devon. Near the mouth of the River Aune, the estuary grows shallow and narrow, which, combined with an outgoing tide, increases its speed. You can feel like Superman as you fly along above the sandy bed, seaweed fragments disappearing fast beneath you, covering giant stretches of ground with each stroke. To end a 6-kilometre swim like that can be to think, 'this is the life, I am bionic.' Then the river meets a rocky headland and bends right, producing a deep, fast channel that swooshes even faster. In this section (tide allowing) swimming is entirely optional – and people take to floating on their backs, snorkelling, or turning to the wet rocks to gauge how fast they are travelling.

Wherever swimmers have located safe places to do it, swooshing is a thing – the current is fast on the Aare River in Bern, Switzerland, for example, and it is wildly popular to jump in and swim or float downstream (bright red markers flag the get-out points).

You need confidence and ability in the water for a swoosh – children can love it, but they are also faster to understand that the water is stronger than them, and feel alarm if they can't swim across the current and get out on the bank.

EDDIES

Eddies are areas of reverse current – so water is moving upstream. They occur after an obstruction to the main flow of the river, such as a bridge, rock or bank that extends out into the channel. Some eddies will be small, some large enough to huddle in and regroup if you're out swimming with others, and others large enough to hamper your downstream progress – metres to tens of metres long. (Bay-wide eddies can occur in the sea, with the tidal race reversing when it hits a headland.)

While a lot of eddies, particularly the small ones (a metre or so in length), have a minor flow within them, larger ones can have a strong current. They can cause minor amusements – going up and down in a circle.

Eddies are good spots for entering and exiting the water, because you won't have to deal with a strong current while clambering in and out.

STOPPERS

If you swim at a weir regularly then you may see people sliding down the structure with no problems at all – the water may just flush them away from the weir. But when water levels rise, the same weir may have a 'stopper' wave at its base. 'Stoppers' are recirculating currents, like vertical eddies, that occur when water drops into deep pools: water falls into deeper water, bounces off the riverbed, rises, and then rejoins the falling water, creating an aggressive recirculating current that can be impossible to get out of. Stoppers can form elsewhere on rivers, for example under waterfalls, or rapids, but bank-to-bank weirs can create bank-to-bank stoppers, which are even more dangerous.

In general be extremely wary of weirs and if you are caught in a stopper try to swim out sideways or down out of the stream of air-filled liquid, and then up.

SIEVES, SYPHONS, SWEEPERS AND STRAINERS

Water has a lot of power when it moves and can hold a swimmer against an object. Sieves, syphons, sweepers and strainers are all versions of water flow being constricted. These are kayaking terms and it is not necessary to remember which is which, just to give them a wide berth:

- **Syphons** – if there's a gap between some boulders or large rocks and water is forced through it, then it's the equivalent of a plug – a swimmer can get sucked in, plug the gap and then not be able to move out again because they are pinned by the weight of the water upstream of them.

- **Sieves, strainers and sweepers** – a fallen tree or roots overhanging a bank can create a sieve, with strong currents pushing a swimmer against it, and the weight of water holding them there. Strainers and sweepers are terms used almost interchangeably, with strainer generally meaning underwater objects, and sweepers something dangling in the water.

The advice for all of them is the same: stay well away. This becomes harder as a river flows faster, and as you approach an obstacle currents intensify and will even pull you towards it. I was caught out recently by a tree that had fallen right across the river. The current in the river was mild and I don't know what I was thinking (not enough, clearly), but I thought I would climb onto the trunk and jump off it into the river on the other side, to avoid the scratchy fight with foliage involved in swimming round the tree's crown. Closer up, things accelerated and as I flung my bodyweight over the trunk I could feel the river try to pull my legs underneath it. It was a good reminder to avoid midstream obstacles. If you do start getting too close to an obstacle, turn to face upstream and swim upriver on a slight angle away from the obstacle – this is a ferry glide and will take you across the river.

If you see a solitary twig breaking the water, remember that – like an iceberg – there is a lot more where that came from under the surface, likely a big branch or whole tree.

Trees are particularly likely to come down on bends where the banks are being eroded – be particularly cautious after floods. Rapids often end with a deep slow pool where storm debris is deposited as water hits the slower pool.

FRESHWATER FIELD GUIDES

'The art is to draw no attention to
oneself but to cruise quietly by the
reeds like a water rat: seeing and
unseen from that angle, one can hear
the sedge warblers' mysterious little
melodies, and sometimes a cuckoo flies
cuckooing over our heads,
or a kingfisher flashes past'

IRIS MURDOCH,
on her approach to swimming
in the Thames

FRESHWATER BIRDS

COMMON KINGFISHER

Alcedo atthis

A kingfisher's colours are flicked on by sunshine. It's often when a kingfisher turns or takes off, when it emerges from the dappled shadows of overhead branches into the light, that we see it: the chest catches fire, an electric blue stripe down its back flashes.

It is possible to swim right up to them if you are integrated noiselessly in the water. Kingfishers are shy birds with bold coats; try to tell another swimmer you have seen one and it will quiver and flash off down the river. But it will return, if you can wait; kingfishers develop favourite fishing posts where they live, alongside rivers and lakes, with 1-kilometre territories. They nest in tunnels and eat their bodyweight in fish a day.

A kingfisher has a jet-black beak the shape of a long dagger, which is part of its success as a hunter. Fish can sense the compression wave of a diving bird (or any other disturbance on the water) and will flee with a flick of their tails, but the shape of a kingfisher's beak means that it can enter the water without a splash.

Sightings are usually so brief, so fleeting, that they are always exciting. I love the sharpness of kingfishers: their bright dark eyes, their shrill silvery whistle, the speed of them as they fly fast and low over slow-moving water. I love their focus as they sit on their sticks, rotating their big heads to hunt for stickleback, minnow, shrimp.

A much loved Gerard Manley Hopkins line of poetry was inspired by this bird: 'As kingfishers catch fire, dragonflies draw flame [...] 'crying "'Whát I dó is me: for that I came."'

CORMORANT

Phalacrocorax carbo

A favourite companion for many swimmers, cormorants are stark and striking birds, familiar from their conspicuous, structural silhouette as they hang their soggy coppery-black wings out to dry. They are often seen adding a Gothic air to dead trees and offshore rocks, but anywhere there is fishing they may be found – on buoys, cliffs and pylons too. Historically a coastal bird, they are increasingly seen inland, by estuaries and lakes. Their huge webbed feet make them excellent divers and swimmers, hunting underwater, and their 'wettable' feathers may make them less buoyant so they can dive more easily.

DIPPER

Cinclus cinclus

Unlike most birds, dippers have solid (not hollow) leg bones, which act like weight belts to reduce their buoyancy, allowing them to walk around under water, hunting for larvae and crustacea to eat. They have plump bodies and a white breast and bob or dip up and down while perched.

Dippers hang out in beautiful wild places, like tumbling streams in upland and moorland areas, but also in estuaries and at the coast. They change the way they see underwater, with a transparent eyelid acting as goggles, and are superb divers and swimmers. Nests have been found behind the curtains of waterfalls, but breeding birds often pick human structures like weirs and bridges.

GREY HERON

Ardea cinerea

Scarcely visible in its stillness, the heron is one of the few big birds we have left ornamenting our landscape. We British are a nation of 'little brown jobbies' – so cherish the elegant heron, standing among the reeds on tall bamboo legs, long black crest feathers blowing softly in the wind.

The heron has the poise of aged gentry but is a killer whatever the clothes. A black stripe marks the trajectory of all the stretched white neck swallows: fish, frogs, ducklings, eels, voles and mice (you will sometimes see them looking for these in fields).

Herons can be found around any type of water – ponds, lakes, rivers and estuaries – with their main hunting times being dawn and dusk. They avoid casting shadows in their fishing territory, and when they tire of you watching them will rise like smoke into the air, wings opening softly and silently as they drift across the water to settle elsewhere, or glide on up with a slow wingbeat.

The neck is tucked in flight, making them harder to recognise. Solitary hunters, herons make messy stick nests in treetops and do so sociably; there can be up to ten nests per tree. The wingspan of a grey heron is slightly smaller than that of the whooper swan or mute swan but bigger than that of the cormorant. 'Cinera' in Latin means 'resembling ashes', after its colour.

2
3
4

GREY WAGTAIL

Motacilla cinerea

That 'yellow wagtail' that you've seen on the riverbank, dipping its tail as you swim by? The surprise is, in the ultimate misnomer, it's a grey wagtail, which live here all year, frequenting fast-flowing rivers and streams in summer but found all over – weirs, millstreams, bridges and reservoirs (their old country name was 'the water wagtail'). The yellow wagtail, which is yellow all over, comes only in summer and is rare. The grey wagtail is grey with a lemon yellow underside and a longer tail. Its wagging tail mirrors the commotion in the water it sits by.

MOORHEN

Gallinula chloropus

One of the most widespread waterbirds (along with mallard ducks), moorhens live near water, not on moors, and can be found around ponds, lakes, streams and rivers. Yellow legs and red beaks lend a cartoonish air to what are often perceived to be humorous birds. They will issue a *kuruk-kuruk* noisy call to warn other birds when swimmers approach, and may hide underwater themselves, holding on to vegetation. Moorhens spend a lot of time bobbing on the water; their feet are not webbed so they are not strong swimmers, but they are not strong fliers either and have to run to take off.

MUTE SWAN

Cygnus olor

The heaviest of all our birds, mute swans live in lakes and rivers. They need a lot of space to take off and land, running across water for 100 metres before becoming airborne. If you are lucky enough to be swimming when they take off, you will experience the avian equivalent of being under a Boeing 747. Swans nest in the banks. I have seen them eat fresh willow leaves, but they feed mainly on water plants, with their long necks reaching to the bottom (so if you see one do this, it is giving you a good indication of water depth). Mute swans have orange beaks, but the UK also has whooper swans and Bewick's swans, which have yellow beaks. Do not get between swans and their cygnets.

SWALLOW

Hirundo rustica

A summer bird with curved wings, a forked tail and long streamers. Swallows will catch insects on the water's surface, particularly at dusk, flying so low you can hear their feathers. Like swifts and sand martins, they are harbingers of summer and fly in clouds, murmuring this way and that over water. A wonderful bird to float underneath with arms outstretched, as it floats above doing the same, but on a thermal.

5
6
8
7

FRESHWATER FLORA

ALDER

Alnus glutinosa

Alder is a water-lover: if you see this tree, water is, or was, nearby. The alder does not rot when waterlogged; instead it turns stronger and harder.

These trees offer something to the swimmer year-round: their bright green leaf-burst and catkins mark the start of spring, while in autumn they remain stubbornly green when other trees turn. Unusually, male and female flowers are found on the same tree: the male catkins dangle pendulously, while the female cones are round and egg-like and sit in clusters.

Alder is an important pioneer species: it can populate places other trees can't go, fixing nitrogen in poor soils so others species may follow. It also stabilises river banks and provides food for caddis flies, stoneflies and water beetles.

COMMON REED

Phragmites australis

A limbo-land plant; beds of these large aquatic grasses are found in the margin between water and land, beside rivers, streams, lakes and across wetlands and marshes. I love the way common reed drains of colour in the autumn, and have such an animated shivering life. Usually reaching 2 metres tall, colonies can dominate to the exclusion of other species but are home to birds including bittern, warbler, cranes and starlings.

COMMON WATER-CROWFOOT

Ranunculus aquatilis

If you have a mental picture of Ophelia in a river, it is likely to be common water-crowfoot you see beneath her. A member of the buttercup family, crowfoot forms mats midstream in rivers, swishing green meadows of streamers bedecked with flowers that look like buttercups, but with five white petals and yellow centres. Crowfoot needs clean, fast-flowing water with a stony bed such as chalk streams. It is a sign of good river health and is eaten by water voles. Once established, common water-crowfoot can change the dynamic of the stream it's in, providing cover for fish fry, larvae and invertebrates, and slowing down a stream so that it drops sediment enabling other plants to take root.

CRACK WILLOW

Salix fragilis

Often found besides rivers, streams and lakes, these large trees like wet ground and can survive months with their feet in the water. The trunk of the crack willow develops deep cracks or fissures with age, and the tree provides a home to nesting birds and food for mute swans, who eat their young leaves. Like their cultivated cousin, the weeping willow, their roots help hold banks in place during floods.

1
2
4
3

MEADOWSWEET

Filipendula ulmaria

Lining the banks of rivers and lakes, meadowsweet has creamy frothy clusters of flowers – a little like elderflowers on cow parsley stems – which appear from May until the first frosts. The scent is variously described as caramel, sweet almond, marzipan, Germolene and Deep Heat, and it used to be (and still can be) strewn on floors for its aroma. It can be used in similar ways to elderflower in desserts or cordials, or blanched (to kill parasites) and made into meadowsweet tea.

ROWAN TREE

Sorbus aucuparia

Rowan or mountain ash are tough little trees that will be found on mountain swims across Europe, often in bent and wizened shapes as they lean over streams and their branches take on the shape of prevailing winds. They can live for up to 200 years, and in Celtic and Druidic traditions have often been seen as protective trees with a positive forcefield around them, so you may find them planted by houses, stone circles and at other auspicious sites, as well as marking the threshold between this world and the watery one.

Dangling clusters of red berries make them easy to identify, appearing in midsummer and sometimes still there on bare branches amidst winter snows, long after all leaves have fallen. In spring the cycle begins again with creamy white flowers, followed by delicate fern-shaped leaves that can provide welcome shade on exposed hillsides in summer.

WATER MINT

Mentha aquatica

Water mint grows on the margins of water, and if you don't see it first, you may smell it as you brush or crush your way past. Has pink globe flowers from July to October, and leaves similar to common mint, with serrated edges, but tinged with purple. The leaves, which can be harvested at any time of the year, are edible and have been used in herbal remedies for years. The young ones have the strongest flavour, and, steeped in hot water, make a fresh mint tea to drink on the banks. (Don't add it to your bankside water bottle without blanching, as wild water plants that have been below the waterline or had contact with grazing-animal poo may be hosting parasites such as liver fluke.)

YELLOW WATER LILY

Nuphar lutea

Some flowers open at dusk and stay open all night (these are pollinated by moths), others stay open all day. The water lily has its own timetable, opening in the morning and closing in the late to middle afternoon, so evening swimmers will miss their full display. The flowers give off a sweet scent that attracts bees and beetles. Damselflies and dragonflies use the spongy floating platforms to lay their eggs either in the leaves or in the water, depending on the species.

A rooted aquatic, water lilies stick their roots into the mud of slow-moving rivers and riverbeds and are a sign of good water health. Will bloom from mid spring to early autumn and, once fertilised, its stem begins to curl. Life goal: to come across a frog, sitting on one.

8

FRESHWATER INSECTS

CADDIS FLY

(from the order *Trichoptera*)

An insect commonly used to indicate aquatic ecosystem health. Caddis flies fly in swarms over the water, and will fly around lamps on the banks at night; but it's their larvae you are most likely to be able to identify as they spin themselves cases out of pieces of tiny stone, gravel and plants, wrap them in silk and live there underwater. There are over 200 species in the caddis fly family in the UK and different species use different materials: larvae in still water choose light materials, while larvae in running water use heavier stones that stop them being swept away by the current. They are also known as sedge flies. They can reach a size of 30 millimetres and at rest their wings are folded back along their body like a moth's.

COMMON BACKSWIMMER

Notonecta glauca

Also known as the great water boatman, the common backswimmer swims on its back under but near the surface of the water, grabbing insects from the water film. They are fast, with powerful hind legs allowing them to whip around in the water while the front legs grab prey. Air trapped in their abdomens helps them to float, in the same way as holding a float to the stomach helps swimmers kicking along on their backs. The lesser water boatman (*Corixa punctata*) rows on its front. Up to 20 millimetres long.

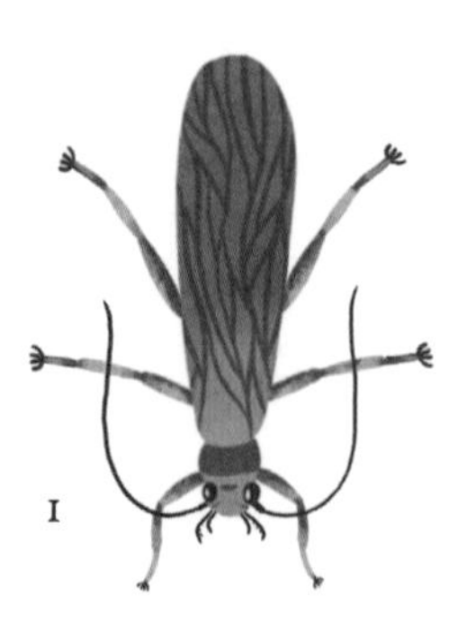

1

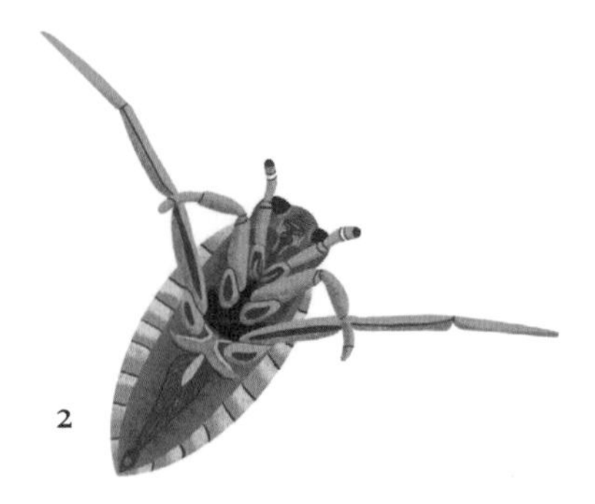

2

ENTOMOLOGICAL SIGNS OF WATER PURITY

I follow a blogger who makes poetic reports of hatches as we go through the season – 'the mayflies are rising with a good number one after another and then another and yet more in a steady flight all afternoon' – but for many of us, identifying insects is not easy, even when we see them clinging to grass stems along the riverbanks rather than buzzing fast about our heads.

There are three particular insects that are useful to learn as they are all super-sensitive to water quality: the stone fly, caddis fly and mayfly. These three bugs (all big enough to be visible to the naked eye) are like the canaries in the coal mine; they cannot survive their life cycle in polluted water, so their presence is a good bioindicator of water purity. (However, absence of them does not necessarily mean that the water quality is poor – there might be other reasons such as flow rate or temperature that make the water inhospitable.)

While I am still a long way away from being able to throw out lines like 'the breeding season for nettle weevils seems to be in full swing', I hope this short field guide will encourage you to join me in the game of 'match the hatch' or 'what's that fly in the sky?'.

DAMSELFLY

Zygoptera

When it's mating season in midsummer, the lily pads on my river start to look like floating platforms full of miniature cranes; the green female forms the base, her tail laying eggs in the leaf while the blue male damselfly acts as the tower, his wings the jib. This is one of the clues that they are damselflies, not dragonflies: female dragonflies lay their eggs alone, dipping their tails in the water. While they share their green and turquoise colourways, other ways to distinguish damselflies from dragonflies are: damselflies are small and rest with their wings folded together on their back, while dragonflies are bigger and rest with their wings spread. Damselflies flutter, while dragonflies show stronger, more purposeful flight.

EMPEROR DRAGONFLY

Anax imperator

A fossilised giant dragonfly with a wingspan of four and a half metres was found four miles from my home in Somerset; imagine *that* fluttering on to your hand after a swim. It was a relic of the swampy Carboniferous period, 359 to 299 million years ago. The dragonflies buzzing around the same landscape now are harder to spot, but are still attracted to the marshy edges of waterways – they like slow-moving ponds and lakes, with well vegetated edges. They are most active at midday; look out for them on warm sunny days (above 16 degrees) between May and October. July is a peak month. You can hear them too: tiny little guiro sounds, like a soft wooden ratchet.

The emperor dragonfly is the most substantial of the UK dragonflies and arguably the most beautiful in colour; the male has an apple green body and sky blue tail with a dark central line, and the female is an all-over more low-profile green. Their average size is 78 millimetres, the length of a little or ring finger. They are hugely territorial and will fly at you to get you to move on, and will often fly back to the same perch and patrol, hungrily, for hours at a time. They have two pairs of independently operated wings that allow them to fly with astounding agility; they can fly backwards, at speed, execute sharp turns and hover like a helicopter.

Dragonfly nymphs can remain in a pond for up to seven years. Swimmers with goggles can track them down on reeds and watch them crawl around underwater.

MAYFLY

(from the order *Ephemeroptera*)

Mayflies are one of three insects that are particularly sensitive to water pollution and, along with caddis fly and stonefly, are commonly used as a biomarker of good water purity. They hatch en masse in the late afternoon and evening and rise and fall in plumes above the water, in swarms that you may swim through. As the name suggests, this is usually around May and June. The mayfly adult can be identified by its three long swooshy thread-like tails and large clear-veined wings that fold together at rest. Nymphs live for a year or two in silt in the water and are famous for living for just one day on the wing – it can actually be longer, but once above water they do not eat or drink, so there is limited time for mating to take place. Found in streams and the edges of lakes.

3
4
5

POND SKATER

Gerridae

Often seen in groups, pond skaters skate over the surface of lakes, ponds and slow-moving rivers, with legs dimpling but not breaking the surface. They eat dead or dying bugs on the water's surface and as winter approaches they produce young that fly away to hibernate, and re-emerge the following April. About 15 millimetres long.

STONEFLY

(from the order *Plecoptera*)

An insect used as a biomarker of a healthy body of water because of its sensitivity to pollution. Stonefly larvae cling to the undersides of pebbles, cobbles and wood on the beds of fast-flowing streams and rivers (do not disturb by turning them over), particularly where there is shade and high dissolved oxygen levels. Stonefly live on the wing for two to three weeks between April and June. There are thirty-four species of the family in the UK and they are usually various cowpat colours: dull, dark, and drab brown, yellow, or sometimes green. They have two pairs of transparent wings with veins that are folded back at rest, and two long tail filaments. They are reluctant to fly and prone to crash-landing. Up to 3 centimetres long.

WATER MEASURER

Hydrometra stagnorum

One of the thinnest insects on earth, the water measurer is found on the vegetated margins of lakes, ponds and slow streams. Eats water fleas and mosquito larvae, for which we can be thankful. (Water fleas themselves you will not see; they are the size of a full stop and see-through.) About 13 millimetres long.

WATER SPIDER

Argyroneta aquatica

An anomaly, this spider lives underwater, in a diving-bell web anchored to plants and filled with air brought down from the surface in the tiny hairs on its legs and abdomen (it is also called the diving bell spider). This gives these creatures a mercurial appearance and a bubble to breathe in underwater. They may be spotted in weedy lakes and ponds, and slow streams. They are carnivores and feed on water mites, water boatmen and various types of larvae, with fangs sharp enough to make dinner from tadpoles.

WHIRLIGIG BEETLE

Gyrinidae

These small shiny black beetles whirl around like mad dancers on the surface of ponds, lakes and slow rivers. The dance is a hunt for small insects to eat; they can also dive to feed but have to cling to plants to avoid pinging back up to the surface. Surprisingly good fliers, they can travel from pond to pond. In winter whirligigs burrow into the mud and they hibernate till spring.

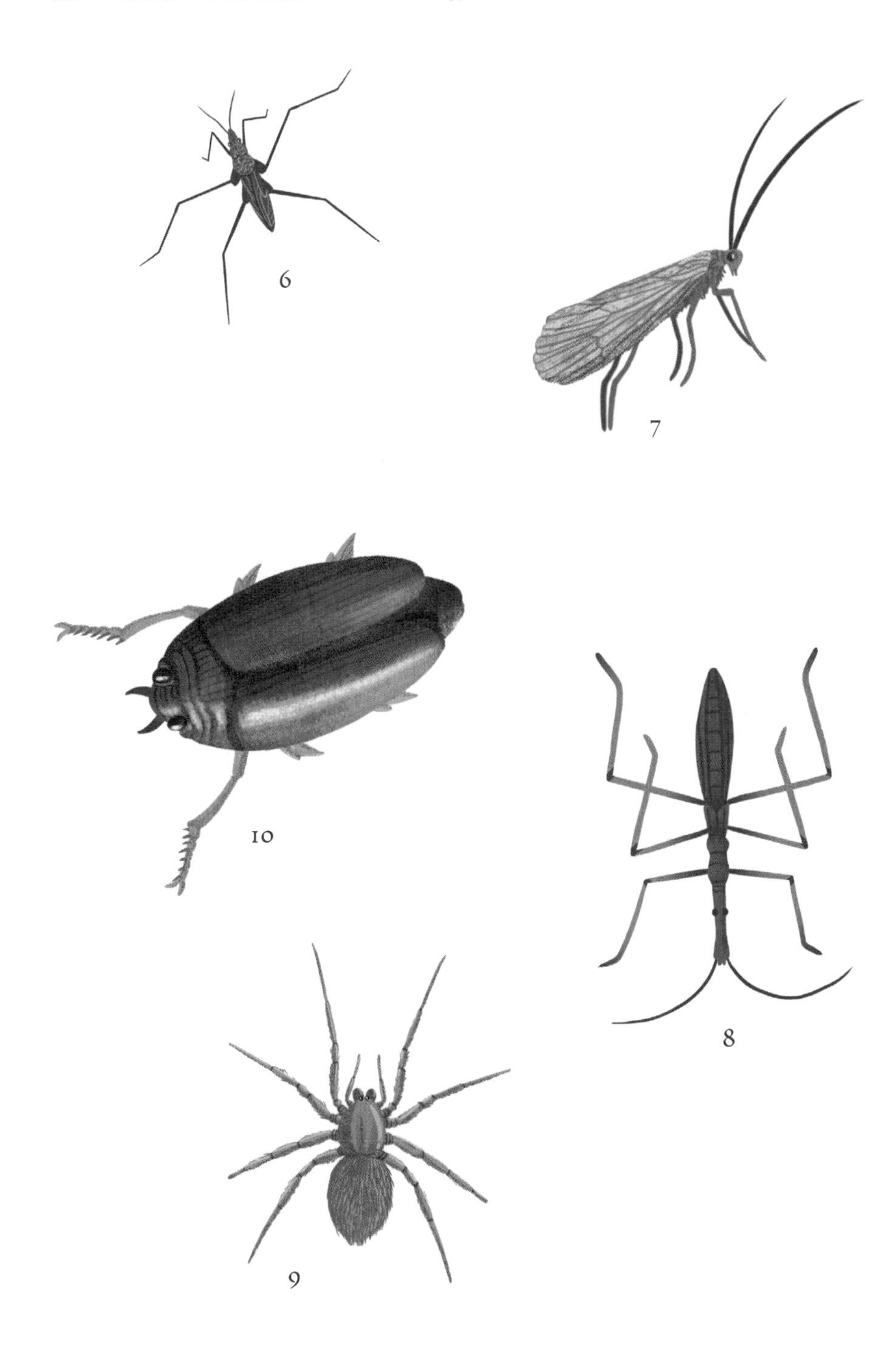
6
7
10
8
9

CHAPTER 3

UNDERSTANDING SEAS

'It has a unique fascination.
It's a living thing. You never know
what sort of conditions you are going
to meet out there'

ALISON STREETER,
43-time Channel swimmer,
on the sea[1]

THE SEA HOLDS SIMPLE joys. Squinting into bright light with sea spray in our faces and the horizon in front of us gives humanity something so strong people have been self-medicating with the sea for ever. The buoyancy of it, the ions in the air, the constant swell and sway, push and pull: people form lifelong relationships with the sea and its uplift.

Beach swimming is not the whole story: the sea is also the landscape of some of swimming's biggest adventures. There are crossings to make, distances to achieve, caves and coastlines to explore and experiences to have: night swimming in phosphorescence, snorkelling over kelp forests and coral. There are animals to meet, sea gardens to cruise over, islands to circumnavigate and rock features to explore. 'Waves can turn the sea into the most spectacular and thrilling of wild swims, a natural fairground ride of wildness and surging energy,' wrote Lynne Roper, an early member of the OSS team. Lynne loved the sea, how it would become unmanageable when a big set came through, or there was a sudden collision between a wave reflected from a reef or cliff with an incoming one. She thrived on having fun on the limits.

Some swimmers embrace its power and unruliness from the start; the feeling of their own insignificance is what they show up for. Being knocked off their feet and nudged about the ocean: it all helps create that sense of awe.

Others struggle with its essential lessons, which are all around control and our lack of it – if you want a practice ground for dealing with the unexpected when it happens, for choosing one thought over another, for adopting a learning stance in the face of disheartening reality, then the open sea is there for you. Whether it's waves chopping up your lovely rhythmic stroke and making it hard to breathe, a tide pulling you crossly sideways, or a huge barrel jellyfish looming up beneath you as you swim across a bay, the sea has many ways to make it clear that it is bigger and stronger than us, and that the only thing in our control is our response to that.

To be a good sea swimmer takes experience that you can only acquire in the water. Big wave surfer (and swimmer) Al Mennie calls it 'time served'. We can educate ourselves on the theory – the tides, currents, waves, chop, races and local weather. But the only way to become good sea swimmers is to serve our time, to develop a feeling for a huge body of water constantly on the bob and swell. Al has forty-one years of experience of his home beach to draw on – and countless other experiences – and says it's still impossible to have enough information to be 100 per cent sure what the water will do when he enters it.

ENDLESS VARIATIONS: SNAPSHOTS AND STORIES

We are in wetsuits at Birling Gap car park in Sussex, grabbing a quick coffee from an otherwise deserted café before we walk across the undulating white chalk cliffs of the Seven Sisters and swim back alongside them. The sea is the colour of bonfire smoke (it's that time of year) and the water is murky: a little chalk goes a long way. The cliffs here recede 30 to 40 centimetres a year, and from the cliff the sea has coloured bands. We are facing a 4-kilometre swim in big swell and we will not complete it, not today – the swim ends with us scrambling out, cold and seasick, a Sister or two short of completion. A wave butting us up the bottom is the final indignity, knocking a few of us on to all fours as we scramble out to clamber home along the narrow shoreline. Our bare feet manage to be both numb and painful at the same time. It doesn't matter, it is an adventure to remember. There are always adventures to be had at the coast; sea swimming allows you to reach places and see perspectives no one else can: around the wild back of islands, underneath rock arches, into caves.

Another day, another swim: this time we are swimming in the lights from a power station, in a brown sea with a grey sky. Not every sea swim is a postcard: this is an industrial sea swim, like swimming through the black legs of a pier or within Dover docks. Colours of cliff, sand and water change around the coast: some beaches are miles of mud at low tide, a lot of the Jurassic Coast is red. I remember one swim off a red sand beach that shelved so sharply mackerel came right to the edge.

The liminal space of the coast is permanently entrancing, with drastic weather and constant surprises like upturned warehouses of sea creatures dumped at random by departing tides: a thick bed of razor clams like giants' toenails, bleached grey hills of starfish and brittlestars, a display of silky furbelows recently torn from their holdfasts, lines of sailors in the wind now dried out and bleached by the sun, like a line of clear plastic bottletops.

Our behaviour changes in this transitional zone. In any car I've ever been in on the way to the coast, 'I can see the sea!' is cried out in triumph; we're on the way to the edge, about to take a dip in our own freedom! We expect it to be glorious. And it is: there is the sheer joyous buoyancy of seawater lifting us and the sheer buoyant joy of swimming in waves and getting it right: diving under, coming up, sweeping the hair out of your eyes. The sea draws us back again and again. Part of the magic is the constant change of light and shape, and the resonances between one form and another. I like smashing through the foamy walls of water at surf beaches, floating on my back and looking at the sky scud past, treading water by a rock with clusters of barnacles like constellations of stars. What swimmer hasn't had a summer day at the beach where they took 'just one more swim'?

Sometimes I've stayed out too long and come home feeling like my nipples have frostbite, or emerged to find bags, dresses and jumpers floating out to sea on the rising tide. In the Scilly Isles the sand is white, the sea clear and the water turquoise: jumping off rocks, we were so fascinated by the whirls of bubbles we created that we didn't notice we were violently shivering. Out and dressed, we flattened ourselves on hot stones, soaking up the sunshine while tuning in to the sound of a blowhole: deep sucky noises and then what sounded like the low bellow of a whale sonar.

Part of the enchantment is that tides constantly change things. The Corryvreckan whirlpool rises and falls with it. On the boat out we saw patchwork water: ruffled patches, smooth patches, strange eddies and patches with fast-running edges. We saw fat seals lying on bladderwrack rocks bleached by sunshine and a stag standing on the skyline. We made it across in the brief 30 minutes for which the whirlpool stills, and arrived at the other side breathless and euphoric, called quickly back to the boat before the tide started running.

As an inland dweller I welcome holiday opportunities to get familiar with stretches of coast and what lies beneath. Birds become companions; I remember one shag riding a green foamy wave past me, looking for fish. Sheltered bays and inlets can make good training grounds: in Greece the only beach 'away from it all' was a naturist one, so, naked but for goggles, I swam back and forth and forth and back, day after day, training for something. On holiday on the Lizard Peninsula one Easter I went in the opposite direction and wore everything as I started work on summer fitness. Over the week the seabed grew familiar with clumps of seaweed and rocks becoming signposts and markers of distance.

The sea holds big marathon challenges for those that way inclined. I supported my friend Colin Hill swimming the English Channel. He was poorly and the day started with him hunched over a short privet hedge in a motel carpark at 3am, in Crocs, cargo pants and an OSS hoodie, being sick. It ended better, after 10 hours 30 minutes of flawless metronomic swimming, his pace not faltering across 26 miles of flat green slate sea. I jumped in to swim the final stretch with him and there might have been tears in his goggles as we hauled out onto the rocks to celebrate.

My point is that while rivers invite A to B swims and lakes invite distance, the sea puts all the ideas out there in front of you: rocks to swim to, things to swim over, crossings to make, times to go. Around the seasons and around the world there are endless variations on offer. There is always the frisson of the unexpected. I am going through a seagrass and kelp phase at the moment: fascinated about where to find them, what they look like, how they might save the planet. And also, simply, how they look and where they can be found on the sheltered side of islands, swaying glossily like the rumps of a team of galloping horses.

UNDERSTANDING WAVES

The first and best thing that you can do when contemplating a sea swim is to take the time to observe the sea and watch a few sets of waves. See how they are breaking, who's out there, what is happening in the sky? Take in the ocean's rhythm, and get a feeling for yourself too: is it within your comfort zone? Arrive somewhere mentally as well as physically.

Once we made it to Portreath, Cornwall so I could have a boogie board. When our boys were small excursions sometimes ended prematurely, the maximum number of hurdles cleared when we'd made it as far as (but not beyond) a car park. We arrived worn out. Outside the car the wind howled and slapped my face with rain and the sea looked hideous: big, grey and surly. I didn't fancy it at all but 'we'd made it this far' and other bodyboarders were in, so, not really paying attention, I strode down to the ocean with a self-conscious breeziness, got in, flung myself round to catch the first wave purely as a defence mechanism against being thundered over by it, and was immediately slammed unceremoniously on the sea floor. I stumbled out as fast as I could, a mess of hair and snot and sand and terror, back past the beachgoers I'd passed seconds earlier, my shoulder feeling torn and my heart hammering.

As I changed and the blood thundering around me began to slow down, my husband got chatting to a guy who turned out to be a pro coach. The coach had come down to watch a training session; 'The recent storm has drawn out a real field,' he said, pointing to all the past and present UK bodyboarding champs on the break to the right of the beach. No, we hadn't seen the sign saying 'Locals Only'. No, we hadn't known there was such a heavy, hollow break bouncing off the harbour wall it had its own name ('The Vortex'). And no, I will never use social cues to overcome instinctive fear again.

That, by the way, was a dumping wave, and it is one to avoid (see page 70).

TYPES OF WAVE

Waves are shaped by a combination of factors – swell, the sea floor, wind and tide – so they are constantly changing from one hour to the next, and one day to the next. Waves occur when swell (an ocean's unbroken waves) hits an obstruction – a beach, reef or shallow sea floor – making the water rise.

Swell is created by wind blowing on the ocean surface. Big storms a long way off lead to swell organising itself before it reaches a shore, and the more organised it becomes, the longer the intervals between waves, and the bigger they become. If you go for a swim in the days after a storm you can still see its effect in the water, an echo of what's passed still present in the bounciness and energy of the sea at the shore.

As a general rule, waves tend to be bigger when the tide is on the push (approaching high tide), and smaller when the tide is falling. Researchers at the University of Plymouth found that, an hour before high tide, wave energy peaks (making them bigger and/or most powerful). Waves are slower and less powerful around low tide. Just bear in mind that a rising tide may have bigger waves but it will push you back to shore; a falling tide may have smaller waves but will pull you away from the beach.

Standing on a beach you will almost certainly underestimate how big the waves will feel when you are in. Identifying wave types gives useful familiarity, but nature is not neat; one stretch of beach can give you three types of waves within an hour, barrelling you in a dumpy one, giving a great body-surf in a fat mushy one, then having several spill past you.

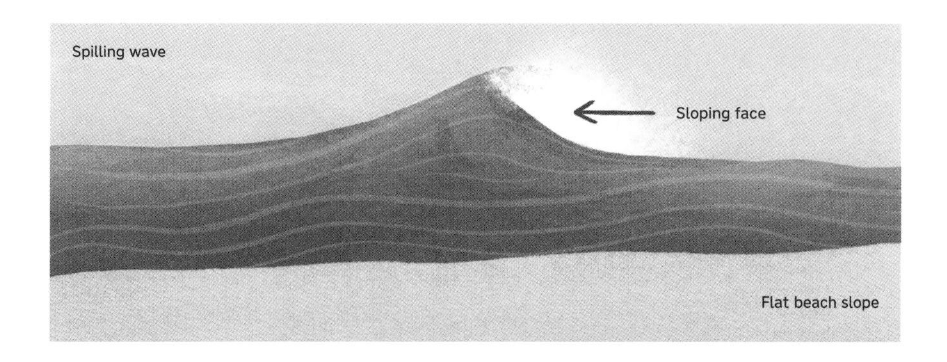

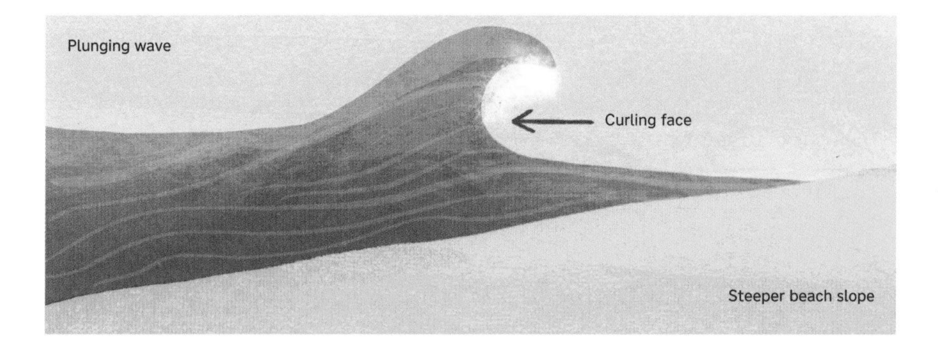

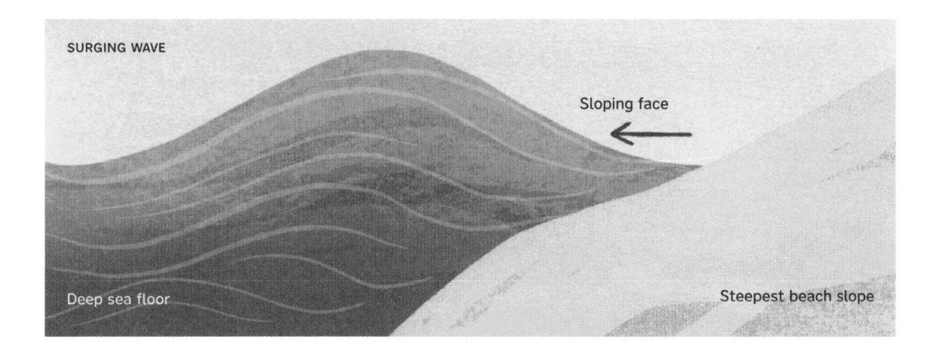

TYPES OF WAVE

SPILLING WAVES

Spilling waves occur on gently sloping beaches, and have little force. They are quite safe, gentle waves to swim in. The crest either spills over as they break or the wave just collapses back down on itself into a pile of bubbles and whitewater. If not too mushy they are good for swimmers and beginner surfers. You can typically bob about in these sorts of waves, ducking under them or swimming through them without much difficulty.

PLUNGING WAVES, DUMPING WAVES AND SHORE BREAKS

Plunging waves take on the classic wave shape seen in surf logos; when big swell hits a reef or shallower water, it rises quickly to a steep crest, with the tip eventually overtaking the base of the wave, dropping into the trough when it breaks. When the wave is at any angle to the beach it will 'peel' rather than break all in one go, creating a good surfing wave (called a tube, barrel or green room).

Plunging waves break with more energy than spilling waves, so are either more intimidating or more fun depending on your viewpoint. You may be able to jump over them, duck-dive under them or swim through them. The bigger and stronger the plunging wave the more it will churn the water underneath it, so if duck-diving beneath them, dive deep enough to be beneath it (see page 72).

Plunging waves become more difficult and dangerous for swimmers in two circumstances, both of which it's a good idea to avoid. If plunging waves are parallel with the shore they may break all in one go, making a 'dumping wave' where all the energy in the wave releases in one violent impact. You can hear a dumping wave from the crashing sound they make. Dumping waves are not safe for swimmers; they break with force and impact and can throw you to the bottom, causing injuries. If you get stuck in one, curl into a ball and hug your knees. As well as breaking with great force, dumping waves can result in a strong and highly localised backwash current as the water returns to the sea. This can make it hard to exit the water.

Dumping waves become 'shore breaks' when the steep rise in the sea floor happens at the shore. In this situation you may be thrown against the ocean floor when the wave dumps, causing serious injuries and spinal injuries. When you walk down a beach for a swim be aware that if you descend a steep shelf or step off a steep shelf into deep water, that sudden change in height could lead to a shore break at a different stage of the tide. Shingle beaches are typically steeper than sand, and the shingle beaches of the south and east coasts, such as Chesil Beach, Shakespeare Beach in Dover and Brighton beach, all experience shore breaks.

ROUGH EXITS – TIPS FOR DUMPING WAVES

Encountering dumping waves when I come to get out of a swim has happened to me more than once. The first time was entering the water at one end of Brighton beach to swim pier to pier after a huge storm. Our primary concern was the difficulty getting in past the breakers and out into swell, where we could start to swim. The secondary concern was the huge rollers coming up behind us as we made our way to the other end of the beach. Both those concerns turned out to be nothing compared to how to get out. When we reached the exit we found waves dumping with explosive force on the pebbled shore, with a deafening backwash raking through the pebbles. We hovered there in the swell, watching the shore and assessing our options.

If you're faced with a rough exit like our one in Brighton, try these strategies:

- Look left and right: is there a more gently shelving part of the beach where it looks easier to exit, and can you get to it?
- Is it an option to tread water and wait for conditions to change without getting too cold? Is it necessary to signal or call for help?
- Are there lulls between big sets?

- What is the surface – sand or shingle/pebble? If there is someone to throw you your shoes in the water, this will help you get out on shingle or pebble.

- Is it possible to land behind the breaking wave? One option may be to wait for a smaller set of waves, and then be carried in on the back of a wave in a vertical position, putting your feet down so it breaks in front of you, not with you in it. Then, run as fast as possible with backwash grabbing at your ankles before the next wave breaks. The key here is to choose your wave wisely and then go for it – this is not a time to process foot pain.

SURGING WAVES

The third type of wave, surging waves, are not safe to swim in, and best given a very wise berth on the shore. A surging wave forms where the sea floor goes from deep to shallow very quickly, for example where big swell arrives at a steep beach, some rocks or a harbour wall. A surging wave does not have time to form a crest, so instead of all that energy rising up it surges forward in a strong swash and then backwash. Surging waves can look quite friendly but they are not: a surging wave can knock people off their feet and pull them from quite high up the beach (much higher than you might expect) into the sea.

Remember waves are not uniform: playing in foamy swash after or during a storm carries the danger of being tugged back to sea when a rogue wave comes in and knocks you off your feet.

HOW TO SWIM UNDER AND THROUGH WAVES

On a beach with surf there will be a 'breaker zone' where waves break. Swimmers commonly look to get through that zone into the calmer water beyond, where they can swim parallel to the shore.

To get past big waves, swim underneath them. When they're 5–6 feet away, take a big breath and dive down beneath the turbulence and swim forward underwater, letting the wave pass overhead – you will be able to feel and hear it pass over. Come up, breathe, and prepare for the next. Keep your eyes on the wave.

In open water races competitive swimmers will hold the sea floor, digging their fingers into the sand and using this handhold to propel themselves forward as a wave passes overhead. Holding on to the sea floor stabilises your position.

Where surf is still shallow, Australian surf swimmers use a technique called 'porpoising'. Leaping forward for the bottom, they hold the sea floor, bringing their knees to their chest and feet to the floor, then when the wave passes they 'explode' back out of the water, over the sea, taking a breath and going back down again, repeating this motion until it's deep and then starting to front crawl.

When making your way back to shore in waves, swim and look back (under one arm every stroke if doing front crawl) to see what's coming. If the wave isn't breaking, it'll move you towards the shore. If it is, it may be better to turn and dive back under a breaking wave.

WAVE PERIOD AND NEGOTIATING WIPEOUTS

The bigger the waves, the bigger the chance that you'll get wiped out. If you do get wiped out, there are some basic principles that will help you to recover:

- Take a breath if there's time.
- Stay calm: relax and go with the turbulence, or, if you prefer, curl up into the foetal position. Don't fight it. Being relaxed will help your oxygen last longer.
- As the turbulence lessens, push up to the surface and be ready to deal with the next wave.
- If there's another wave on top of you, grab a quick breath and dive under the wave.

Waves come in sets (although not necessarily in fives or sevens or twelves). If you're in the middle of a big set, stay calm; a smaller set will appear and give you the chance to get back into control. If you feel shaky after a wipeout, get out of the water and relax on the beach till you get your strength back.

Where there is a good amount of time between waves (the wave period) you can recover between breakers, but if headed away from shore you can get caught in the washing machine zone, where you are tumbled over by one wave and just coming up for air when the next is upon you. In this situation, take control, and very purposefully head one way or the other: back to shore, or out the back, beyond the breakers into calmer water. Just don't stay in the hectic zone with waves breaking on you, being churned about by them, taking on water, growing panicked.

SWASH, BACKWASH AND MOVING SAND

When a wave breaks, water is washed up the beach. This is called the swash, and it's often a foaming layer of water. When the water runs back down the beach, that is called the backwash. Backwash runs along the bottom, seawards, beneath the incoming waves – when you stand on the shore and waves excavate the sand beneath your feet, this is backwash in action. The strength of the current depends on the volume of returning water.

Backwash might be what's meant when people refer to 'undertow', but it won't literally pull you under – it runs along the bottom of the shore, but you are buoyant, and will pop up to the surface.

Swash and backwash keep beaches and sandbars permanently on the move. Waves tend to come in at a slight angle to a beach, while backwash flows straight back to the sea, drawn by gravity. So in effect, materials are being zigzagged along the coast. When lifeguards put flags up and down the beach they are marking the safest area. One reason this area moves is because the sandbanks themselves are moving – they can stay in a similar area for a few days or a week, or change from one day to the next. They can also collapse, causing flash rips. Storms can remove and relocate whole beaches.

ROGUE WAVES

'Rogue waves' are unusually large waves, and it's good to remember that these can occur – a serene post-swim moment perched on a rock looking at the water coming in and out of Zawn Pyg at Land's End had a very uncomposed finish when a rogue wave came in, scattering three of us over barnacled rocks. The British National Institute of Oceanography has suggested that 1 in 23 waves will be twice the average height, and one wave in 1,175 will be three times the average height.[2]

LOCATING PLACID SEAS AND SURF BEACHES

Surf is unequally distributed around coastlines. The size and frequency of waves are due to the distance the swell has travelled, so any coast with a protective land mass between it and open sea is likely to be more favourable for swimmers. (Conversely, anywhere uninterrupted ocean meets land is likely to have the greatest swell and possibly the biggest surf).

In UK terms, this translates to more placid swim conditions being found on beaches on the east coast and facing the English Channel, all of which have smaller tides, smaller waves, and flatter seas. Some of our biggest surf beaches are on north coast of Cornwall (exposed to great Atlantic swells that roll in from as far away as America), and the east coast of Scotland, with its North Sea swell exposure.

TIDAL POOLS

Tidal pools are often found in places where conditions are rough. In the UK many were built in the 1950s, but some go back to Victorian times. The pools can provide a window into the great ocean, and you will likely share your swim with seaweed, sea anemones, starfish, crabs and maybe the odd fish, carried in by the tide. The Cape Peninsula in South Africa also has a stunning chain of pools built and expanded at similar periods, and the pools are now maintained as wild spaces. Many have resident octopuses, and swimmers also find psychedelic nudibranchs on the pool walls, and swim with starfish, flamboyant anemone, and fanworms that look like purple feather dusters.

Tidal pools will generally be invisible and unswimmable at high tide because they're submerged, chaotic and confused when the sea is level with their edges, and then exposed and swimmable at lower tides. On neap tides water might not be refreshed with the tide, and you may find cloudier water.

Tidal pools are also found on beaches that have a very shallow profile, where swimmers would otherwise have a very long shallow walk to reach anything deep enough to swim in – Walpole Bay Pool at Margate and North Berwick in Scotland are examples of this.

UNDERSTANDING TIDES

'What if there were no moon', asked poet and astronomer Rebecca Elson, who had a galactic view of life, where 'space might cup itself around a planet, like your palm around a stone.' I struggle with mental rotation; imagining multiple planets spinning on their axis while they spin around each other with the ocean lurching towards them makes me as dizzy as a ride at the fairground. However, I have learnt (by rote) to embed some simple connections between space and the sea so I am able to look up at the night sky and picture high seas on a distant shore.

HIGH TIDE, LOW TIDE, SLACK TIDE AND EBBING AND FLOODING TIDES

The sea is generally either rising towards high tide or falling towards a low tide. A sea at low tide is very different to the same sea at high tide. For one thing, the view changes: you may see miles of damp sand and exposed rocks versus, at high tide, a tiny beach of dry sand.

The water itself is different: it can seem sparser and flatter at low tide, while high tide seas 'swell and billow like the sails on a galleon'.[3]

Tides are particularly important to UK swimmers as we have one of the biggest tidal ranges in the world, with the seas rising and falling up to 15 or 16 metres twice a day. In some locations in the world the sea remains in the same place all the time (the Mediterranean, Baltic and Caribbean seas). Not here: the beaches of the Bristol Channel are near my home, and there the sea retreats 1.5 miles (2.4 kilometres). As the tides move in and out swims change: islands are drawn closer and then moved further away, rock arches uncovered and submerged, the seabed itself drawn into snorkelling distance then lowered away again. Offshore rocks may protect a coast from larger swell, until such time as they are breached, when suddenly conditions may get more exciting. In Greek mythology, the saying 'between a rock and a hard place' refers to a space between a cliff and a whirlpool – but it could equally refer to a swimmer at the base of a cliff who suddenly finds themselves in untempered swell.

Here are some general rules, but *everything* varies with location – the length of slack tides, when rips appear, when there are dumping waves or periods of calm. 'What state is the tide?' is a sea swimmer's first question, not an answer to anything.

KEY TIDAL TERMS

High tide or high water is the highest point of the tide. High tide (HT) may mean a considerably shorter walk to the sea, which is a real bonus in cruel weather. In summer, an afternoon high tide can also mean an appreciably warmer sea, where the tide has travelled across sand or pebbles warmed by the sun. Where a high tide collides with a cliff base, conditions can get swirly as incoming waves boomerang off solid surfaces, colliding with incoming swell and creating lurching chaos.

Low tide or low water is the lowest point of the tide. Low tides (LT) may be the only phase of the tide where a beach has sand. It can mean exposed caves, rock features, tidal pools and accessible bays (if you can walk around headlands that are otherwise sea-locked). Low tide generally means lower, flatter water conditions, which may be the optimum tide to swim across a bay and back. Islands that are offshore at high tide may now be connected to the mainland by a tombolo or sand spit, and closer to you (meaning a shorter swim). Rock outcrops may emerge from the sea, good to swim around and snorkel beside.

Slack tide or slack water is the period of time either side of high and low tide when the water – which is generally always rising or falling – is 'slack' and barely moves in or out. Slack tide may mean there are fewer currents, which can be preferable for swims. For a short island or offshore rock feature, I will generally swim at slack low tide, timing it so that by the time I reach the island and am on my way back the tide is starting to rise and push me back to shore again.

A flooding tide is when the tide is coming in. A flooding tide pushes you back to shore, but is associated with bigger waves. Something to consider with a flooding tide is getting back to where you started – if you walk around a headland to a bay via wet sand and the tide rises, you may not be able to walk back.

An ebbing tide is when the sea is falling, and the tide is going out. An ebbing tide tends to be quieter, with smaller waves, but will make it harder to get back to shore than to swim out. Falling tides can intensify currents around the corners of islands and rocks, but will also reveal seaweed and underwater features.

Tidal range is the difference between high tide and low tide. It is a factor in wild conditions and varies around the world but the more water that is sloshing in and out, the more powerful currents will be. Smaller ranges have the potential to lead to calmer swimming.

TWO TIDES A DAY

Most places have a 'semi-diurnal tidal range', which means they experience two high tides and two low tides a day.

Our tides are tied to the moon and a lunar day (the time it takes for a specific point on the Earth to rotate to the same point under the moon) is 24 hours and 50 minutes, while a solar day (the time it takes for a specific point on the Earth to rotate to the same point under the sun) is 24 hours. The moon causes two tidal bulges in a day, when it is either side of the Earth, and they are 12 hours 25 minutes apart. What this means is that successive high tides are generally 12 hours 25 minutes apart.

So if you want to know what the tide will be tomorrow a useful rule of thumb is to add 50 minutes (so today's high tide at 6 a.m. will likely be tomorrow's 6.50 a.m. high tide). There will be some local variation but it's a good basic guide.

MONTHLY CYCLES: SPRINGS AND NEAPS

The planets have monthly as well as daily spin cycles: it takes the moon 27 days, 7 hours and 43 minutes to orbit the Earth.

During this orbit there are two points when the sun and moon line up with the Earth, at which point their gravitational pull on the oceans combine to give us spring tides. 'Spring' here means spring forward, not the season. Spring tides occur at full moon and new moon, approximately every two weeks.

Neap tides happen seven days after spring tides on half-moons. I remember this as 'full moon, full tide'. When a full moon is shining in my bedroom window at night, I like being able to picture what the sea is doing elsewhere, brimful on springs. The half-moon is a halfway house, giving wishy-washy neaps, while no moons are as committed and absolute in their being as full moons, so bringing about the same full (spring) tides.

Spring tides are like slightly exuberant friends: their highs are higher and their lows are lower than your more moderate, balanced neap tides. With more ground to cover, spring tides give the sea wilder, more volatile excitement and energy. They also expose more of the beach at low tide if you are beachcombing.

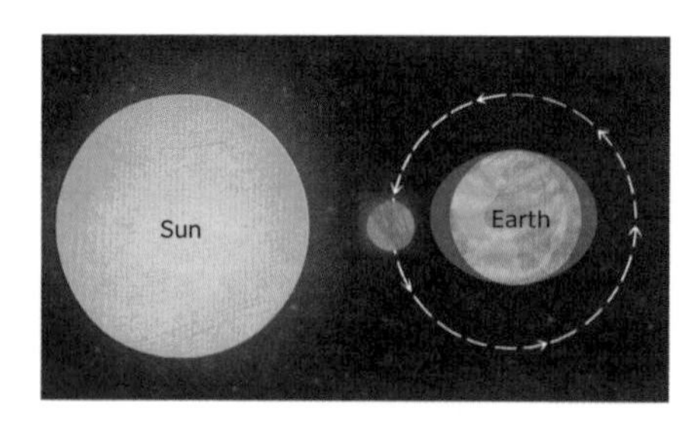

NEW MOON, SPRING TIDE

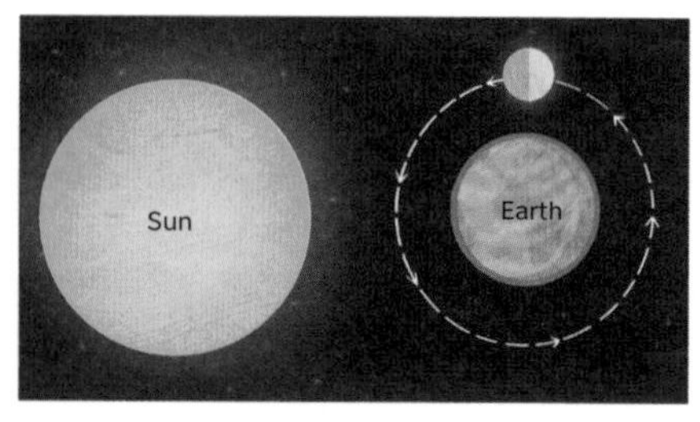

THIRD QUARTER MOON, NEAP TIDE

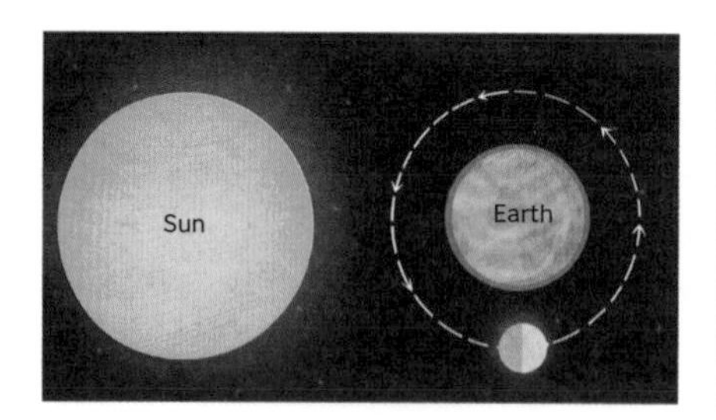

FIRST QUARTER MOON, NEAP TIDE

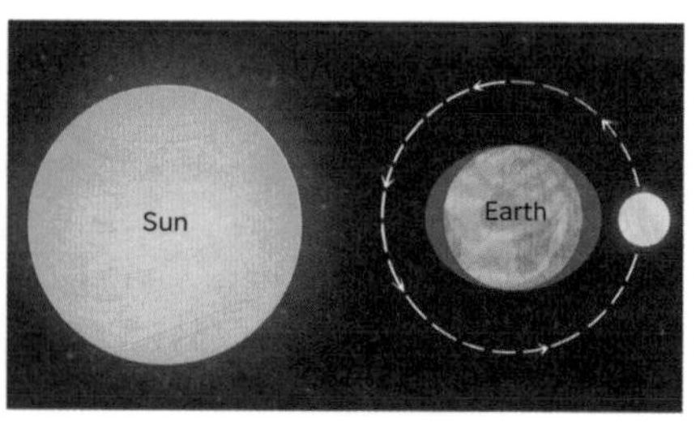

FULL MOON, SPRING TIDE

SPRING TIDES OCCUR ON THE FULL MOON AND NEW MOON

EQUINOXES AND SUPERMOONS: ASTRONOMICAL EVENTS AND ASTRONOMICAL TIDES

The equinoxes, defined by day and night being equally long, give us the biggest springs of the year.

At the spring and autumn equinox the sun is directly above the equator and closer to the Earth than at other points in the year. These 'equinox tides' give us 'astronomical tides' (boom boom): very high springs that run faster than others, and reach places others don't (they can, for example, pull debris into the water from higher up the shore and banks). At the equinoxes day and night are equally long.

The summer and winter solstices do not have the same effect on the tides. The solstices mark the longest and shortest days of the year, and at this point the Earth is at maximum tilt in relation to the sun, so there is less of a line-up between sun, moon and Earth, and spring tides are not so big.

Supermoons also give us astronomical tides: they occur when the moon is closer to Earth, when as well as looking bigger it exerts a stronger lunar pull.

RULE OF TWELFTHS

Another thing you may want to consider on a sea swim is what phase of the tide it is, which alters how fast the sea is moving in and out. The 'rule of twelfths' expresses the fact that the tide does not ebb and flood at a linear rate, but moves at different speeds at different stages.

Starting with a low tide, the tide starts flooding slowly and then picks up pace, reaching maximum pace in the third and fourth hour, and then slowing back down. Once it has reached high tide, this process reverses: the ebbing tide starts slowly, reaches maximum pace in the third and fourth hours, and then ebbs more slowly before becoming slack around the second high tide of the day.

The rule of twelfth is useful to know as a swimmer:

- When the tide is running slowly – around either high or low tide – conditions will be more settled, as the sea is at its most stable with less current, making a more approachable swimming window. It is almost still at slack water, the length of which varies around the coast, it can be 20–30 minutes or an hour.
- The middle hours between high and low tide are when the water will be rising or falling the fastest, and more water moving results in stronger currents. This will be even more dramatic when there are spring tides.

THE RULE OF TWELFTHS

ALL THE EXCEPTIONS TO THE RULES

• Tide charts use generalised locations, but the tide at a specific place will be influenced by its shoreline – for example, a tide may be magnified in a funnel-shaped bay or estuary.

• Some places have double high tides – where high tide is reached, ebbs slightly, then peaks again – and some have double low waters, where low tide is reached, floods slightly, then drops again. Double high tides are found in the Solent and Southampton; at the Beaulieu River on the Solent the second high tide is two hours after the first. Double low waters are found at Weymouth.

• Tide charts are guidelines, not absolutes. Barometric pressure (high and low pressure, given on weather forecasts) affects tide heights: extremely high pressure systems literally press down on sea levels, leading to lower tides than predicted, while extremely low pressure allows tides to rise higher than predicted.

• Strong offshore winds can push water away from the coast, exaggerating low tides and holding back high tides. Strong onshore winds push water on to the shore, virtually eliminating low tides and exaggerating high tides

• Not everywhere has two tides a day (semi-diurnal range). There are parts of the world with one high tide and one low tide each day (a diurnal tide range e.g. the Gulf of Mexico), and some with two tides but of very different sizes (a mixed semi-diurnal range e.g. the west coast of the USA, parts of Australia and in South East Asia).

A GUIDE TO USING TIDE TIMETABLES

Tide timetables and surf forecasts are available as apps, websites and pocketbooks. Many online tide times will only give a week at a time, but include weather, surf data and webcams. A physical book allows easier long-range planning and can be used in conjunction with weather forecasts. A physical copy can be invaluable back-up – tide times can be hard to mentally retain, and you might be out of reception.

Tide charts are based on predictions: actual tides can be higher or lower and a margin of error of at least ten minutes is to be expected with any forecast. The quality of data varies by port and country – tide charts for remote fishing villages in Asia are going to be less accurate than western ports.

There is a lot of information on tide charts and surf forecasts, and realistically most of us use very little of it to go sea swimming, more often just pitching up and going from there. But here is a quick guide to filtering a forecast to get the information you need to go sea swimming:

1. **Locate your date.** You can either look for a specific day that you are going to the beach or look for a specific tide you want to swim on (e.g. neaps) and work out what days they occur.

2. **Look at high tide and low tide times.** Check whether these are given as BST (British Summer Time) or GMT (Greenwich Mean Time). It's quite common for tide timetables to use GMT, which means you will need to add an hour to the times between March and October when the UK is in BST.

3. **Look at the size of the tide** – is the sea on springs or neaps? Tune in to how conditions may change at the same place between a big blowsy spring tide, or a neat(er) little neap.

4. **Look at wind direction, speed and gusts.** Wind is typically given as a steady speed and then gusts. Gusts confuse the sea, leading to messy conditions. What is the speed – is it light,

fresh, strong or very strong (usually presented by the colour red)? What you experience locally might be slightly different: beaches may be protected from winds by their headlands, but equally, they may funnel winds. The wind can also affect which direction you swim in. Onshore is safer for swimming as winds blow you back on to the beach and flatten waves, but with an onshore wind you are likely to want to breathe to the beach to avoid mouthfuls of water. Sea breezes (see page 149) are not captured by weather forecasts, so are another reason that what you find when you arrive may not match the forecast.

5. **Check sunrise and sunset time** – first light and last light may also be listed, so you don't (unintentionally) plan a swim in the dark.

6. **What's the surf height?** Waves are measured from the trough to the peak in feet. We are used to thinking of heights when we're standing up (as surfers themselves are doing while stood on their boards on the sea). But when we swim, we are just bobbing heads, which means that a 1-foot wave, a height that would generally be at our knees, is as big as our heads. And a 6-foot wave may be intimidating.

7. **What is the swell height?** A big swell can be fun to swim in, as you join the sea in a slow-motion bounce, but you can also lose your buddies fast – them in a trough when you're on a crest – and it can be harder to swim.

8. **What is the swell direction?** This is the angle at which swell (and waves) are coming at the beach. Swell direction allows you to predict which coves on a headland will be rough and which may be sheltered on a particular day.

TIDAL STREAM AND TIDAL RACES

The tide does not move in and out of a shore, but along the coast.

> **Tidal stream or tidal flow** is the direction and speed of moving water caused by the tide. Tidal stream will help or hinder your progress – if you swim back and forth on a beach, one way will be easier than the other.
>
> **Tidal race** is a strong tidal current, and occurs where a fast-moving tide passes through a constriction.

Anything that gets in the way of moving water changes its direction and speed – headlands, islands, bays, reefs, narrows, stacks, caves. (Wandering into a sea cave on an early swim with my husband Tim, it took just one wave to put 6 feet between us – him at the top of a wave, and me in its trough. We made a very quick exit.)

Any static object – for example a buoy or boat – allows you to see the direction and force of a tidal stream, and also watch it changing direction. Watch moored boats and you will see the moment that they all turn around with the tide.

Tidal streams pick up speed around exposed coasts and straits, so venturing out of a bay or along a steep rocky cliff of coastline requires extreme caution – boat cover is a really good idea as currents will often be stronger than you, and getting-out spots may be infrequent or non-existent.

A strong current in the sea is very similar to a strong current in a river, in terms of the dangers of being pinned against an object by it. In an open expanse of water you will often not feel how fast the tide is travelling unless you sight on something. Be very cautious around moored boats, which may come up faster than you think and which you will not want to be pushed into or under. I have taken part in the famous annual swim on the Bosphorus, a tidal strait between Europe and Asia. The water moves so fast that swimmers start heading in to the finish beach 1 kilometre away from it – leave it any later to tack right and you may be swept straight past, to the pick-up boats beyond it.

USING A TIDAL STREAM ATLAS

A tidal stream atlas or tidal flow atlas is a map of the coastline which shows the direction and speed of tidal flow hour by hour (HT +1 hour, HT +2 hours etc.). They are mapped for sailors, and will show (for example) when the streams run clockwise or anticlockwise around an island.

The more committed a swim – meaning the fewer places you can exit easily – the more important tidal stream atlases become. I have used tidal stream atlases for swims such as the Seven Bay Swim from Botany Bay to Ramsgate in Kent, and the Seven Sisters swim from Cuckmere Haven to Birling Gap in Sussex, and swims that go along a cliff rather than across a bay and need to go with the tide, not against it (which is virtually impossible). With epic marathon swims – crossing the English Channel, Lewis Pugh swimming its 530-kilometre length, Ross Edgley swimming around the coast of Britain – tidal atlases become a bible, allowing swimmers to time swims for the most tidal assistance.

Even if you are not using a tidal stream atlas you can make some simple predictions: the strength and speed of any stream will increase with the size of a tide, and be at their strongest in the middle of any tide.

One thing to note is that atlases show currents on a big scale, but tucked into the coast you may experience something quite different (to either an atlas or what you thought you observed from a headland). My friend Kari and I once made extensive plans to swim into a limestone slot called Huntsman's Leap in Pembrokeshire, which entailed a short swim along some tall cliffs. We timed the swim around slack neap tide in calm conditions, with the idea that if there was any current then it would push us out on the way out, and bring us home on the way back. The swim into the narrow, 150-foot-tall slot in the cliff went well, but when we emerged for the swim back the current was very firmly against us. I had packed flippers in our tow floats 'just in case' ('Really?' wailed Kari) and with those on our feet we powered home, which was just as well as there is nowhere else to get out and without them we couldn't make any progress. What we surmised from the experience is that there is a bay-wide eddy: when the tidal stream met a headland a small local eddy must have sent some of the current back the other way.

TIDAL RACES

A tidal stream becomes a tidal race where a fast-moving tide passes through a constriction or over an obstruction, which speeds it up, and results in waves, eddies and hazardous currents.

Some tidal races have become magnets for swimmers because of the excitement of trying to make it across in a calm window. The Gulf of Corryvreckan between Scarba and Jura in the Outer Hebrides is one of the most well known. The race there reaches 8.5 knots, and is caused by the combination of the two islands channelling the water between them, while meeting a 95-foot pinnacle underneath the water. It is mostly unswimmable, and home to a whirlpool; swimmers (with experienced local pilots) dare to cross in a 40-minute window when the race stops running. The Menai Strait can run at 8 knots but is a swooshy swim on any tide.

SWIMMER VERSUS TIDE

Tide speed is measured in knots. 1 knot is 1 nautical mile an hour, which is the same as 1.9 km/hr, or 1.15 mile/hr. Uninterrupted tidal streams may flow at around 2 knots, while a fairly average crawl pace is 1 knot, so it's easy to see how in a swimmer versus tide situation, the tide will generally win:

- 1 knot: a swimmer who swims a 34.5-minute mile (64 lengths of a 25m pool)
- 2 knots: uninterrupted tidal streams rarely flow at more than 2 knots

- 3 knots: typical flow of a mature river
- 4 knots: a world-class swimmer travelling at a sprint speed
- 8 knots: Menai Strait, between mainland Wales and the island of Anglesey
- 8.5 knots: tidal race in the Gulf of Corryvreckan in the Outer Hebrides

WIND OVER TIDE

When wind is going in the same direction as the tide, water will be bouncy but smooth. If the wind stream is going in the opposite direction to the tide, then water will be choppy with standing waves, making for heavy swimming.

UNDERSTANDING RIP CURRENTS

Rip currents are narrow localised currents that can appear on the coastline, where water moves rapidly back out to sea. As waves break on the shore, water is pushed forward on to the beach (the swash), and then starts to drain back into the sea, pulled back by gravity (the backwash). The water is looking for an escape, and its path back is impeded by the sandbar or reef that it went over (the one that created surf). If there is a gap in a sandbar, or the reef, the water flows towards these deeper channels and pours through them, speeding up in that channel. What then develops is a narrow, localised rip current flowing out to sea, directly away from the shore. It cuts through the line of breaking waves like a river. It is strongest and fastest near the surface of the water, exactly where you are as a swimmer.

When a stream, run-off or a waterfall crosses the beach and enters the sea, this can cut through the sandbar and create a flow. If the stream is always there you will probably find that at some stage of the tide, even if it is a small stream, a rip will appear.

Both man-made and natural coastal features such as groynes, harbour walls, piers, storm drains, breakwaters, headlands and estuary mouths are associated with rips at certain times, depending on tides and weather conditions, or usually a combination of the two. This need for a certain set of conditions for a rip, which are unique to each coastal location, is the reason why they are sometimes not very regular occurrences.

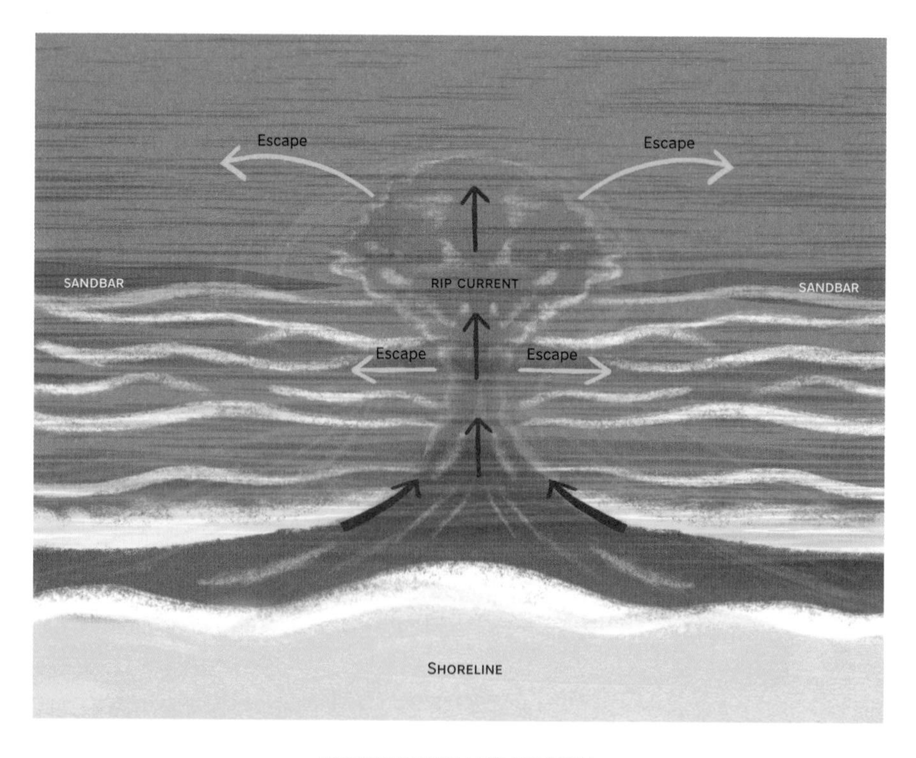

HOW TO ESCAPE A RIP CURRENT

They are not tidal ('rip tides' is a misnomer) but their strength and time of appearance are tide-dependent. If you watch beach lifeguards moving flags around for the day, they will generally move them to the side as well as up and down the beach, and this may be partially due to the formation of rips at different stages of the tide.

Where there are breaking waves, there are usually rip currents, and on surf beaches there will be some fairly hefty rips if conditions are right. Rips might be narrow and short but in extreme cases can be 100 metres wide and 500 metres long. In the latter case, the amount of water needed to generate the rip is huge; here you would be looking at the kind of conditions where swimmers – and most surfers – would not want to be. But rips can be powerful, pulling you off your feet.

HOW TO SPOT A RIP

Rip currents form most commonly on surf beaches, and people get into trouble because they choose the flatter, calmer area of surf to get into, thinking that part of the beach is safer than the rough whitewater – when actually, the flatter and calmer water can mean a rip.

It takes practice to be able to see rips, so ask local lifeguards, swimmers or surfers to help you spot local ones and share where and when they are most likely to be. Spend time looking. Some will be 'fixed', some move over weeks or months, and others appear suddenly and unpredictably as 'flash' rips, where one minute you're standing happily in foamy waves and the next you're heading out to sea at speed.

Stand and watch them to grow familiar. Signs to look out for:

- Area of deeper, dark-coloured water between waves
- Area of fewer breaking waves – lower and less whitewater than surrounding areas
- A rippled surface surrounded by smooth waters

- Anything floating out to sea

- Foamy, discoloured, sandy or silty water flowing out beyond the waves

HOW TO GET OUT OF A RIP

So one minute you're swimming or snorkelling along, and the next you're disappearing out to sea. There are the three things most people do in this situation: panic like hell, fight the current, and swim against it for all they are worth. This is the exact opposite of what you should do, but time after time seasoned swimmers bring back stories of how, with the beach receding from view, they couldn't control the urge to pitch themselves against a rip and try to swim back to shore.

If you are in this situation, remember that the rip will, at some point, run out of steam and stop pulling you out to sea. Rips typically only extend to the back of the surf, rarely more than 100 metres, often less. Rips also slow down as they get further from shore. Some rips run out at more or less 90 degrees to shore, some run at odd angles almost parallel to shore. Some curl round and return to shore.

So if you are caught in one, this is what to do:

- Don't panic. Float (if possible on your back), and concentrate on your breathing and taking a series of slow, calming breaths. Revert to floating and breathing at any point in this process if you feel panic rising.

- Don't try to swim against the rip. Decide whether you're happy to try to swim out. If you think you are, head for the nearest whitewater. This might be perpendicular to the rip, but it might not. Swim calmly, don't panic. When you exit the rip, swim back to shore.

- If you have 'gone with' the rip, once you're beyond it, if it hasn't taken you back to shore, swim wide of it then go back in, or if there are lifeguards or people in the water or on the beach, float and raise your arm to call for help.

- If at any point you want help, float and raise your arm until you're sure someone has seen you. Surfers will always help people in trouble, as, of course, will lifeguards. Remember, you can float or tread water for a long time! Seawater makes you very buoyant.

If someone else is in trouble in the sea, it's better to call for help. Only go in after them if you know how to effect a rescue and you understand the sea and the conditions at the time – this is particularly true if you are a swimmer, as you have no aid to help you rescue them (i.e. a surfboard). If you do find yourself rescuing someone in a rip, it might be better to float with it and signal for help. Keep them calm and stay where you are.

Calm is not always the same as safe. Beach lifeguards will tell you that some of the hardest days of lifeguarding are not when the seas are big and stormy but when the surf is 2–3 feet. To the untrained eye, conditions look inviting, but there are two risk points: one, when waves are smaller it is easier for swimmers to get behind where the waves are breaking – and then struggle back in. And two, on the calmest days it can be harder to see rips.

OBSERVATIONS FROM THE SEA SHORE

• Coves and bays can offer some of the safest swimming conditions – indented into the coastline, they are protected from tidal currents.

• Seas reflect what's around them, so a gently shelving beach, smooth sand (not rocks), settled weather (no storms), low wind (no gusts), flat water (no surf) and slack tide (little water movement) all promote tranquillity and mellow swims.

• The centre of a beach is often the most benign place to be, as swells and currents tend to wrap themselves around islands, rocky outcrops, headlands and rivers.

• Restrictions – piers, groynes, harbour mouths, estuary mouths, islands, caves – all increase currents.

• On most beaches there will be some kind of current pulling you along the shore, and the more open the coast, and wider and longer the beach, the greater this sideways pull.

• Stretches of coast other swimmers have colonised often have nothing to do with mild and docile seas, and everything to do with land-based reasons like being the most viable place to swim in a busy town. Swimmers have swum in 'the scrotum-tightening sea' (to quote James Joyce) at Forty Foot, Sandycove, Dublin since the 1800s, irrespective of the fact that when a storm comes through here it has the same deleterious effects on swimming conditions as anywhere else: strong waves that hurl themselves against rocks and walls. And conditions for Brighton Swimming Club (established 1860) are similarly sketchy: with winds coming from multiple directions the coastline can be dangerous, and the steep shingle beach can make it hard to enter or leave the sea (particularly in the four hours after high tide.)

• Lifeguarded beaches use flags to demarcate areas for swimming and surfing. A split red and yellow flag denotes the swimming zone, a black and white chequered flag the surfing zone, a red flag no swimming. An orange windsock means no inflatables. Swimmers must keep an eye on themselves in relation to the flags.

• Some coastal areas have dedicated 'swim zones' marked out by buoys. As well as excluding strong currents, boats and jet skis are either not allowed in these areas or only allowed at restricted speeds. If you live in a port area, you may be relieved to know the swim zone also excludes ferries and submarines (!). It is still necessary to remain vigilant that you are not drifting outside the buoys, but there are fewer hazards to worry about and look out for, and there is often good company to keep.

• It is always worth talking to locals: lifeguards in the area who have done a few seasons, other swimmers, owners of beach huts, the local harbourmaster, surfers, paddleboarders and sailors.

TEMPERATURES

The sea operates within a narrower band of overall temperatures than fresh water, and progresses more slowly between them. Wintertime sea temperatures rarely go below 6 or 7 °C (6 is very cold, and 8 or 9 about average) and summertime sea temperature is typically 16 °C. In a warm year you may get 18 or 19 °C, and in the North Sea you might find temperatures below 5 degrees, but these are both rare.

There is around a six-week lag between the shortest day and the coldest seas, and the longest day and the warmest seas, so the coldest sea temperatures are found in February while the warmest are found in August. The sea loses its heat very slowly to the atmosphere but, conversely, takes a long time to warm up.

UK swimmers enjoy far warmer water than our Latitude 50 North neighbours, who live the same distance away from the equator in either the Americas or Europe. The Gulf Stream (called the North Atlantic Drift by the time it reaches UK shores) keeps the sea here much warmer than it would otherwise be. Newfoundland shares our latitude, but has the colder Labrador Current, and their wintertime sea temperatures go as low as –0.7 °C, leading to floes of sea ice.

AT THE COAST, WHERE IS THE WARMEST WATER?

The sea might not be as capricious as fresh water but it does still have factors that affect temperature locally and in the short term.

The sea will stratify into different temperature bands, with the warmest water on the top. Anything that mixes the water column up will cool the water down: a strong tidal flow that pulls cold water up from the depths, wind or surf that breaks up the surface, spring tides, an estuary. Tidal races mix water dynamically and constantly, leading to lower temperatures – bathing areas next to them may reflect this. Warmer water will therefore often be found at sheltered coves and beaches protected from prevailing winds, and on beaches where there is less surf.

Good temperature gains can be made on neap tides, when there is less movement. Anything heated by the sun at low tide – rocks, estuary mud, sand – will heat the water that travels over it at high tide, making mid-afternoon swims possibly warmer than dawn ones.

Shallow water will heat faster, with white sand acting a bit like snow, reflecting the sun back into the water so the water is being heated from both above and below.

SEA-WATER QUALITY

Local sea-water quality is influenced by the coastline. Permanent factors that may degrade local water quality include coastline urbanisation, big rivers and estuaries carrying urban and agricultural run-off from upstream downstream, and the presence of a port or shipping in the area. (Three times as much oil is carried out to sea via run-off from our roads and rivers as enters the ocean via oil spills.)

Temporary factors that may degrade sea-water quality include storms and heavy rainfall, which may bring with them run-off, sewage overflow and leakage from septic tanks. Sewage is generally treated before it is pumped into the sea, but when rains are heavy there may be releases of untreated sewage.

There are different systems that track sea-water quality in the UK, such as Designated Bathing Waters (managed by the Environment Agency) and Blue Flag awards (run by Keep Britain Tidy).

Designated Bathing Waters sites are tested and rated by the Environment Agency during the 'bathing season' (defined as 15 May to 30 September), with that data giving rankings from Excellent to Poor. Only a fraction of beaches are tested, though, and as a swimmer you may well be entering the water outside this season.

Blue Flag awards are only given to lifeguarded beaches that meet other facilities and management criteria, which may only be in place at resort beaches. So while a Blue Flag gives an assurance that there are no industrial, waste-water or sewage-related discharges nearby, there may be nearby coves that are cleaner or just as clean.

MARINE FIELD GUIDES

'Beneath the waves lie calm,
silent forests of weed.
The swimmer cruises just above them,
free of time and space'

GEOFFREY FRASER DUTTON,
Swimming Free

JELLYFISH

(and what they are like to swim with)

BARREL JELLYFISH

Rhizostoma pulmo

The largest jellyfish in UK waters, these are gel-like and heavy. Fans say they only stay for a short window of time; while one swimmer I know enjoys spending time chasing these 'wobbly underwater aliens', another described encountering them as being 'like swimming into a dead body'. At least they don't sting.

BLUE JELLYFISH

Cyanea lamarckii

These bright violet jellies are often the first to appear and a sign we're heading towards summer. Can be colourless when young, and similar to lion's mane (see below) in shape: a dome with white tentacles underneath. Fans marvel at the beauty in a colour contrast of indigo-ink jellies, white sand and turquoise sea. Avoiders take comfort from knowing the sting is like a nettle rash. Occur all along the UK coast.

BY-THE-WIND SAILOR

Velella velella

By-the-wind sailors are transparent discs with concentric rings and sails – washed up they can look like discs of plastic on the shoreline. They float and have sails that are orientated to the left or right and put them at the mercy of the wind. During a 'blue tide' they may be beached in huge numbers, graded in size by the wind and tide. Usually the violet-blue is the colour of Quink Ink but after time on the shore they bleach. These tiny forms are not true jellyfish – like the Portuguese man o' war (see below) in colour and nature, they are made up of small creatures. No sting.

COMPASS JELLYFISH

Chrysaora hysoscella

A beige jelly with brown compass-like radial markings on the bell, and a brown trim around the base. They appear from June to September. The sting can hurt 'quite a bit', and the bigger the compass, the worse the sting.

LION'S MANE JELLYFISH

Cyanea capillata

Scourge of swimmers, lion's mane have long, snot-like tentacles (the mane) that trail behind them and have a way of delivering glancing stings to your wrists, shoulders and face before you've seen the body to which they are attached. The mane can also get tied up in goggles and costumes, stinging repeatedly long after it's been separated from the body. The body, when viewed, is no comfort: a gelatinous, orangey-brown mass expanding and contracting as it pulses along.

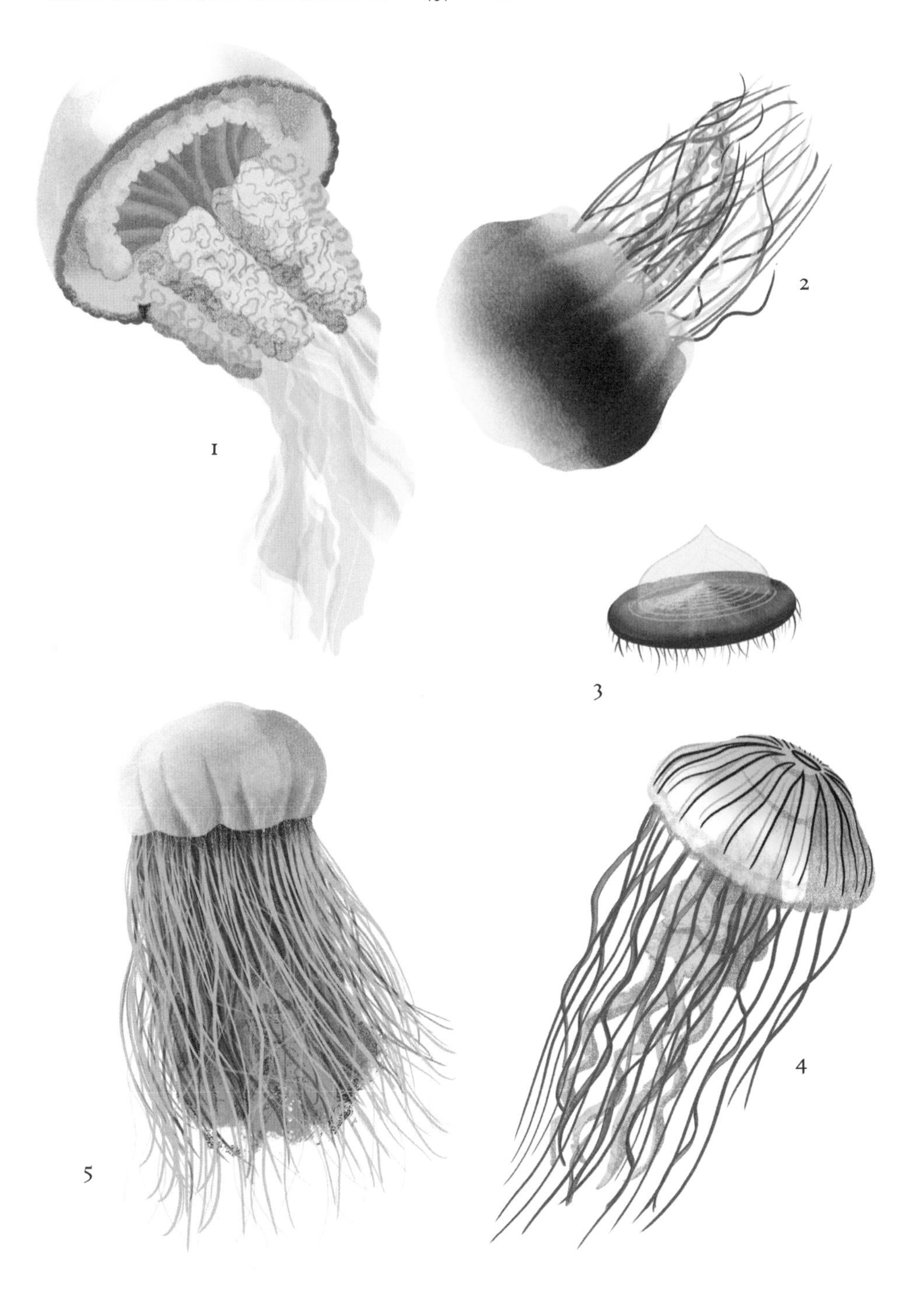
1
2
3
4
5

The bigger the jelly, the stronger the sting: they can grow to 2 metres across, but even smaller ones leave a nasty sting from a cocktail of toxins that leave cycles of burning, itching skin and throbbing pain that can last for ten days. Treat as soon as possible after being stung. Lion's mane are so common that we all have to make our peace with them: their key upside is that they are food for leatherback turtles.

MOON JELLYFISH

Aurelia aurita

Moon jellies are common and appear all around the UK coast, from May till September. Swimmers see them washed up on beaches and catch them in the cup of their front-crawling hands. Fans like swimming in swarms of them and say they look their best when the sun's rays shine straight through the centre, illuminating the four purple rings that are their gonads. More cautious individuals comfort themselves that they have such a mild sting that you can't feel anything.

PORTUGUESE MAN O' WAR

Physalia physalis

Like *Velella velella* (see above), *Physalia physalis* is blue, floats and is not a jellyfish but a 'siphonophore', a colony of organisms. Stings are painful and can be serious; seek treatment straight away. Fans find them 'intriguing and stunning' and say small ones with short tentacles are easier to navigate while snorkelling.

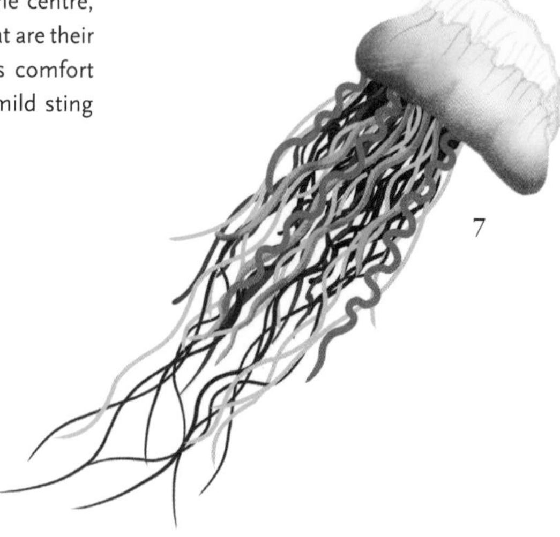
7

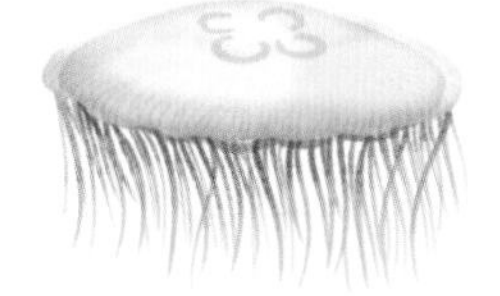
6

HOW TO TREAT A JELLYFISH STING

Jellyfish sting treatment is evolving – encounters are increasing (perhaps because warmer oceans mean more jellies), and as they do, so does practice on best first aid. Most stings are like a nettle sting, but some are worse. Scraping stings, using tweezers, and pee are no longer recommended.

The same treatment is recommended for lion's mane, box jellyfish and Portuguese man o' war (even though the toxins are different): rinse with vinegar for 30 seconds to remove tentacles and inhibit cells on the skin, then immerse in 45-degree (or as hot as can be tolerated) water for 40 minutes. A heat pack can also be used.

Exercising will also pump toxins faster round the body and the team from NUI Galway and the University of Hawaii that researched this treatment found that both seawater and cold packs increase venom delivery - all of which suggests that if we carry on swimming, the sting will become worse.[1] Try not to scratch; it spreads the sting.

The toxins from stings enter the bloodstream and can mimic an allergic reaction, block airways, cause vomiting and cause shock; seeking emergency medical treatment is appropriate if concerned. If a sting surrounds the trunk of a young child, ring 999 and act quickly.

SEAWEED

Always best viewed in the water but frequently displayed on shorelines after storms, and infrequently displayed on dinner tables.

BLADDERWRACK

Fucus vesiculosus

The air bubbles or bladders of this common weed help it to float, and make it instantly recognisable around the UK coast, where it may buffer your bumps among shallow rocks. In bladderwrack the air bladders are opposed: on either side of the frond. There are two other common wracks: egg-wrack has bladders along each frond, like a snake that has swallowed a series of giant eggs. Serrated wrack, as the name suggests, has a saw-like edge.

Bladderwrack is rich in vitamins, minerals and phytochemicals, and there is a long folk history of it being used to treat joint pain, urinary tract infections and thyroid conditions. To make bladderwrack tea, dry it and simmer 1 teaspoon in boiling water for 10 to 15 minutes. For those inclined, armfuls can be used to make a skin-nourishing super-slippery bladderwrack bath. Can also be used as a dye for wool, giving tan and rust colours.

FURBELOWS

Saccorhiza polyschides

A spectacular kind of kelp. When torn from the sea and marooned on the shoreline furbelows look like small trees, and they get their name from their ruffled stems, which look like the folds in ornate dinner shirts. The stormier the location, the longer and more divided the fronds, and the whole kelp can reach 4 metres tall. The ruffles are there to dissipate currents. A fast-growing, annual species.

OARWEED

Laminaria digitata

Oarweed is a type of kelp, and like other kelps (such as sugar kelp) it has a satin-rich lushness underwater. It grows in dense swaying forests attached to rocky seabeds by single strands that branch out into ribbony fingers. It provides a nursery for fish and home for crabs and brittlestars. Fingers shredded by storms may be replaced by new ones the following spring. Washed up after storms, it can be collected to make a good garden fertiliser – first rinse and then chop up and dry. Grows quickly and is part of kelp reforestation projects designed to restore ecosystems and lock in carbon.

PURPLE LAVER

Porphyra purpurea

Silk-thin but strong, purple laver changes colour over the year, reaching darkest purple at the end of the summer. Widely spread across our shorelines in shallow water, and popular as nori – dried edible seaweed.

1
2
3
4

SEA LACE

Chorda filum

Also called mermaid's tresses and dead man's rope, these single fronds are hollow, so have sufficient buoyancy to stand upright underwater, like very tall brown spaghetti. Most often found in sheltered bays with rocky substrates, in relatively shallow (less than 20-metre) water, it grows up to 8 metres but 2 to 6 metres is more common. Disappears in winter. Wrap them around a chosen pebble to make an unusual gift: as it dries, the lace will tighten.

SEA LETTUCE

Ulva lactuca

Emerald green and fragile-looking, sea lettuce is found all around the UK on rocks and in rock pools. It is robust to pollution, thrives on nitrates and is not as tasty as its cousin purple laver, but if the traditional cream tea is not your thing, a Devonian swimmer dries it then adds a large handful to make 'Gutweed and Sea Lettuce Scones'. Yum. Yum?

SUGAR KELP

Saccharina latissima

Also known as sea belt or weather weed, the twirling solitary strands of this conker-brown kelp look like crinkled leather belts tied to their rocks by a thin stipe (stem). Often found swaying lushly in shallow water and rock pools. Once out of the water, a strand of sugar kelp can be nailed in a sheltered spot and used as a (not entirely accurate) poor man's barometer: if the kelp stays dry, the forecast is sunny and dry; if it becomes wet and flexible, rain is coming. When it dries out a sweet white powder (mannitol) comes to the surface. Can be chopped up and baked to make crisps, and the sweet and salty flavour is currently used to add a sweet and salty taste to artisan rum and gin.

HOW TO PRESS SEAWEED

Seaweed hunting was a popular pastime in Victorian times, and specimen pressing is an easy skill to acquire. Collect from shorelines after storms, rinse and cut to size. The most natural shapes are achieved by floating the weed on to paper. To do this bring a piece of paper up underneath it in the water. Then add a piece of paper on top (kitchen roll, brown paper, whatever is to hand) and place your seaweed and paper sandwich under something heavy. I have whole collections pressed under tent carpets and doormats – high-footfall areas where over just one week the samples are both dried out and squashed. Can be framed or made into cards. Take just what you need.

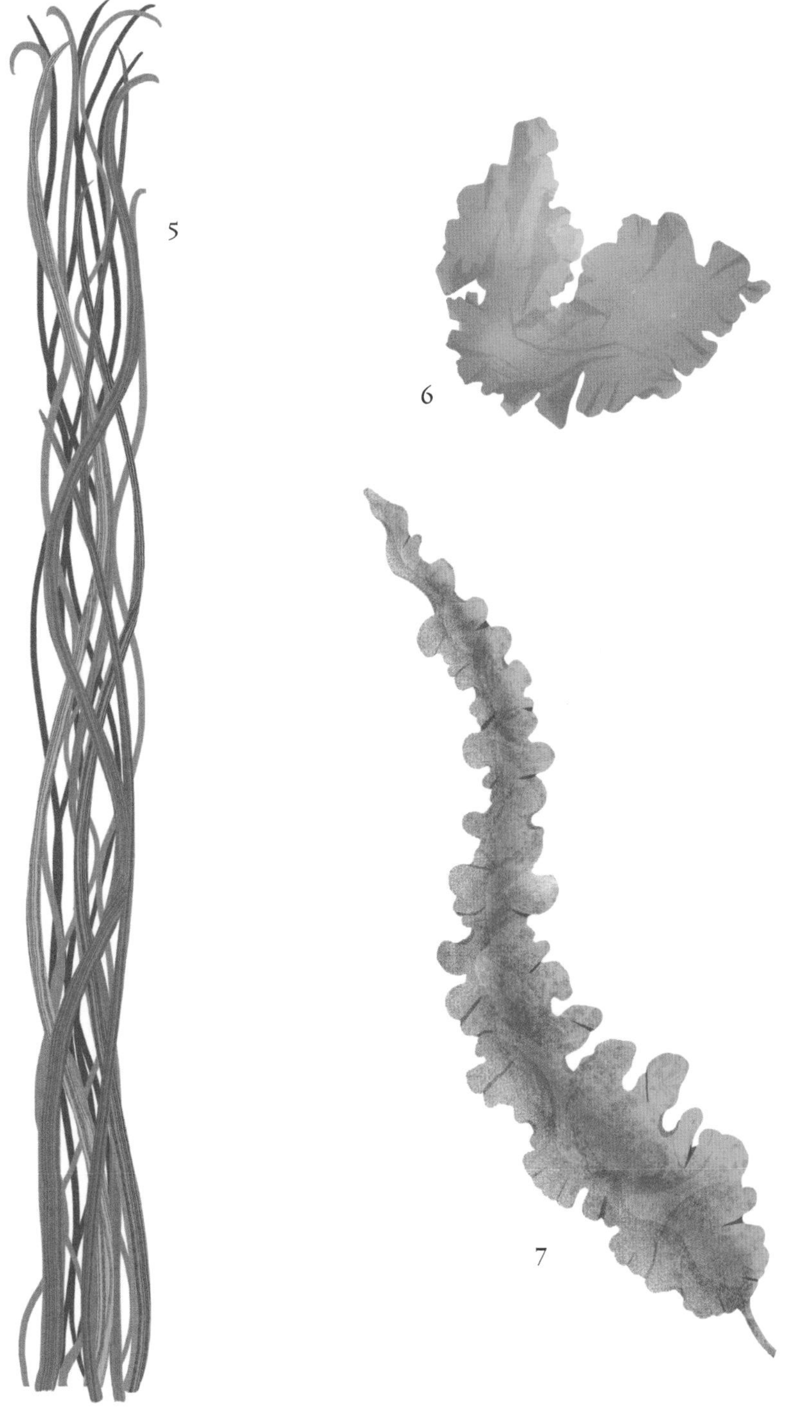
5
6
7

SEASHORE

Put on a snorkel and embrace being one of many living things in the water.

BEADLET ANEMONE

Actinia equina

Beadlet anemones are found all around the coast of the British Isles, all year round, in sheltered and exposed places. Most commonly rusty red, but they can be brown, green or orange. With so much coral around the world now bleached, these are our new colours and flowers of the sea.

COMMON LIMPET

Patella vulgata

Even rocky seashores with pounding waves will harbour life. Limpets hold fast to their rocks when the tide is out but when covered by the tide they set off to graze seaweed, an action you may catch, alongside the limpet trail behind them on the rocks. They will graze up to a metre away from their home base, then return to their scoured-out groove. They live for up to twenty years.

ORANGE-CLUBBED SEA SLUG

Limacia clavigera

There are over 3,000 species of nudibranchs around the world, soft-bodied gastropod molluscs – a branch of sea slugs, with the Latin *nudus* meaning 'naked' (without a shell) and 'branch' a derivation of the Latin word for gills. Many of these are psychedelic shades of turquoise, mauve, orange and yellow. They eat anemones, corals and barnacles. One of the UK's brightest is the orange-clubbed sea slug, which is a translucent white with orange 'clubs'. Up to 2 centimetres long, and found living on kelp and rocks in shallow water all around the coast of the British Isles.

PEACOCK WORM

Sabella pavonina

Although they can be up to 30 centimetres long, you will only see the top 10 centimetres of these long slender worms, which are topped by a crown of feathery tentacles, somewhere between the magic of a dandelion clock and a peacock. Widely distributed around the British coasts in muddy sea floors and rocky reefs. The tail extends out of the tube at high tide (at low tide it withdraws back, looking like a grey tube). The tube is built of mud or sand particles held together with mucus, while the crown catches food particles in water that flows past.

1

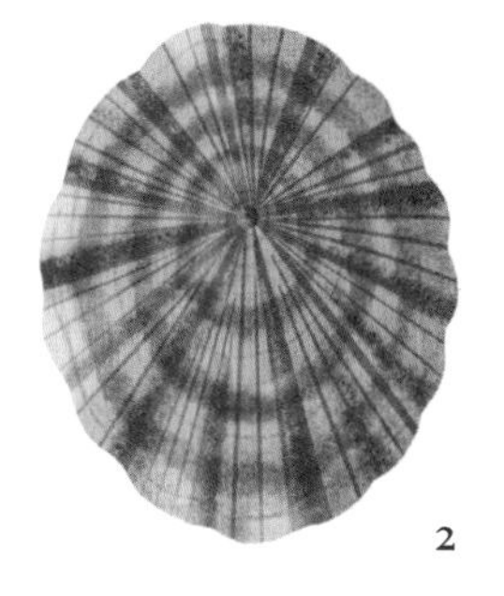
2

4

3

PIPEFISH

Syngnathidae

Beds of seagrass like underwater lawns are being regenerated around the UK coast and if you can locate one (they favour shallow calm, sheltered areas of coast such as estuaries and bays) then you may find pipefish, which swim among them, well camouflaged by their shape. The pipefish is similar to a seahorse but with a straight body. Not strong swimmers. They suck up minuscule crustaceans such as shrimp with their snouts.

SHORT-SNOUTED SEAHORSE

Hippocampus hippocampus

One of two seahorses found around the UK, the short-snouted seahorse is a close relative of the pipefish and is found in shallow muddy waters, among seaweed and seagrass meadows. They are weak swimmers and use their tails to cling to plants, and their noses to probe nooks for small shrimp and food, which they suck up like vacuum cleaners. Up to 15 centimetres long, they eat small shrimp and plankton. Found mainly around the south coast of England, Channel Islands and Ireland, but with sightings on the Thames and east coast. The Latin name means 'horse caterpillar'.

SNAKELOCK ANEMONE

Anemonia viridis

Like limpets (see page 108), snakelocks move along their rocks – albeit slowly. Snakelocks like sunny water, and are found at depths down to 12 metres in the south and west of the UK all year round. They are quite large – up to 8 centimetres wide with 15-centimetre tentacles – and are capable of capturing and eating a prawn after stinging it insensible.

SPIDER CRAB

Maja brachydactyla

With huge long spidery legs and hairy shells that can attract seaweed, spider crabs are both easy to recognise and an annual event: they start arriving on the shores in the south and west of the UK (coming up from depths of 100m) between April and June, and can be seen mating in kelp, and sometimes forming heaps, to breed or moult.

5
6
7
8

CHAPTER 4

UNDERSTANDING ESTUARIES

'Now the tide is out... and well out.
Afon Mawddach is a feeble trickle in
the midst of that expanse of sand.
Like the Dart at low water, it seems
almost inconceivable that it will ever
again be full enough for 200 ragged
idiots to swim up.
Surely we'll end up walking...
(some of us will, but not for that reason
and not here, in the wide expanses
flashing past on my left)'

PAUL SMITH
observing the Hurly Burly swim course
on the Mawddach Estuary at low tide, 2017

Estuaries are between-land places, not quite land, not quite water. There is something supernatural about them, with swirling clouds of birds and the ultimate trick: a tidal reverse, where the river flows both ways. Wide and flat, quiet and wild, with sea skies and the silence of salt marshes and mudflats. At low tide the eerie piping of curlews, and the steady work of wading birds with long legs and long beaks looking for worms in the mud. One minute empty – a feeble trickle in a vast expanse of sand or mud foreshore. The next full to the brim, tickling the branches of overhanging trees. Which way is the tide tugging you as you bob among oak leaves and bladderwrack – this way, or that? Does it taste of salt water, or fresh?

Wide as a lake, flows like a river, tastes like the sea: I cannot decide which I like more, swimming down estuaries on a flood tide, as they empty towards the sea, or swimming up them on an ebb and seeing the landscape narrow and change as I go – from the bright brine and sand of the coast to pastoral green rolling-hill softness.

When I started running swim events my self-imposed standard was that they had to be swims that would be difficult to organise yourself. (The OSS is the home of empowering *free* swimming, after all). It turned out that the experience of being in a contentment of swimmers (our chosen collective noun) is justification enough for operating and attending an event, but it remains true that most of the swim routes I've been part of inventing are in estuaries – the 10k down the Dart Estuary in Devon, a 10k on the Mawddach Estuary in North Wales (the Hurly Burly), and a 6-km Swoosh on the Aune Estuary to Bantham. For a few years we ran a river lido at a festival – it opened when the tide came in.

Estuaries are difficult to predict, so here's what I have learnt. Learning this has involved many hours swimming the same three estuaries over and over, and many boats getting stuck.

WHAT IS AN ESTUARY?

An estuary is a transitional zone where a river meets the sea and fresh water and seawater are mixed, becoming brackish. In an estuary a river loses its integrity and becomes a wide tidal slosh, snaking through channels, creeks, shivering reed beds, salt marshes and swamps.

Estuaries are dynamic environments with water continually coming in and out, and the distance of tidal influence varies – some estuaries are just a few kilometres, others go on for hundreds of miles. The world's longest estuary is thought to be the St Lawrence River, which connects the Great Lakes in Canada to the Atlantic Ocean, and where the tidal influence is 1,197 kilometres.[1]

They are commonly (but not always) muddy places, with mud and silt being carried down rivers and deposited when a river loses momentum. Tides bring salt water, sediment and sea life – sand, but also seals, weever fish, crabs, cockles and phytoplankton. Bioluminescent bacteria may also be present – setting up in the dark on Dart10k weekends, one of the safety crew would often find a light wave ahead of his kayak, and sparkles dripping off his paddles.

Birds are a big feature, rollercoasting through the sky at feeding time, grubbing in the mud. Waders will be present all year round, and during spring and autumn migrations huge flocks come to feed. Low tide or recently flooded mud is in general the best time to see them feeding, although birders say it depends on the estuary whether high tide, low tide, falling tide or rising tide work the best.

PLANNING AN ESTUARY SWIM

Estuaries are complex, combining the hazards of rivers, the logistics of seas, and some risks all of their own. If you like a swim without elaborate logistics, estuaries are probably not for you. But if you do want to get to know an estuary, here's my methodology. Understanding an estuary is so tied up with planning a swim in one that it's all covered together here.

EASING FACTORS	COMPLICATING FACTORS
The speed of the tide can help you swim a distance faster	Long gaps between access points and exit points may be muddy
The water can be warmer, as water flows over extensive mudflats	Tides make conditions difficult to predict, creating constant changes in depth, flow and currents, and eddies. The flow changes direction as well as speed.
There is legal access to tidal water (with a few exceptions)	Silty or muddy water – organic material and pollutants can accumulate and concentrate in estuarine mud
	Debris and obstacles include flotsam, jetsam, other water users, anything that comes downstream in a storm, and obstacles (such as tree trunks) lodged in the mud (which may be hidden at high tide). On OSS events the estuary bed is always checked by a paddler at low tide, before it's swum at high tide.
	Neap tide or spring tide? A spring will give you more depth, but empties out faster and further than a neap.

ACCESS:
WHERE ARE YOUR IN AND OUT SPOTS?

The simplest estuary swim route is generally an A to B swim that starts upstream at high tide and finishes downstream, so first you need to identify locations where you can get in and out and then measure the distance between them. This is your possible swim route.

You will need to check whether A and B remain accessible all through the tide or whether they shrink away from you behind metres of sinking mud. An exit point somewhere near the mouth of an estuary, with a handy beach car park, is generally easy to find; it's the upstream get-in point that may be harder. But everyone likes water, so there may be pubs with jetties upstream, or someone with a slipway or pontoon who will let you use it. Pontoons and jetties are generally only accessible at some points of the tide, not always.

You may need to visit A and B and watch the water rise and fall at the times of the tide you anticipate being there. If you are driving around doing this, pay attention to signs announcing 'tidal road' or 'causeway'. A causeway is exposed at low tide and submerged at high tide. I have swum past more than one car and sprinter van semi-submerged on tidal roads, with a stricken owner watching from the banks.

FIELDWORK:
WHAT TIME IS HIGH TIDE UPSTREAM?

There will be a delay between when it's high tide at the coast and when the river stops filling. Some upstream places may have published tide times, so you can take high tide at the inland location from those. Local estimates are often contrary. You can look for a satellite image time series (SITS) on Google Earth. Most commonly, though, you will need to confirm inland high tide times by personal observations.

High tide at narrow river necks is not pretty: the rising tide lifts the sediment from the surface of the sand or mudflats, so it can bring in a mix of organic scum and floating litter. Often only the first part of a swim looks like this, and once you get down to the wider estuary with more water, things clarify. The simplest way to work out the time of high tide upstream, and whether there is a period of slack water, is to sit watching the water rise on a flood tide, and record when it turns relative to high tide at the coast – look for a leaf or floating straw to change direction (beware of conflicting winds), or a line of something – seaweed, scum, leaves, twigs – being left behind as the tide retreats from a high water mark. You are looking to come up with a rule of thumb: 'High Tide at [Upstream Place] is twenty minutes after High Tide at the Coast.'

The exact turning point will vary slightly: if a river is high from recent rains, that may turn the tide earlier, while if the tide is coming in with a strong following wind, high tide may be reached earlier and there may be a longer period of slack water. What you are really doing is working out the variables, not expecting hard and fast rules. Unless you are getting 800 people in and trying to get them all out before they are grounded on mudflats, it's unlikely to matter precisely.

FIELDWORK: WHEN IS IT SWIMMABLE AND WHAT ROUTE TO TAKE?

A flooded estuary at dawn is hard to beat. Some estuaries are deep and easy to swim when flooded, but not all. So, once you have identified possible get-in and get-out points, the next thing to do is get a sense of what size tides the estuary needs to be swimmable. By this I mean deep enough to actually swim in rather than wade, so guidelines might be 'on any high tide', 'only swimmable on springs' or 'swimmable on tides over 4.7 metres'.

On some estuaries the problem is a simple one of receding depth: you need to get to B before you are grounded. Whether you are swimming on springs or neaps can make a big difference if you are planning an estuary swim, where 1 metre can make the difference between being able to continue a front-crawl journey downstream or being marooned on mudflats. A spring tide will provide more depth at high tide (tick), and more tidal assistance (the current as it fills or drains will be stronger), but that doesn't necessarily mean it's the tide to swim on, as on springs the estuary will empty out faster than it does on a neap. The only way to work out the perfect tide in these places is to start with educated guesses, and follow it up with trial and error. The speed at which an estuary rises and falls also depends on local topography. On a wide flat estuary on the flood nothing happens, and nothing happens... the tide has such a vast width of land to cover it seems to come in on a trickle... and then BOOM, once the whole channel is covered the tide starts to move upstream at speed (the extreme version of this is a tidal bore, see below). Be warned: it will empty out equally fast.

Another issue may be finding the channel to swim in. At low tide the channel will announce itself clearly, a narrow river snaking through acres of sand or mud. But at high tide you can see nothing: once a layer of water is over the top of it, what lies beneath is hidden from view. Finding the moving water, or the deeper water, is a science and an art. If the estuary is used by boats then buoys may mark the deeper water, but you may want to swim out of this area to avoid collisions.

Ways to address the 'when is it swimmable' question include asking people (such as harbourmasters and other water users, like boat clubs or rowing clubs) and observation from the bank and in the water. I have done a lot of repetitive personal observation, first looking at the estuary at low tide to see where the channel is, then (for example) paddling out at points in the tide, sticking a paddle in now and then to see how deep it is, and finally swimming it. Like sandbars at the coast, channels move – often massively – from year to year.

If it's a sandy-bottomed estuary, wear aqua shoes; you may be able to wade if it becomes too shallow to swim, but weever fish may be buried in the sand and are extremely painful if you stand on them.

Swooshes – where the flow speeds up – will appear on an estuary wherever there is a constriction in the channel, because it narrows, grows shallow or both.

BOAT SUPPORT

You might want and/or need boat support on an estuary swim because there is often no viable exit between point A and B, so if you are in doubt about making it, having someone in the water who can help you home (paddleboard or boat) is a wise idea. Boats also increase your visibility to other craft and offer protection from them.

From a higher vantage point a boat may be able to help you read the currents, find moving water, and avoid mudflats, sandbanks and eddies. They can also help with the bigger problem of finding the way at all: creeks and inlets that look tiny on maps have a way of looking, in real life, just as big as the dominant channel that you want to swim in. As with rivers, what you see in the water is not what you see on the water: when sunk to water level, it is often hard to work out which way to swim. On the Dart 10k, near the start people often swim into a small dent in a reed bed thinking it's the main channel, even with all the other swimmers and safety crew around them.

UP, DOWN OR BOOMERANG?

Which way to go? As described, the starter swim plan is generally to start your swim upstream at high tide and then swim down as the tide ebbs. A swim upstream with an incoming tide is harder to plan, as you will generally need to time your arrival at the top precisely to avoid being faced with mudbanks.

A boomerang swim makes use of a change in flow: going upstream with a rising tide and then turning around and swimming downstream when it turns. The only thing to notice here is that once you start, you are committed: there is no way out and no way home until the tide turns. Kari and I once planned a 10k boomerang having not been able to see each other or swim for months because of lockdown. I felt cold almost instantly, which was judged as mental weakness (#thestoics) until about forty minutes in, when she took a proper look at me and said, 'Oh you are cold, aren't you? Your lips are blue.' The problem was that the tide wasn't going to turn for another two hours or so, and we couldn't swim against it as it was shooting up the estuary behind us with a force 4 (30 mph) wind behind it. We were in a mobile blackspot, so attempts to ring a friend with a boat to come and get me failed, but we had my husband Tim (heroic, stoic, trusty Tim) on a paddleboard beside us. The decision was made for us to swim to the top of the estuary and get out, while Tim paddled back against the wind and tide, got the car, and came to rescue us. Four kilometres of very stiff paddling ensued, zigzagging across the estuary and tucking under trees to try to get out of the wind. We were located later shivering in a car park in our wetsuits, with the rain heaving down. Kari was stood in a puddle 'to warm up'. I had flip-flops in my tow float, and was faring very much better stood there in those: go calibrate that as a luxury.

VARIATIONS IN WATER TEMPERATURE AND TASTE

The water temperature in an estuary will often change along its length. It is likely to be colder at the neck, where there is more river water, and then grow warmer towards the sea. A swim will commonly drop or rise a few degrees as you travel. The taste of the water will also change from fresh to salty.

Water temperature is influenced by the temperature of the estuary bed as the water floods. If the ground is cold (for example because you are swimming on a high tide early in the morning), it will bring water temperature down a few degrees. But if the sun has been on the estuary bed all day, it will increase water temperature by a few degrees when the channel floods.

Salt water is denser than fresh water and sinks underneath it. Which is why there may be a part of the estuary where you can stand and feel like your upper and lower body are in different temperature waters.

SCUM, SCUM LINES AND EDDIES

On an early swim in an unfamiliar estuary, Kari and I swam into a cloud of something brown and bitty. We stood up, looked at it swirling on the surface, swam on, felt revolted, stood up again, looked at swirls that were denser. Eventually we looked at each other: is there a sewage outlet? We didn't know. Eventually I freaked us out enough that we decided to get out, and slipped and skidded over thick mud to land, where we found ourselves on the wrong side of a hedge. There was a footpath that could take us back to our car – if only we could reach it. The sight of Kari's wetsuit-slick and steaming rump wedged into a badger run as she disappeared through the hedge is one I will never forget.

The surface scum was, I now believe, tree pollen. You may also encounter bubbles encased with mashed-up organic matter, sea foam and debris. Scum lines can be a useful way of working out where the eddies are. On bigger estuaries, be aware that they may contain driftwood, which can hit you. And be aware that after heavy rainfall, they can also contain branches. Eddies may come and go with the tide, and can be either small or large areas of reverse flow.

UNDERSTANDING TIDAL BORES

It was back in the time before Google was a search engine, and some friends and I were on a self-created 'cider cycling' tour somewhere in the Cotswolds. On the Friday night we met a man in the pub who said the Severn Bore was rising the following morning. Swimming a bore! That sounded exciting. I knew literally nothing about bores other than they are waves that come up rivers, but I was ready to find out more.

Cut to the next day, where I pulled everyone who had a wetsuit out of bed too early, someone fried eggs, and we drove to a pub garden that was a possible get-in point. The man in the pub was blurry about tide times, so we went early, as I didn't want to miss it. There we stood, under an overcast sky, sweating lightly in our wetsuits and feeling a bit queasy. The water was not, to use that infallible benchmark of swimmers, 'appealing'. It was milky brown, and moving slowly downstream. There were big things floating in it. Our feet were bare and cold while our bodies were cold and clammy. I looked for a place we could hurl ourselves over the reed bed and into the river when the moment came.

Catching-up chat and grogginess occupied more than an hour, as we watched the water continue to flow slowly downstream. You are supposed to be able to hear the bore coming, so we listened out: was that it? Or was that the rumble of a lorry? Increasingly large pieces of debris floated past. A wooden pallet, a 10-gallon drum. Someone opened the pub kitchen's door and pans started to rattle. Then a whole raft of planks and sticks with an estate agent For Sale sign in its middle passed by, like a nest for a pterodactyl. Eyebrows rose.

But not as much as when the nest reappeared and passed by the other way.

'Is this actually safe?' Emma asked me. I had, I admitted, absolutely no idea.

The Australian surfer among us started excavating dormant knowledge about waves, while I rushed to the kitchen to ask what they knew before the bore arrived. 'Is it safe to swim it?' I asked.

'I don't know,' said one of the kitchen staff, in a very broad West Country accent. 'All I do know is when people drown they sometimes don't find the bodies.'

And so it was that we lived to learn that a bore could kill you. We watched it go by instead. A small and startling miracle: a river that looks like any normal river, until the wave happens: a heapy brown slow low wave going upstream, spanning the river. Oh yes, said the surfer, more awake as it passed, 'without a beach to hit to dissipate the wave energy, if you got stuck in it, it could just spin you round and round endlessly.'

WHAT IS A TIDAL BORE?

A bore is a tidal phenomenon that happens in about sixty places around the world. They occur where there is a large tidal range (at least 6 metres) and a wide estuary that funnels these big tides into the neck of a shallow river that is increasingly narrow, creating a clean wavefront that moves upstream.

As a result of our huge tidal range, many of the bores in the world occur in the UK. Bores appear on the River Dee (Wales and England), River Mersey, River Severn (Wales and England), River Trent and other tributaries of the Humber Estuary, River Parrett, River Welland, River Kent (Arnside Bore), River Great Ouse (including the 'Wiggenhall Wave', see below), River Ouse (Yorkshire; like the Trent bore, this is also known as 'the Aegir'), River Eden, River Esk, River Nith, River Lune (Lancashire), River Ribble (Lancashire), River Yealm (Devon) and River Leven (Cumbria).

Bores tend to appear on spring tides, particularly on the vernal and autumnal equinoxes, which are the largest of the year.

They rumble. 'When the wave or tide comes it is steep as a mountain, roaring like thunder, a horizontal flying bank of water,' says a thirteenth-century reference to the Qiantang River bore.[2] More recently, engineer Hubert Chanson (University of Queensland, Australia) was motivated to study the low-pitched rumble of a French bore, and concluded that the sound comes from 'collective bubble oscillations', with air trapped in the bore roller making some of the sound and forming part of its 'acoustic signature'.[3]

ARE ANY TIDAL BORES SWIMMABLE?

The world's tidal bores come in different shapes – some are large, with a single breaking wave; others are undular, like a large ripple travelling upstream followed by smaller undulations known as whelps.

A moving wall of water, advancing rapidly, has the power to break and destroy what lies in its path, so I would say in the main, no, they are not swimmable.

Bores have been surfed, for 10 miles or more. But surfers, kayakers and canoeists all have big floating objects to keep them on top and in front of waves, and to help them surface or get kicked out of the wave if they fall. The risk for the swimmer of getting caught in a wave that doesn't fade out is that you end up in the dark barrel of the bore, and held underwater as the wave pushes upstream.

The second danger is that you are spun around in the barrel with objects. Bores scour the estuary bed as they travel, a turbulent mixing of water, sediment, mud and anything else the wave picks up. Big debris is a known feature of the Severn Bore, with obstacles – dead farm animals, fridges, beer barrels – an articulated hazard among the community who surf it. The comment about 'not finding the bodies' on the Severn we interpreted as the risk of becoming jammed in underwater debris.

The risks are clearly real, and the water murky, but there are swimmers who have got to know their local ankle-biting bores and given them a whirl; for example, the 'Wiggenhall Wave' on the River Great Ouse in the Norfolk fenland. This would seem to involve getting in when it's so small that you need to swim to keep up with it, rather than it being big and strong enough to push you along and about.

CHAPTER 5

WEATHER

'As I swung my head to the side for air
I could make out the dull moaning
of foghorns in the distance'

KARTEEK CLARKE,
Sri Chinmoy Marathon Team

PART OF THE WONDER of swimming outdoors is becoming part of the weather. When hoar frost crystallises the trees and fields around you, when a morning river fog makes a familiar spot mystical, when the sun makes getting in seem essential: as a nearly naked swimmer on the banks, you are skin to skin with all this.

The wind, the rain, the sun, the changeability of it: weather has a huge effect on water conditions and is one of the things that makes every swim different. It's when the sea is made into mountains that we truly experience 'storm force'. In water, rain stops being one thing and starts feeling like many, as it drums on the surface around us, creating patterns of force and abundance: is it pelting, sleeting or pattering? More than once I have been caught out by hail on the shoreline. Would you rather: have your naked skin shot at by ice air pellets, or plunge your shoulders under a freezing sea before you can breathe?

Weather tracks loosely with the seasons, and over time we become seasoned too: knowing full moons look biggest when they rise in autumn, looking out for snowdrops, sheep, birdsong and bud when we move back into spring, planning long downstream swims in summer, joining fish in the shade of overhanging branches as we wait for our swim buddies.

Ultimately we are looking for new reflexes so we connect weather with swims – choosing the best clear night of the week for a swimming stargaze, for example. Weather also affects what kit you may want to wear and take.

THE BASICS OF WEATHER AND WEATHER FORECASTS

In the UK our weather is constantly altering. Above us five different air masses clash and tussle it out, causing swift changes in temperature in water and air – sunshine one moment, freezing hail the next. The seasons bring their own changes. Across the year we can be very different swimmers, with a range of swimming experiences available to us that we wouldn't get in other countries.

Weather that was already fickle is growing more extreme with climate change. Extreme weather events – heavy rainfall, longer dry periods and big storms – have all grown more common as a result of global warming and have real effects on us swimmers. We are in a locked-in period now where whatever we do the climate is changing to some extent for the next fifty years.

As swimmers we need to pay attention to the weather that's just been, as well as the weather that's coming. When we are looking at forecasts we are noting what is likely to happen, not knowing for sure that it will. When we get to the water we may need to plan again – which is what water safety guys call making 'dynamic risk assessments'.

There are thousands of apps you can use, extracted from different datasets and algorithms. But the old-school way – watching a live weather forecast – can be better for understanding weather patterns and likely changes than reading data from a grid. If you are using an app, you may wish to choose one that shows tide times, wave height and swell at the coast.

There is also folklore. Before we had 1.2 billion Met Office supercomputers we still had ways of estimating what weather was coming. Folklore and proverbs based around predictions aren't always right (neither are the supercomputers) but they do suggest ways to start tuning in to the weather around you. Growing up I could sense rain coming, perhaps because I spent so much time outside in one place.

HIGH PRESSURE AND LOW PRESSURE SYSTEMS

If the goose honks high, fair weather
If the goose honks low, foul weather

WEATHER PROVERB

You may not have a formation of geese to hand, but geese do change their flight height with air density and the proverb is an easy way to remember what type of conditions high and low pressure systems (as given on weather forecasts) give you. High pressure systems are associated with clear sunny days – crisp, dry weather in winter and warm sunny weather in the summer. Still days and settled weather may create good water clarity and calm conditions; good for snorkelling and underwater photography.

Another sign of high pressure is spiders out and spinning, getting ready for a good few days of hunting: spiders are sensitive to humidity, so if they're out and active it may mean a few good days of dry air and good weather. 'If dew is on the grass, rain will never come to pass' is partially true: dew is more likely to form during periods of high pressure.

Low pressure systems lead to wet and unsettled weather. When air is rising, as it is with low pressure, it is cooling and condensing, which means it forms clouds and can't hold as much moisture. When there is a big low-pressure system over the Atlantic it's a bit like a pebble being thrown into the sea: low pressure produces swell, waves and rougher water on the shores.

Isobars are pressure lines that join equal areas of air pressure. Wind is air moving from high to low pressure: the closer the lines are to each other, the faster the wind is moving. If it's coming over the Atlantic, it will generate bigger waves.

INSHORE WATERS FORECAST AND THE SHIPPING FORECAST

The Shipping Forecast gives mariners information on offshore waters, too far out (generally) to interest us as swimmers. The Met Office Inshore Waters Forecast is more relevant. This divides the coast of Britain into nineteen large sections, each of which is given its own forecast. The forecast contains details of wind direction and force, sea state, weather and visibility. This forecast provides a more holistic way of looking at sea conditions ahead than forecasts where phenomena like surf have been isolated.

The inland forecast starts with a general overview: for example, 'A series of weather fronts and a mainly southerly flow will continue to affect coastal waters during the next couple of days, with occasional gales or severe gales in the north and west.' If you then home in on a stretch of coast, more detailed information is available. Through this forecast I have learnt that Lyme Bay is often the most sheltered and swimmable bay on the stretch of coast near me: it is part of area 8 (which runs from Land's End to Lyme), and Lyme often has winds described as 'occasionally moderate' while elsewhere in area 8 conditions are being described as 'rough or very rough'.

Again, these are only forecasts – sea state near the shore, where we swim, is highly variable, and the best way to assess conditions is to look at them from the headland or shore. Local webcams are useful for remote surveillance. Data that says 'swell of 4–6ft in 24 mph strong winds' might not create a mental picture for you of what to expect – the webcam will show you exactly what those conditions look like (inhospitable).

THE BEAUFORT WIND AND SEA STATE SCALE

'Gale Force 4,' says the forecast. Can you swim in it? That depends on lots of factors – your ability in rough water, your appetite for being out of control, the location, and the type of swim you want to do (long-distance or just surviving and bobbing). How long the storm has been raging also makes a difference: if the winds have been blowing for days, then it will have created bigger swell than if they have just started.

As it gets rougher, waves grow as well as becoming more unpredictable: the water beneath you starts to sway and roll. Wave crests start to break and blow apart, creating a foaming sea with spray coming in with air as you try to breathe. Water becomes stronger, and harder to move through. Sometimes you can relax and find a rhythm with the swell, other times it is chaos. Waves can hit you hard, knocking you off course, and all this while you start to swallow water as well as aspirate spray. There is no chance to stop and gather yourself as the mayhem is relentless, whether you're being hit by rollers or battling a headwind. It becomes harder to sight, and the calm rhythm of swimming, the steadying act of breathing, both of which can calm and suppress natural anxieties about being in a sea that's bigger and stronger than you, are blown apart – leaving a much more exposed feeling of terror. You start coughing, you can't breathe, the waves are crashing over your head. Then BOOM. It's all too much and you want to get out. Or not; because this kind of messy water is exactly what some swimmers love in a day out. Everyone has their own version of 'too rough'.

Gale Force winds are typically described in marine contexts and measured in knots (nautical miles per hour) – it's the open ocean where winds pick up unimpeded and drastically change the terrain. The number rating comes from the Beaufort scale, which was originally devised by a Royal Navy commander as a way of classifying sea state in 1805.[1] In 1805, looking at the sea state came first, translating it into a number second (the scale would have enabled mariners to compare conditions and generate procedures for them). Now we are swimming in numbers and left looking for ways to translate them into understanding of conditions.

UK wind forecasts can be delivered in the form of the Beaufort scale, miles or kilometres per hour, or knots. Mass participation events and swimmers crossing the Channel will be hoping for breezes of Force 3 or below on the Beaufort scale; however, 'You should hope for Force 1 or 2 but be prepared for Force 4 or 5,' say the Channel Swimming Association. Wind affects the ability of safety crews to operate on the water so it's well worth thinking about whether rescues will be possible in stronger winds, not just whether you can still swim in them. It's also worth noting that the Beaufort scale makes its sea observations (such as 'moderate waves') from the perspective of being in a boat, whereas 'moderate' 3 to 4 metre waves will feel massive to a swimmer in the water. (See pages 138–9.)

WIND CHILL

A further metric you will hear in forecasts is wind chill, which is a measure of how air temperature feels.

There are various versions, and the UK one is an index of how fast heat is lost from a bare face, if walking around with it uncovered and facing the wind. Lucky winter swimmer then, walking around with far more than the face uncovered. Long marches to withdrawn seas can be bitter.

Wind chill will be most rapid when skin is warm, and finding a sheltered place to change will stop the wind robbing you of body heat quite so much. Swimmers prepare for this meaningfully when it matters – changing into swimming kit before arriving at a shore, wearing a windproof changing robe, storing clothes in a bag to both retain any warmth and make sure the wind doesn't blow them away. Wind cools us down faster than still air, and wind and wet skin chills faster still.

The wind chill index is only used at air temperatures below 10 °C and winds above 4.8 kph/3 mph.

WIND

If I'm off to swim around my local open water lake I try to move my mind outside before I get there – and noticing the wind is always a part of that. If I can see leaves skittering across the road and trees bending in the wind on the drive I'll be ready for a swim that requires a bit more effort when I arrive, rather than feeling like a calm 'time-out swim' that isn't on offer.

PREVAILING WIND AND WIND DIRECTION

If you are planning a longer swim, a location's prevailing wind direction (the predominant direction where wind in that area comes from) may be used for far-out planning, with plans tweaked when five-day forecasts become available. Wind is defined in terms of where it is coming from – a northerly wind is coming from the north (and is cold, though easterly winds can also be bitter).

Prevailing winds change across the seasons, and data on average wind speeds and direction is available so you can find out what winds you can expect. The English Channel, for example, has no prevailing wind; winds blow from all directions in different percentages. The average wind strength on the Channel is 13 mph (Force 4).

- **A headwind** is when the wind is blowing towards your head. It causes chop and waves to come directly towards you, and can be a beast, making the whole action of swimming difficult. 'A headwind of twenty miles an hour would nearly double the time a swim would take, if it did not cancel it altogether', says Gerald Forsberg in his book *Modern Long Distance Swimming.*[3]

- **A crosswind** comes from the side, and can take you off course as your arms act like sails and you can get

THE BEAUFORT SCALE

BEAUFORT SEA SCALE	DESCRIPTION	WIND KNOTS (MPH)	WINDS (KPH)	SEA OBSERVATIONS
0	Calm	0–1	0–1	Flat. Sea like a mirror.
1	Light Air	1–3	1–5	Sea rippled, smooth with no crests.
2	Light Breeze	4–7	6–11	Small wavelets on sea – glassy-looking, no crests.
3	Gentle Breeze	8–12	12–19	Large wavelets on sea, crests begin to break, scattered white caps. Chance of spray. Swimming becomes harder.
4	Moderate Breeze	13–18	20–28	Waves becoming bigger and longer, fairly frequent white horses, breaking crests, chance of spray. Experienced swimmers only: the waves are now taller than you.
5	Fresh Breeze	19–24	29–38	Moderate waves, many white horses (i.e. crested waves), unpredictable water, spray.
6	Strong Breeze	25–31	39–49	Large rolling wells begin to form, extensive foam, crests, airborne spray.
7	Near Gale	32–38	50–61	Huge heapy sea, white foam from breaking waves blown in streaks across the sea. Moderate amount of spray.
8	Gale	39–46	62–74	High waves with breaking crests that break into spindrift (spray that is blown by the wind). Foam is blown in streaks across the sea.
9	Strong Gale	47–54	75–88	Colossal rolling waves that ferries bump off. Wave crests topple over, airborne spray affects visibility. Dense foam blown in wind direction.
10	Storm	55–63	89–102	Sea white with foam, huge and heapy, enormous waves with overhanging crests.
11	Violent Storm	64–72	103–117	Mammoth waves. Sea covered in white foam, visibility seriously affected.
12	Hurricane	Above 72	116+	Gigantic waves. Sea completely white. Air filled with foam and spray.

LAND OBSERVATIONS	PROBABLE WAVE HEIGHT IN OPEN SEA (M)
Smoke rises vertically.	0
Direction shown by smoke drift but not by wind vanes.	0.1
Wind felt on face; leaves rustle; wind vane moved by wind.	0.2–0.3
Leaves and small twigs in constant motion; light flags extended.	0.6–1
Raises dust and loose paper; small branches moved.	1.0–1.5
Small trees in leaf begin to sway.	2.0–2.5
Large branches in motion; whistling heard in telegraph wires; umbrellas used with difficulty.	3.0–4.0
Whole trees in motion; inconvenience felt when walking against the wind.	4.0–5.5
Twigs break off trees; wind generally impedes progress of pedestrians and cars.	5.5–7.5
Slight structural damage (chimney pots and slates removed). Branches break off trees, small trees blown over, construction temporary signs and barricades blown over.	7.0–10.0
Seldom experienced inland; trees uprooted; considerable structural damage.	9.0–12.5
Very rarely experienced; accompanied by widespread damage. Medium-sized ships lost to view behind waves.	11.5–16.0
Devastation. Air filled with foam and spray, very poor visibility.	14+

A note on the table: The original ratings scheme described sea states and was not correlated to wind speeds; two attempts to correlate the scale with wind speed and the addition of land-based observations came later, so you may find slight variations between the numbers. These are drawn from the Royal Meteorological Society.[2]

battered by chop and waves from the side. You will want to breathe away from the wind direction so your head is sheltering your mouth from filling with water. If you have a boat, it may well position itself to protect you from a crosswind.

- **A tailwind** is the easiest wind direction to swim in – the wind drives the top layer of water forward, and you with it. If you have a choice on an A to B swim, choose to swim with the wind behind you; it will push you along and you'll be going with the waves. If the waves are big it can still be difficult. Going offshore with a tailwind can lead to difficulties coming back. Forsberg estimates that 'the most advantageous following wind is about 10 miles an hour, more than that tends to chop up the water too much for efficient stroking.'[3]

Out in exposed water you are interested in gusts of wind, not just average wind speed.

WIND, CHOP AND FETCH

Wind affects lake state as well as sea state. Are you looking for a swim when the lake is glass-flat and glossy, or when the water is choppy and chaotic?

Wind picks up speed along a lake's length, as water has a smoother surface than surrounding vegetation, land and mountains. Wind creates waves, and wave height builds with wind duration – if a storm has been blowing for a good two to three hours you will see bigger waves than if it has just started. The shore furthest from the wind is often where the roughest water and the sharpest exposure is. On some lake shores you can even find freshwater surf; the Great Lakes in Canada have recorded waves of up to 8.7 metres in autumn, when harsh storms and strong north-easterlies blow.

- **Fetch** is the distance over water that wind blows in a single direction.

- **Chop** is the word for small messy waves that form on the water surface when it is windy. Choppy disorganised water is more common than waves, as waves rebound off the sides and end of a lake and crash into each other. (Wind may also rebound against landforms at the end of the lake, causing further confusion.) Chop will increase in height with the distance along the lake and get messier and more challenging.

Lakes in mountain areas will have multiple disturbances – lakes are often located in depressions, such as valley bottoms and corries, which syphon wind. The best (sometimes only) way to find out what is going on locally is to get there and see it. Local breezes may create winds blowing in different directions to the forecast and the edges of a large lake (outcrops, coves, river mouths and jetties) can provide shelter as well as stir up local disturbances. Calmer water is generally on the lee side of obstacles, and the taller the obstacle (e.g. a row of tall trees), the larger the area of water that will be protected.

Wind on large water bodies (sea, lake or other) can cause surface mixing of the water, so where water has previously stratified into a lovely warm surface layer and a colder underlying layer, after the wind blows it may all be mixed up. This can lower temperature by several degrees, changing a swim from a warm summery one to cold and autumnal even though it may only be a day later.

STORMS

So, there's been a storm, and now time has passed – the weather has settled.

Is that the end of the effect of a storm surge on your swim spot? No. Offshore storms bring a trail of swell that can last for days, and where there has been rain water levels in a river can take some days to return to normal. When surf is high because of storms, it is likely to be most approachable at low tide.

Storms can reshape rivers and beaches, moving sandbars and mudbanks, relocating rocks underwater and throwing debris of all sizes around. Storm surges often dump flotsam and jetsam, leaving behind litter, plastic debris and driftwood. On the coast you will also find ripped-up seaweed and mashed-up crab moults. The effects can extend to removal and relocation of sand and shingle. Be aware that a swim that has had the same character for decades may change if a big rock or a sandbar is moved by a storm.

Not all debris is weather-related: some things just fall or get thrown in. Marathon swimmer Lynne Cox tells an unforgettable story (trust me, I've tried to forget it), about hitting something with her hand on a swim and finding she had punched through the rib-cage of a dead dog.[4] UK swimmers find dead livestock only rarely, although we do come across some sheep down here in Somerset. If you see a carcass get out upstream, or swim wide of it, and contact the Environment Agency for removal.

WIND AND CAT'S PAWS

'Cat's paws' is what sailors call dark patches of tiny waves, observed on becalmed seas. They are caused by small gusts of wind.

If you are standing looking out at a relatively calm lake (or sea) assessing a swim, you may see patches of dark, ruffled water. If they're not cloud shadows, then they're signs of wind ruffling the surface: the ripples do not reflect as much light as the smoother surroundings, leading to water that looks dark.

If you are surrounded by mountains or trees that create dark reflections, then the cat's paws can be lighter, rather than darker, than the surrounding lake.

RAIN

Rain adds endless variations to the swim experience. There is nothing like seeing a mist of rain above the water or raindrops roll like pearls across a calm surface; or watching it change the water's surface, flattening waves or percussing.

I have a whole history of loving rain. There are lots of places where flood water stonking along would make for an appalling swim plan – count the ways to hurt yourself: fallen trees, strong eddies, debris, sewage... but while most of the time flood water should be avoided, a high river is not always out of bounds.

Visiting my orthodontist, the conversation turned to his local river. 'There's a tree-root jacuzzi at high water levels,' he said. Who had ever heard of one of those? Cut to the next morning, when we traipsed across a sodden September field in trainers and swimwear, to enter a slight swollen, slightly brown river. The tree jacuzzi wasn't, it turned out, running that day, but what an experience to watch out for.

RIVERS AND RAIN

The key fact to retain is that rivers vary with rainfall, so the fact that you have swum here today doesn't always say enough about how you will find a swim there tomorrow. Rain can:

- create eddies to play in
- lower water quality
- lower water temperature
- add debris (surface and underwater)
- alter water level
- increase speed
- alter force – which can drive you into rocks and debris, creating impact injuries
- create hazards such as sieves and syphons

A word on snow: for snowfall, the same issues around raised river levels will occur, but when snow thaws, rather than when it falls. Snow also has the potential to decrease a river's temperature by a greater amount as it makes its way into the river. If snow has stuck around for a period of time (a week to months) it may bring with it a higher amount of debris, as it will have been deposited on the snow through wind and then flown into the river with the snowmelt.

FLASHY RIVERS AND FLASH FLOODS

Flashy rivers are ones that go from calm to chaotic in a flash after heavy rainfall. The time it takes for river levels to rise after rain varies between a few hours and a few days. The Dart and the Wye are flashy rivers, with the former said to rise 4–6 hours after rain, although after heavy rain one swimmer watched one location rise 45 centimetres in 30 minutes.

Flashiness is a guide to both how long it takes a river to swell, and also how long it takes for storm water to flush through and water levels to drop. I find it interesting, when swimming in rivers and estuaries, to look at where floods have been: litter and silty tidemarks (warp) are often left behind in high branches, a visual history of high water marks that can be surprising.

For the scientifically minded, public information on the 'lag time' of water for every spot does exist, via river gauging station data. In my home patch the Frome rises eight hours after rain, for example, whereas the Avon upstream takes about a day, and the Avon around Bath (further downstream) a day and a half.

Factors that affect how long it takes for a river to rise after rainfall include how close to the river the rain fell, how steep surrounding slopes are, whether the surrounding land is forested, grassland or urban (the harder and less vegetated the surrounding landscape is, the quicker water will 'run off' and reach the river), and how saturated the land is already.

If it has rained for days or weeks prior then the land will already be waterlogged and so additional rain will flow over land and reach a river more quickly.

But equally, land that is baked hard by drought can become impermeable and this can also leads to flash floods, which is why flash floods are often associated with desert canyons, where water is funnelled and rises fast.

RAIN, RUN-OFF AND SEWAGE

Ah, sewage: swirling, whirling thoughts of sewage: scourge of swimmers, surfers and all other water users.

Sudden heavy rain or prolonged rain can change a swimming place (river, lake or sea) from a pure clean swimming experience to a potentially polluted one, and is likely to downgrade the water quality of a place from very good to good, or good to poor.

Soil and underlying bedrock absorb and filter water before it enters courses. Run-off occurs when there is more water than land can absorb and it runs down the hills, and into rivers, lakes and seas. As it runs, it picks up pollutants from the land's surface such as cow manure, pesticides, fertilisers, oil from car parks and car exhaust particles, and carries them straight into rivers and streams. This can cause floods and lead to polluted water bodies.

Untreated sewage can also enter waterways after big storms, via storm overflow systems and leakage from septic tanks. Our sewage and drainage systems are linked, so where there are heavy storms untreated sewage is sometimes discharged via 'storm overflows' straight into rivers.

It is worth knowing where sewage outlets are on a river; there may be options, like swimming upstream of them. Sewage outlets can be identified on OS maps, and online, where you may also find live data on storm overflows.

Real-time water quality data, and information about storm sewage overflows, is available in some places. Common sense can also provide you with some data to work out whether you want to swim or not. Upland water, closer to source, is likely to be purer than water further downstream or in urban areas.

Measures reversing land management practices of the past

– re-meandering rivers that have been straightened, reintroducing beavers, restoring floodplains, restoring hedges and forests – are among the countryside restoration projects going on to moderate floods and assist ecology. Introducing wetlands and re-wetting bogs are another way to provide a buffer between land and water, the primary benefits being flood protection and river health; but these moves will also stabilise and improve swim conditions.

A word on getting sick from sewage: to create sickness and ill heath, the pathogens of polluted water need to find a pathway to enter your body, for example, as a result of your swallowing water, entering the water with an open cut or burst blister, or eating before washing your face and hands. Polluted water that comes into contact with your eyes, nose and mouth is not necessarily enough to create infection and swimmers might be less likely to swallow water in the course of a swim than someone falling in from a boat or paddleboard. Anecdotally, reports of seasoned swimmers getting sick from polluted water are rare, with cases often involving those doing marathon swim challenges. This is likely to be because marathon and novel challenges place a stress on the immune system, and may lead to swimmers becoming cold, tired, weak and more vulnerable to infection; also, these kinds of swims involve greater overall pathogen exposure due to the extended time spent in the water; and finally, they may lead to swimmers being in the water at times when others might stay out and let things settle for a day or two, or (for example) change their swim route to avoid inhaling spray. Being new to open water may also increase vulnerability: it's possible new swimmers swallow more water as a result of being unfamiliar with swimming in chop, for example. Whether we build up tolerance or immunity with time spent in the water is less clear.

The decision to swim is always personal, and whether you feel robust or that you have 'a weak stomach' can be part of your decision-making. But whenever and wherever you swim: wash your hands and face before eating, and again after handling wetsuits or kit. Make sure to dry your ears (tip your head on one side and use a cloth) and take a shower when you can afterwards. A nose clip will reduce exposure of the mucous membranes in the nose, carrying antibacterial hand gel or using ear plugs are further preventative measures. Some paddlers and surfers suggest drinking but not eating straight after being in polluted water, to flush through anything they have swallowed.

SUMMER RAIN

Your river may react differently to summer rain. If there has been a period of a few weeks or longer of very hot weather, the ground may have dried out and become hard. This will mean the water will flow straight across the surface and not sink in, and an amount of rain you might think will take x hours to reach the river and bring the level up may take much less time.

Summer rainfall can have a larger impact on water quality than the same amount of rain in winter. During dry spells debris, litter and man-made pollutants can build up on the land surfaces. Farmers will also have been fertilising their fields, and livestock will have been out on the land, so there may be larger amounts of effluent and agricultural run-off flowing into the rivers. All this means that in summer, it's possible that a relatively larger amount of nastiness may reach the river for the same amount of rain. You may want to give summer storms a few days to flush through the river before entering it again.

DRY SPELLS AND DROUGHTS

Dry spells are associated with lower flow, which can also lead to lower water quality in rivers, lakes and reservoirs, as there is less dilution of any pollution. Drought also increases the risk of lower oxygen levels. Rivers can feel murky and thick, lakes can experience algae bloom and show signs of distress – fish gulping in the shadows, limpets on the surface. Damage to aquatic ecosystems leads to a downward spiral in water health.

During low water levels we may also end up knocking our knees, wading and adjusting our stroke to swim in shallow water (aqua shoes are handy).

Low flow can lead to injuries where jumpers attempt jumps that are no longer safe as water is too shallow, and they hit rocks, objects, or the riverbed with force.

Low flow in rivers is an increasingly frequent summer event due to climate change, but dry spells can come in winter and spring too. In 2020 winter floods were followed by a long dry spell. For England and Wales, it was the driest May since records began (in 1910), with just 17 per cent of the average rainfall, and some regions receiving below 10 per cent. Some rivers recorded lower flow levels than they had seen at that time of year since records began.

LOCALISED WEATHER PHENOMENA

Your location will have a direct effect on the sort of weather that you are likely to experience when you swim outdoors.

MOUNTAIN ENVIRONMENTS

Mountains are renowned for their effect on the weather – the fact that they protrude higher into the atmosphere means they upset air patterns. Mountain weather is faster-moving and more tempestuous: rain of biblical proportions, scudding clouds and light rapidly changing the weather around you. Bleak can be beautiful but you need to be more prepared than in the lowlands.

Relief rainfall is a common occurrence around mountains; the air has to rise over the mountain, and cools, then as it drops over the other side it warms and releases the water vapour it had collected as it travelled over the seas, as rain or snow. If you're in a mountainous area in the UK the eastern sides of mountains are likely to be wetter (and therefore where you find the lakes).

The glacial hollows that hold lakes and tarns (corries in Scotland, cwms in Wales) are often the coldest part of the mountain, below the summit – glaciers form where air temperature is lowest, and often receive a relatively low amount of sunlight compared to the surrounding landscape. They may also be exposed to wind.

Air temperature drops 1 °C with every 100-metre ascent, and wind speeds pick up. So, if you want to swim in mountainous lakes be prepared for colder conditions than at lower elevations, and for windy conditions with little sun to warm you up.

LAND AND SEA BREEZES: ONSHORE AND OFFSHORE WIND

Forecasts do not include local breezes. Big bodies of water, even still ones, can create winds that vary with the time of day.

Early morning tends to be a calm time. Anyone who lives near a large lake may have discovered that the 'first in' millpond moment, where water is glassy and unruffled, is more often found at sunrise. This is because at some point overnight – normally around 5 a.m. – the land and water surface areas will have become equal in temperature, and any wind effect from one to another will have dropped.

But as land warms up in the morning sunshine wind can pick up, with cooler air being drawn in from the sea, or funnelled down a valley over a lake. Lake or onshore breezes are more common around midday and in the afternoon on warm days in spring and summer, but the warmer the climate, the earlier onshore breezes will develop. They may drop off in winter, when there is less temperature difference between land and water.

At nightfall, this flow of air reverses; the land cools down faster than the sea and a localised breeze may be offshore. At some point parity is achieved, winds drop, and all is calm.

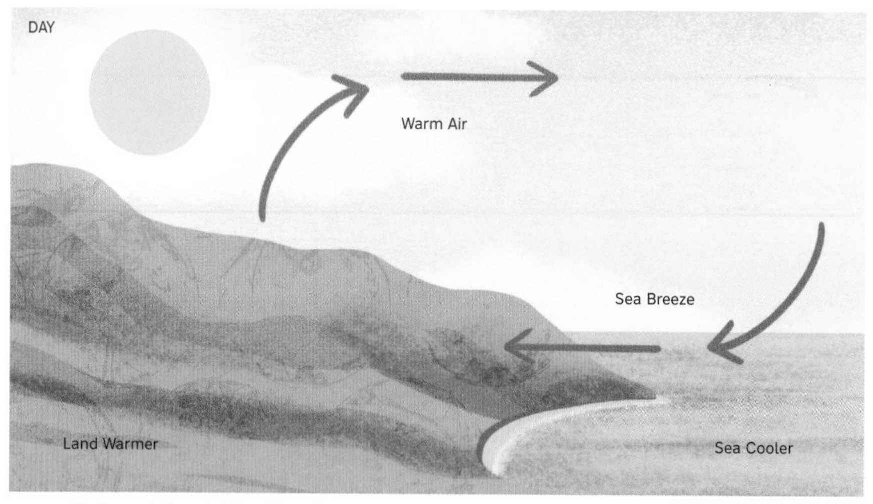

Onshore wind: a wind that blows from water on to land. Also called a sea breeze or lake breeze. Sea breezes can be 10 to 20 knots (12–23 mph), a wind speed that will sufficiently alter a swim. More common in spring and summer when days are warmer.

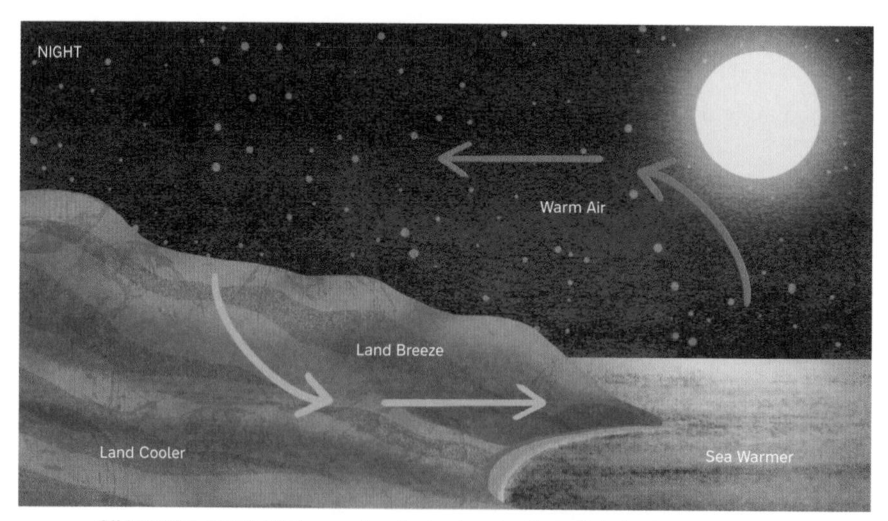

Offshore wind: any wind that moves from land on to water. Also called a land breeze. They tend to occur at night. Land cools down faster than water after sunset, and as the air above it cools it sinks, and is pushed offshore over large bodies of water, where the comparatively warmer area rises. Offshore winds tend to be weaker than onshore, with their pace spanning from 5 to 8 knots (6–9 mph). Most common in autumn and winter when nights are cooler.

ONSHORE AND OFFSHORE WINDS

KATABATIC WIND (VALLEY OR MOUNTAIN BREEZE)

If you are swimming in the mountains, or in a river or estuary on a valley floor, then you may come across other local winds: katabatic winds. These are downslope winds, and occur where there are steep valleys. As the slopes cool overnight, the tops are cooler than the valley bottom, and the cool air sinks into the valley, sliding downhill.

Katabatic winds can be sudden and quite violent, and are not shown on a forecast. If you were expecting an estuary swim with a following wind from the forecast but arrive to find a headwind, it could be a local katabatic wind at play.

SEA FOG, STEAM FOG, RIVER MIST AND OTHER LAND-BASED CLOUDS

The difference between mist and fog is how far you can see through it. Both are caused by fine water droplets hanging in the air. With mist you can see more than 1 kilometre away, with fog the visibility is less than 1 kilometre.

Will they affect you as a swimmer? Possibly, as river valleys and large bodies of water such as the sea and large lakes can all help to create mist and fog. Some people are looking for it, a swim where no one can see them and they can only see peeks of the world as the fog parts. Others may need to see other swimmers, support crew, the way, or other water users for safety.

Many swimmers get up early in autumn to take a misty swim in valley fog – leave it later and the sun may burn it off. This type of fog is created when the ground cools rapidly at night, chilling the air. The moisture in it condenses to form mist or fog. This will usually dissipate after daybreak as the land and air warm up, but radiation fog can settle in a valley for several days if there is no wind to disperse it. One year valley fog settled in on a corner of river at the Dart 10k and an anxious delay occurred, with swimmers hopping from foot to foot by the start pen while downstream the water safety team sat and waited for it to burn off.

Coastal and lake fogs happen when the wind blows moist air over a cold surface. Coastal fogs are more common on the east coast of the UK, over the North Sea, in spring and summer. If there is no wind and little warmth to disperse them then they can sit on the coast for a long time.

Swimmers may also be familiar, by sight if not name, with 'steam fogs'. Ever gone to your local lake first thing on a summer morning to see it steaming like a hot tub? This effect occurs when very cold air flows over warmer water. Water vapour evaporates into it, producing wisps that look like steam.

CHAPTER 6

UNDERSTANDING COLD

'I dived in.
Blue shock.
The cold running into me like a dye'

ROBERT MACFARLANE,
The Wild Places

The most common experience of outdoor swimming in temperate climates like the UK, United States, large parts of Europe and South Africa is that the water is cold. There may be a few months in exceptional summers where water temperature rises to the 20s and is experienced as warm, but this is rare. The most common experience until you get into the swing of things is brrrr. Huh-huh-huh, fwaw-fwaw-fwaw and brrrrrrrr. Having your breath taken away is a noisy business.

Forming a relationship with cold is one of the subversive things about outdoor swimming that many come to love. Cold is an adverse condition for humans; it hurts, it's the opposite of what we spend our modern lives doing (getting comfortable). And therein, ultimately, lies the wealth: cold taps us back into our wild wordless selves. Bit by bit, over the year, the temperature rises and falls, and, submerged in the water, we move with it, up and down the thermometer of experience.

HOW COLD WATER FEELS

Water temperature in the UK and much of the world is low enough year-round to lead to getting cold when you swim. If the water is below 35 °C then you can get hypothermia; it's just a matter of how long that will take. (I have had a friend take to the shade in Greece, feeling funny after a swim, not realising she was suffering from cold, not sunstroke.) Swimmers experience water temperature in the following bands:

0 to 6 °C: Baltic

This is winter swimming temperature. In the words of Lewis Pugh, the endurance swimmer, water in this temperature bracket is a 'violent physical assault on the body'.

Getting in is likely to impair breathing in the uninitiated, as breath comes in big jolting gasps and it feels like someone has clamped on an ice neck brace. Water has bite, skin smarts and burns. Exiting, you may sport what swimmers call a 'Scottish tan': skin taking on an orange/purple/red colour, burnt by wind and cold rather than sun.

6 to 11 °C: freezing

Much like Baltic, but not quite so painful, nor so breathtaking. Swims in these temperatures are likely to remain short and be therapeutic. 6–10 °C is the average winter sea temperature in the British Isles, and spring and autumn swimming temperatures in fresh water generally. Fresh-water temperature tracks land and air temperatures.

12 to 16 °C: fresh

The International Triathlon Union rules state swims must be cancelled where water temperature drops below 13 °C,[1] but in a wetsuit, you may find you can swim comfortably for a while. Without one, the water is 'fresh' – doable for the brave, and not a problem for hardened open water lovers.

This is 'face in' territory (people do put their faces in below 11-degree water and swim front crawl, but it is not as popular).

British outdoor swimmers have to embrace 12 to 16 °C as their home territory – from May to October this is the river temperature in the UK – and mass open water swim events such as the Dart 10k in the UK, Robben Island swim in South Africa and Escape Alcatraz in San Francisco have always operated in whatever temperature water nature provides (frequently under 15 °C).

17 to 20 °C: summer swimming

Lakes and more mature rivers reach this temperature over summer during hot spells. The water still feels fresh on entry but makes for comfortable lazy-hazy summer swimming. Multiple dips within a day have an easy appeal and kit dries outside without a problem. The seas, which have been the warmer option over winter and spring, may now be a few degrees cooler than rivers and lakes.

Even committed wetsuit wearers may start to leave them behind at this temperature. One downside: algae can start to bloom.

21 °C plus: warm

You'd think that 'warm' would be a good thing, but on the rare occasions that river pools and shallow lakes reach these temperatures during hot spells, there can be an odd sense that something is missing – the exhilarated feeling when you get out, that cold water 'tang'.

On the plus side, longer swims in togs take on a whole new ease.

28 °C: pool temperature

So warm, you're likely to be in an Icelandic hot spring, or the warm seas of the Caribbean, Maldives or Thailand. Or (gasp) an indoor pool.

For regular outdoor swimmers, these temperatures may feel arguably unpleasant.

Experience of cold is quite different depending on whether you are a marine or freshwater swimmer. Inland bodies of water are much more volatile than the sea, with a wider band of overall temperatures, and more dramatic changes between them. Freshwater temperatures in the UK start at 0 degrees and can climb up to 27 °C (very rarely), and are capable of changing overnight in response to cold air, ground temperature and rain. We once had a late September Dart 10k event on the Dart Estuary in Devon where early autumn ground frosts and cold air lowered the water temperature five degrees in one week pre-event, from 17 °C to 12 °C. Feet that had been happy bare the week before suddenly wanted insulating from the ground. Bodies had no way of acclimatising pre-event – swimmers just had to add extra neoprene (or not) and give it a go.

Even when it is down to 6 degrees, most swimmers will tell you that a 6 °C sea feels considerably warmer than a 6 °C river – no, we haven't found a physiological explanation either, but experience bears it out. The sea varies between 6 and 18 °C.

COLD SENSITIVITY

Baseline cold sensitivity is as widely distributed as any other physical trait. Just as there are people who can run marathons in the desert, and people who feel unwell on a hot day in summer, people arrive at cold swimming with different baselines. There are fast coolers and slow coolers. Put a group of similar-weight friends in any kind of cold situation, whether that's a draughty kitchen or icy water, and they will grow cold at different rates: some will be fast coolers and lose body heat and grow uncomfortable quickly; others will be slow coolers and have warm feet for much longer. You will probably know which you are: my lips going blue first in a group (a sign of falling body temperature) surprises people, but there we are. I was not born with cold tolerance as a gift.

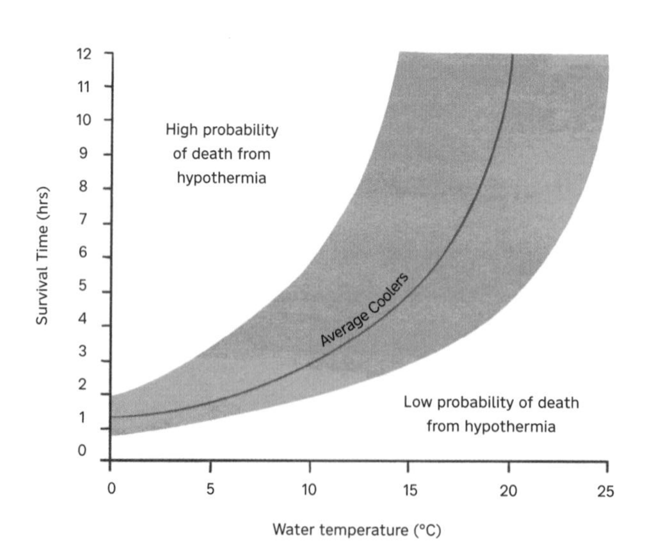

CALCULATED SURVIVAL TIME DURING WATER IMMERSION

Dealing with cold as a swimmer is a personal journey, in which you will get to know your own signs of cold, what you can (and are prepared to) tough out, what is trainable, and what you need to watch. This is the variation in predicted calm-water survival time (defined as the time required to cool to 30 °C or 86 °F) in lightly clothed, non-exercising humans in cold water. Body size, build, body fat percentage, physical fitness and state of health will all affect where you sit on the chart. Wetsuits slow down cooling significantly. In a survival situation huddling together, stationary, is more advantageous than swimming, which cools people down faster.[2]

BIOPRENE, BODY MASS AND BODY FAT

The winning physique for marathon and endurance swimmers is quite different to that for other sports. 'You can't be too vain to gain' is a maxim in the Channel-swimming community, where the acquisition or maintenance of body fat is part of the journey.

There are three dimensions of body size and shape that increase resilience to cold. Overall mass matters; large objects take longer to cool than small ones, and similarly a big person will take longer to cool than a small one. The ratio of surface area to volume is also important. A tall slender person will cool down faster than a shorter stockier one.

An individual's level of body fat (measured via 'skin fold thickness') also assists the retention of warmth. When you get in cold water, blood withdraws from the surface of skin, turning this fat layer into 'bioprene'; it's like having an internal wetsuit that helps insulate your core. Women naturally hold more body fat than men, and a more even distribution of subcutaneous fat, which provides some insulation, but swimming perfuses muscles with blood close to the skin surface, so if you are exercising in water body fat is not as advantageous as it would be if you were stationary.

FITNESS AND WARMTH: KEEPING MOVING

Lynne Cox is one of our cold-water and endurance swimming pioneers, and one of the swimmers who scientists have studied to see how she achieved what others could not. What they found was that during long swims – for example after a four-hour swim in 10 °C (50 °F) water – Lynne was warmer than she was at the start, with a core temperature of 38.3 °C (101 °F). They discovered that she had the right level of fitness and fat to create more heat than she lost.

When doing a swim (rather than bobbing about), being fit is one of your defences against cold; a fitter person can maintain a higher level of energy expenditure and heat production than a less fit person, and this can help keep their temperature stable in colder water. When I'm getting cold on a longer front-crawl swim (over an hour), I often kick more than is strictly efficient to generate more warmth, and keep snacks in the arms and legs of my wetsuit to supplement my energy reserves so I can afford to 'waste' energy in this way.

One surprising thing about water is exactly how fast you can start to feel cold if you stop – less than a minute's pause for a chat, or a snack, or a photo can leave you feeling chilly. Water cools you twenty-five times faster than air. In terms of being stationary in water, Heather Massey at Portsmouth University researches cold water immersion and survival physiology and has found acclimatised swimmers cool more quickly than the non-acclimatised.[3]

GETTING IN, STAYING IN, GETTING OUT

Entering the water, I have a ritual of putting my hands in it and then splashing the cold water on my cheeks and face, the back of my neck and my pulse points – the insides of my wrists and elbows – to help me acclimatise, but it's more about how much surface area you cover with cold splashes than where on your body you splash. Here follow some tried-and-tested tips on the best ways to get into the water and to enjoy the experience safely once you are in.

THE BEST WAY TO ENTER WATER: DEALING WITH COLD SHOCK

The term 'cold shock' refers to the gasp reflex that happens when the body enters cold water. All swimmers will be familiar with this 'takes your breath away' moment, and a wetsuit does not protect you from experiencing it. There are, though, various ways to reduce and manage the response:

- **Enter the water slowly,** in a controlled way, dabbing water on your skin to help take the gasp away. Some people stand waist-deep in water while they settle, and duck their shoulders in the shallows, so they have brought their breathing under control while their feet are still on the floor. You may want to bend over and put your face in, maybe blow bubbles, if you want to set straight off doing front crawl. You will find what works for you at different points in the year and in different situations. If need be, stand up and walk back out, then try again.

- **Control your breath.** If you feel like the cold has punched the air out of your lungs and you can't breathe, exhale with a strong 'fwaw'. It's all about the out-breath. This may feel counterintuitive but if you puff the air out the next breath will come back in. Then concentrate on steadying your breathing rate, taking slow steady breaths and relaxing. The cold shock response involves an elevated heart rate and increased blood pressure and can breed a sense of panic and lead to hyperventilation. Consciously controlling your breath helps – rapid breathing can increase panic, controlled breathing can induce a sense of calm.

- **Finally, habituate.** All aspects of the cold shock response – the initial gasp, rapid breathing, increased heart rate and blood pressure – dull in habituated swimmers so that they can get in with no obvious disturbance. Swimmers can subdue this response very fast: as few as five or six three-minute immersions where the whole body (not the head) is immersed in cold water will halve the cold shock response. Research shows that these dulled responses are conserved for a period: if you miss a couple of weeks in cold water, you don't start all over again. Half of this cold-water shock reduction is present fourteen months after the initial batch of cold-water immersions. Habituation is not completely temperature-specific, either: repeated immersions at 15 °C will help dull the response to cold at 10°C. But being able to control your first gasps says nothing about how long you can stay in.

Cold shock can get people into trouble in the water. If a person is under the water when this gasp reflex takes place (because they have jumped in, or a wave has come over their head), they may inhale some water, and not much water needs to be inhaled to cause a serious problem with breathing. There can be a chain reaction of problems – first the initial gasp, perhaps some inhalation of water, then a period of uncontrolled hyperventilation leading to a feeling of panic. Incidental and new swimmers tend to go upright in the water when any (let alone all) of these things are happening; in this position they are less buoyant, and panic can really set in as they struggle to stay afloat as well as draw breath, increasing the chances of drowning. The first gasp is always the worst, so I always try to get my children in and out of the water in the shallows before any jumping into deeper water begins.

As cold shock affects breathing and heart rate, swimmers with conditions like asthma or heart disease can experience additional difficulties and may wish to be cautious and discuss this with their doctor before they go swimming.

STEALTH CHILLING: COLD INCAPACITATION

'Will I get too cold?' is a question that may rarely leave you. There is 'too cold' as in 'not experiencing a high level of thermal comfort'. And then there is too cold as in the physiological phenomenon of 'cold incapacitation', which is what is described here. Stealth chilling (to describe it more accessibly) is a risk for any swimmer on a swim away from the shore or bank, or trying to complete a distance.

Stealth chilling affects both physical and mental ability in the water. When the body becomes cold, blood is shunted from the extremities to the core to preserve core temperature, and in the process swimming becomes more difficult: we lose muscle strength, manual dexterity and may have problems coordinating our movements. We may also become mentally impaired. It might take some time for the effects to be noticeable, but in really cold water it can happen quite quickly – I have experienced this crossing a small tarn. I was entertaining thoughts that the rock I was swimming to was exerting a polarised force that was pushing me away from it, and it wasn't until I turned back and felt equally weak that I reappraised what was happening.

The cold-incapacitation phenomenon explains how cold makes even a strong swimmer weak – even if a distance is no trouble at all to you in a pool, if you get cold swimming across a lake, say, and your arms and legs grow weaker and you grow less coordinated, then you could be in serious trouble. Stealth chilling leads to a more upright position in the water, which leads to sinking – over time everything gets harder, including getting out. If exiting the water involves a climb or holding on to things, you may struggle to pull yourself up or hold on to things. Mental impairment can get worse, to the point that the swimmer is unable to coordinate their breathing with, for example, gaps in waves and spray.

To stay safe: be aware of the phenomenon, swim along shores rather than away from them (unless you have boat or paddleboard support) and, if you start feeling cold or incapacitated, take the fastest route to land. If there is any current or flow, swim against it first, so it will assist you on the return. If you find yourself distressed and beginning to panic or sink, turn on to your back to float. Breathe, yell for help, calm yourself and then propel yourself back to the beach or bank.

THE CLAW

A common experience among outdoor swimmers is losing control of your hands – first the little finger separates from the pack, in a one-finger Vulcan salute, and then in time the whole hand may separate and claw. The surface area of your hands (and feet) is what propels you in the water, so splayed fingers therefore make strokes much less efficient. The claw happens because muscles contract as they get colder, pulling the tendons in the fingers apart.

If swimming in a wetsuit, your hands may go numb and the little finger separate even if your body is warm. Keeping the thin-skinned area of your wrist a bit warmer with longer wetsuit sleeves will give the blood travelling to your hands a better chance of staying warm. So will neoprene gloves, but they do take away feel for the water.

For swimmers just in costumes or trunks, large muscles will be experiencing the same contraction seen in the hands, making the swim stroke shorter and less effective at the same time. Steven Munatones is founder of the World Open Water Swimming Association (WOWSA, an international association dedicated to the promotion open water swimming), the International Swimming Hall of Fame (ISHOF) and 'Oceans Seven', a marathon swimming challenge that involves seven big open water swims. When observing long swims he uses a combination of a 10 per cent drop in stroke count with clawed hands as signs that a skin swimmer is now 'survival swimming' and should be asked regular questions (e.g. 'what are the names of your children?') to establish hypothermic state and decide whether to call it a day.

IF IT'S X DEGREES, HOW LONG CAN I STAY IN FOR?

Urban myths abound on this one. At some point, someone, somewhere, said, 'For water temperature above 10 °C, double the degrees to get the time you can spend in the water.' Soon the 10-degree part was forgotten and it became 'one minute per degree' or 'double the temperature to get time in the water' and some swimmers started treating these as goals or points to surpass rather than points to aim for.

There *are* no good universal guidelines on long you can stay in for, that depends on your particular body and what you enjoy. Start out with small dips, see how you are after you get out and extend your time in the water gradually. What someone else is capable of is not a good guide.

People rarely get competitive about being able to endure heat in a sauna, so it seems slightly bizarre that we're almost geared up at the moment to be competitive around enduring cold.

DO I NEED A THERMOMETER?

Whether or not to use a thermometer is an entirely individual choice. For some, a thermometer is unnecessary and may get in the way – there is nothing we can do about temperature, so on one level we might as well just embrace what we're presented with. And bodies do not function like machines – we can swim longer on some days than on others, so it's monitoring how we feel that is important.

For others, thermometers are interesting and may form part of keeping a logbook and making a science of their own body when training for an event, with a target time they want to be able to spend in the water, for example. Some swimmers opt to take the water temperature on the way out rather than the way in, so they swim according to how they feel, but still build up a profile of progress – logging temperature, time in the water, and how they felt afterwards.

Shore surface temperature is often a few degrees warmer than water you will be swimming in further out.

AFTERDROP AND THE SUBTLE ART OF WARMING UP

'Afterdrop' is common after swimming in cold water; you get out feeling fine, and then ten to forty minutes later you feel really messy: colder than you were when you got out, shivering, unwell, perhaps faint. This is as a result of your body temperature continuing to drop.

Immersed in cold water, the body conserves heat by shutting down blood to the skin, and eventually to the muscles. But when you exit the water, the cooling process does not stop straight away. At this point, even if you're dry on the bank, this cold layer of skin and fat continues to chill you – the insulating jacket is now part of the problem. According to Mike Tipton, from the Extreme Environments Laboratory at the University of Portsmouth, on the bank, depending on how you warm, you can lose up to 2 to 3 °C from your core temperature, bringing on shivering, hypothermia, or feeling faint and unwell.[4]

For the science nerds: another urban myth is that afterdrop is circulatory, a result of blood returning to the cold skin and cooling as it travels. It isn't; it's 'conductive' cooling, like wearing a cold, wet coat.

It is important to warm more from the inside than the outside. If rewarming occurs too quickly from the surface, blood pressure can fall, which is dangerous.

Warm showers or baths are no good if you have cooled the deep body beyond the skin. They can make you feel colder, dizzy and a bit sick, will reduce the shiver response (which you need), and may accentuate afterdrop and cause hot aches and chilblains.

WARMING UP

Here's what you can do to help yourself or another swimmer who is cold or hypothermic. The key is to get warm and dry as fast as possible:

1. Get out of the water.

2. Remove ALL wet clothes as soon as possible.

3. Stay out of the wind – a changing robe provides a portable shelter.

4. Pat skin dry, don't rub. Right now your skin is cold, so you don't want blood coming back to it in a rush.

5. Dress in dry warm clothes; you will want to dress one season colder than the season you are in (and if it's winter, imagine a snowy day): thermal base layers, wool jumpers, insulated jackets, hats, gloves, coats. Speed is of the essence here. In cold and wet weather skin may not dry well enough to pull on tight clothes, so you may wish to switch your jeans for joggers. You might think that you will never be reduced to this level of coddling, but if you move to being a foul-weather swimmer, there will come a point, bent over your clothes with inoperable fingers in a strong north wind when it all feels very relevant.

6. Arrange clothes in advance so you can dress quickly. Turn them the right way round. If you put them in your kitbag in the order the items come off, it'll be faster to reverse this process when you put them back on.

7. Skipping underwear and going straight to thermal base layers is a popular move when seriously cold.

8. Reflective space blankets will not help, except around the outside of layers to keep the wind off – use wool ones instead. You are not radiating enough heat for the space blanket to trap.

9. If the ground is cold, stand on something to insulate the soles of your feet. Swimmers take all kinds of objects with them: car mats, squares of old carpet, wooden shower trays, changing mats, IKEA bags (useful to stand inside). Or, they balance on their shoes.

10. For really cold people, it is safer to have them lie down or sit down rather than stand up, but do insulate them from the floor.

11. Take in warm drinks and a snack (no alcohol or caffeine). Small sips are best.

12. Shiver (shivering is very good – as you rewarm you will shiver less).

13. Covered hot-water bottles can help; stuck between clothing layers they donate small amounts of heat to the body – but be careful they don't burn cold skin (when skin is very cold, it will not be able to judge what is burning hot and what is not).

14. Seek out a warm, dry and wind-free place, such as a car or café.

15. If symptoms are mild, some gentle activity (walking) can help warming.

16. Keep yourself and others safe by waiting until you have warmed up before driving.

THE SCREAMING BARFLIES

Known elsewhere in the world as the 'hot aches', and well known to winter climbers, this is how these sensations are referred to in Australia, which gives you some idea of their unpleasantness. Seventy-five per cent of people put them at 3 to 4 on a 1 to 5 pain scale.

Sensations include wanting to scream and be sick, pain, extreme pins and needles, throbbing, irritability, dizziness, a whirling in the ears and in extreme cases a transient loss of vision and hearing. They generally last from one to five minutes. They occur most often in the hands and feet when these are perfused with blood again after becoming extremely numb and cold – which may happen when immersing in warm water or taking a shower after a cold swim. They can also occur on entering a warm room.

The best way to avoid them is to avoid hands and feet becoming so cold in the first place, and warm up gradually (for example, by staying outside for a while after your swim and avoiding warm water immersion). The intense itching sensation of the 'hot aches' can also occur on slivers of skin between wetsuit and gloves, or wetsuit and boots – here the easiest remedy is to buy longer boots and gloves, and tuck them under the wetsuit to help minimise this problem.

HOW TO ACCLIMATISE TO COLD WATER

> *'No black magic is required to adapt the human body to immersion in cold water. Essential requirements are merely time, inclination, a reasoned scientific approach, and one other big thing: the conviction that the mind is the master of the body'*
>
> GERALD FORSBERG,
> *Modern Long Distance Swimming*

Whatever base level you start with, whatever natural talent you have for cold, you can train from there.

'Acclimatisation' is the process whereby the body becomes able to deal with longer periods of cold water without suffering (overmuch). Polar explorers and mountaineers are among the groups well known to harden in response to the cold. Alongside farmers, anglers, soldiers and everyone living without central heating.

If you are swimming in temperatures like those we see in the UK the acclimatisation process is relevant year-round.

There is only one way to acclimatise: regular persistent exposure, or putting in the 'cold hard miles' as endurance swimmer Ross Edgley calls it.

Swimmers who want to achieve longer swims at any time of the year, in costumes or wetsuits, need to acclimatise by doing regular longer swims in training – swim at least once a week, and preferably two or three times, gradually extending the time that you stay in the water. Get out if you are not comfortable, and don't set time goals for staying in. It is necessary for your core to cool in order to start acclimatising, but it is not necessary to push acclimatisation to the point of hypothermia. Regular exposure will lead to acclimatisation.

Lynne Cox recommends making the cold a way of life: wearing lighter clothing, having colder showers, training in cooler pools, sleeping with the windows open. Some swimmers at the Channel-swimming, marathon-challenge end of the spectrum go as far as sleeping without blankets or duvets, even in winter. This spartan approach is not for everyone but it is likely that exposure to warmth may counteract cold-acclimatisation work being done in the water.

Spring swimmers who want to get fit for outdoor summer events have a balancing act between using warm pools to achieve longer training times, and not being made soft by them. If it is longer summer skin swims you wish to master, then you could start spring swimming in a wetsuit (with accessories such as neoprene vests, hoods, boots and gloves), then shed neoprene till you are in a costume or trunks only.

INSULATIVE ADAPTATION

When you get into cold water the vessels supplying blood to the skin are temporarily reduced in size, a skin-wide 'clench' in circulation that limits blood flow to the surface of the skin and extremities. This peripheral vasoconstriction is one of the reasons why cold water puts pressure on the heart and why swimming makes people want to pee. The same volume of blood moving through less space in your body leads to a rapid increase in blood pressure, which the body relieves by filtering fluid out of the blood into urine (a job for the kidneys). This phenomenon is called cold diuresis. It can happen year-round in temperate waters, and is dehydrating. (Be conscious of this and rehydrate after a swim.)

Scientist Heather Massey has found that this response where blood supply is moved to the deep tissues of the body, retaining heat, is quicker to happen but slower to reverse in acclimatised swimmers. In acclimatised swimmers the skin, hands and feet may cool to a greater extent than those who have not been cold-exposed, and take longer to rewarm. The blood vessels in the hands and feet appear faster to close and slower to open.

SHIVERING

Shivering is an involuntary muscle movement that the body uses to warm itself back up.

While useful for generating heat, it makes movements like swimming difficult to coordinate and is generally a sign to get out.

Shivering is an unreliable witness to the body's core state. While shivering is a sign of getting cold, not shivering says nothing about being warm. There are several reasons for this:

- it is possible to suppress mild shivering
- people shiver less when they're older
- stopping shivering is one sign that a person might have moved from moderate to severe hypothermia. Far from being better, they could in fact be worse

- most mystifying of all: research has shown the shiver response kicks in at a lower core temperature in regular outdoor swimmers

What Massey has found is that adapted swimmers don't shiver when others would. This enables them to carry on coordinating movement at the expense of core temperature. It preserves energy for swimming (shivering burns through energy reserves quickly), but the cost of that is core temperature dropping further. In short, what this means is that shivering kicks in closer to clinical hypothermia than it would in the non-acclimated.

Massey's research has found that the reduction in the shivering response is core-temperature specific – if a swimmer drops below core temperatures that they have experienced before, shivering will be triggered again.

BROWN FAT

Brown fat (or brown adipose tissue – BAT) insulates our core and breaks down blood sugar and fat molecules to create heat and help maintain body temperature more effectively than white fat. Recent research indicates that there may be an increase in brown fat in cold-exposed swimmers. This is an adaptation, but the extent to which it contributes to thermoregulation when cold-water swimming is likely to be very slight, and swamped by other responses such as generating heat through movement, and preserving heat by losing blood flow to the skin.

THERMAL (DIS)COMFORT: THE DISCONNECT BETWEEN HOW YOU FEEL AND HOW YOU ARE

Cold acclimatisation is partly about what you are happy to tolerate. We can all develop a barometer of what's right for us and may learn from how awful we feel after getting out what counts as having 'overdone it'.

Anyone looking to push themselves to extremes may be interested to learn that science's answer to the question 'can I tell if I'm too cold?' is surprisingly 'no'. There is a poor correlation between thermal perception (how cold you feel) and thermal status (how cold you are), and cold acclimatisation makes this already poor relationship worse. Not only do acclimated swimmers not shiver, paradoxically they feel more comfortable as their deep body temperature falls.

Two of the first physiologists to look at cold water immersion were Griffith Pugh and Otto Edholm. In the early 1950s, they put two people in 16 °C water in a cold immersion tank and measured their core temperature and responses. One these men was Pugh himself, while the other was a leading endurance swimmer of his generation, Jason Zirganos, who had crossed the Channel three times. Where Pugh was tall, lanky and unacclimatised, Zirganos was stocky and acclimatised, and 20 kilos heavier than Pugh despite being 19 centimetres shorter.

The authors measured the discomfort and the core temperature of the two men in their tanks. Mike Tipton found out more about the study in private correspondence with the researchers: they discovered that while static in cold water Zirganos cooled at the same rate as Pugh, but he neither shivered nor reported discomfort – in fact, he sat there happily, reading his newspaper. At the same time Pugh, thinner, taller and unacclimatised, was in an adjacent immersion tank desperately uncomfortable and almost tetanic with shivering. (Tetanic means having spasms or contractions).

What the study showed was that Zirganos lacked insight into his thermal state, a phenomenon Tipton dubs 'undetected or insidious hypothermia', where people drift into unconsciousness on a swim. Zirganos drifted into unconsciousness in 1953, in a four-hour swim in the 8 °C Bosphorus, and again a few years later as he attempted to swim the 22-mile North Channel of the Irish Sea. He did not feel cold prior to this. He was hauled from the water and pronounced dead at the scene. A tragic and cautionary tale – and one which isn't, according to Heather Massey, wholly uncommon.

HYPOTHERMIA

The difference between feeling cold and being hypothermic is numbers. Normal core body temperature is 36.1 °C to 37.2 °C, mild hypothermia is a core temperature of 32.3–35 °C, moderate hypothermia is 28–32.2 °C, and severe hypothermia is below 28 °C.

The best way to avoid hypothermia is to be cautious. There is a sliding scale that goes from too cold to hypothermia and things that will push a swimmer down the slope faster include inexperience, peer pressure, not paying attention, being competitive (with yourself or others) and misadventure (mistiming how long a swim will take). Also, lack of sleep, stress, lack of food, hangovers, feeling ill and external factors such as wind chill.

Marathon swimmers refer to 'The 'Umbles' as a way of remembering what to look for. A hypothermic person may appear drunk, and show some or all of the following:

- **Grumbles** – negative mental outlook
- **Fumbles** – slow reaction time, drops things, poorly coordinated. Fine motor movement lost first, i.e. cannot do up buttons or move fingers properly when asked
- **Mumbles** – slurs words

- **Stumbles** – appears stiff, loses coordination, eventually unable to walk without help

Be aware that cold people often become very withdrawn or introverted, and can also become angry. Coupled with any tendency to 'not want to make a fuss', this means that you are better quietly taking charge of a situation where you feel someone needs assistance rather than asking for permission or waiting to be asked for help. Approach it from the 'let's get you out of the water and into your clothes' perspective. Take all the steps listed in the 'warming up' box above and, if you have any serious concerns about a swimmer being hypothermic, including any alteration in their breathing, call an ambulance sooner rather than later while you are doing so.

A visible sign that someone is cold is when blue appears around the lips, creeping in from the corners. The mental incapacitation of hypothermia leads to errors of omission, plus not making sense and talking gibberish. A moderately hypothermic person will struggle to tell you their name: hard to believe, maybe, but this is the most common check that ice swimmers use on each other. Try asking questions that require some processing – not, what year is it, but what year was it two years ago?

Even if their temperature does not fall into the hypothermic range, swimmers may still feel ill. Age matters: children are more prone to hypothermia than adults, but the risk of it starts increasing again at the other end of our lives, with 65-year-olds thought to be more prone to it than younger adults, and 80- and 90-year-olds even more at risk.

THE DANGERS OF HYPOTHERMIA (AND HYPERTHERMIA)

Physically, the body has one overriding mission: to keep the vital organs at a temperature at which they can function. The body is so keen on staying at a regular core temperature that in a head-to-head battle of 'what is more important', all other physical systems will lose. For example, you could be dangerously dehydrated in a hot desert and still your body would sweat in order to try to cool down. Similarly (as described) when swimming the body will rob the arms and legs of blood and strength in order to stop itself from cooling, however much you need strength to stay afloat.

When Operation Stable Core Temperature fails, as it does with hypothermia (and hyperthermia – overheating), your heart, nervous system and other organs can't work normally. Left untreated, hypothermia can lead to complete failure of your heart and respiratory system as well as unconsciousness in the water, all of which can be fatal.

RECOGNISING HYPOTHERMIA IN YOURSELF

It is hard to recognise hypothermia in yourself because thought processes slow down, making it difficult to gauge your own condition. Cold is a continuum. Feeling cold, shivering and phenomena such as your fingers splaying and drifting apart will continue to worsen, and signs that you are on the hypothermic spectrum include:

- hands becoming claw-like and being less able to control them
- uncontrollable shivering and numbness
- weakness in arms and legs – may feel sluggish
- clenched jaw and some difficulty speaking freely
- loss of simple coordination – swimming stroke changes, swimming position may become more vertical

With more severe hypothermia you can start feeling warm, and have the paradoxical urge to undress – this is not the same experience as the surface heat that you may feel at the start of a wintery swim, a glorious burning surge.

A MIND–BODY PURSUIT

Cold water has been converting people and used as a tonic for 600 years or more. In the fifteenth century, swimming in cold water was recommended for contagious diseases and poisonous humours; it was thought to rid the swimmer of headaches, dropsies, scabs, small pox and leprosies. In the Victorian era, claims were even bolder: the sea air and water were marketed as a match for every disorder. Appetite, spirit, strength: they could all be found at the sea, with resorts full of bathers being wheeled across the beach in small wooden cabins and helped into the water by 'dippers'. It was an activity thought to offer a potential connection with the sublime.

In the twenty-first century there is an almost unquestioned ideology that cold water is good for you. While swimming is an all-body workout that builds muscle strength and cardiovascular fitness in a low-impact way, improving flexibility and posture, it's the benefits of cold water as a tonic that really fascinate some people. Anecdotally, cold water is currently recommended for all sorts of things that can make life suck: arthritis, pain (neuropathic as well as joints), PTSD, depression, grief, anxiety, migraines, fatigue, menopause, psoriasis, Seasonal Affective Disorder, issues metabolising sugar. To anyone who feels unhappy, lost or forgotten the call is going out: oh come all ye faithful to the cleansing power of cold and transcend your difficulties.

The science is some way away from backing up all these purported health benefits but, from a swimmer's perspective, I'm not sure it really matters whether these things are proven or not. For me, one of the real gifts of swimming is the chance to quieten down inside those moments in the water, close to the banks, when we are part of the planet, not separate from it. Or to liven up inside those moments, shrieking and ridiculous, when we are innocent again and could be any age. Or to plough on in those moments when it's all desperate, but we haven't given up. All of which come from wanting to do it, not feeling that we should. If nature and swimming are commodified as yet more things we 'should' consume for a health benefit, we might deprive ourselves of the point.

SCHOOLS OF THOUGHT ON COLD

As we have seen, cold water makes some people feel very, very high, and extremely happy to be alive, with even short dips turning them into good-to-go champions among champions.

But it doesn't have that effect on everybody – some people just find it deeply unpleasant and don't want to. These people happily hang up their trunks after the summer and won't be seen again till May.

What's the difference? Expectations. Mental and physiological responses are two sides of the same coin: the mind is in the brain is in the body, our physiology, psychology and philosophy are all intertwined. The euphoric swimmers expect pleasure when they get in, and they find it. Their anticipation and enjoyment of the cold cause their brains to release all sorts of neurochemicals when they take a cold plunge (sometimes even before it); they have conditioned themselves to take pleasure from the cold and over time that's exactly what happens. It's a powerful placebo. They are convinced that cold creates euphoria, and that conviction is so deep that it does.

Other people get in expecting suffering – and find it. They have not overridden the natural human response to cold. They expect to have a miserable time and do, feeling cold and threatened, freaking out, feeling stressed, feeling drained, resenting the time it takes to warm back up again.

This span of responses is no different from some people associating running with pleasure while others associate it with being tiring and a waste of time. The world is broad church where people have trained themselves to find a pleasure response to all sorts of things others find painful – piercings, tattoos, S&M, ultra-marathons and eating ghost pepper chillies.[5]

If you want to move from one camp to the other, you can – with training: immerse yourself in cold water more, change your attitude, expect health, well-being and vibrancy, and you will eventually condition your response and be able to achieve this feeling of euphoria. Some people's physiology and life experience might give them a head start when it comes to loving the cold, but for most of us our autonomic nervous system can be trained if we want to train it. Here are some popular frames of reference others use on that journey.

STOICISM, SADOMASOCHISM AND MINDFULNESS

When do you start feeling sorry for yourself – when you get out of the car, out of your clothes, or when the water reaches the top of your thighs? According to Charles Sprawson's book *Haunts of the Black Masseur*, eighteenth-century poet Algernon Swinburne was among the 'so cold it hurts' school of swimmers who relish the punishment and pain of cold. Flogged at Eton, Swinburne found that beatings, icy water and violent waves all steadied his nerves and helped him maintain his composure. He remarked in a letter to a friend that it was a pity that the Marquis de Sade had not been aware of the tortures that could be inflicted by the sea.

Beyond the sadomasochists who like the pain are the stoics who bear it: those who give themselves harsh experiences to build character. Stoicism is a rich theme for swimmers, who can make a regular practice of 'not minding' as a preparation for future hardships. 'It does not matter what you bear, but how you bear it', according to the Stoic philosopher Seneca. Nothing teaches calm resilience like getting into really cold water again and again.

Mindfulness teaches people about the twin arrows of suffering (originally described in an ancient Buddhist parable). First arrows are the things that happen to us in life over which we have no control – injury, loss, people being aggressive or annoying, pain from the cold. The second arrows are our reactions: the thoughts we create that generate further suffering and go round and round in our heads, creating festering misery. Framed this way, swimming can become a practice ground for bringing down those second arrows: yes, you are cold (or terrified of pike). Are you freaking out that it hurts, or beating yourself up for not being tougher? No. You are not. You are calm. You are bearing it. Your thoughts are under control, and no panic is happening. You cannot control the temperature of the water but you can control your thoughts about it and you do not have to react.

RECOVERY – FROM ADDICTION, DEPRESSION, ANXIETY AND MORE

While some cold water swimmers are suffering nobly, others are getting high: endorphins, adrenalin, dopamine, oxytocin, serotonin – physiologists still do not know for sure what is released with the shock of immersion, but, high as they are, who even cares?[6] This is the 'elated for hours and calm for days' brigade. People talk about it as a 'cold shock treatment' or 'physiological reset'. Some people start to crave cold water, and this can lead to extreme behaviour: being sad when it's summer, for example, or booking holidays where the water is cold so they can get their fix. Having to stay in longer and longer to flick that physiological switch.

We can be pretty sure there will be a release of adrenalin on immersion that will wake you up and give you a buzz, says Massey, but, at the time of writing, proof that swimming helps addiction, depression and anxiety remains still anecdotal and the physiological pathways undefined. There's one case study, from 2018 by the University of Portsmouth, of a woman who had had major depression disorder (MDD) since she was seventeen, and during the study she started swimming once a week between April and September.[7] The researchers found that cold-water swimming 'led to an immediate improvement in mood following each swim and a sustained and gradual reduction in symptoms of depression, and consequently a reduction in, and then cessation of, medication'. Two years later she was still swimming, and still medication-free. This is astounding; but it is just one case study, and swimming was not the only change in her life at that time: other changes included being supported during the study, having a new child and so a new role as mother, taking up this new hobby, and pride in a new achievement.

One theory on the anecdotal evidence of cold water swimming having mental-health benefits is that by exposing yourself to a physical stress – cold – the brain and body cross-adapt in ways that make them better able to deal with other stresses in your life. Inflammation is thought to be the physiological link between stress and chronic diseases in the body, including anxiety and depression. So the thinking is that perhaps cold lowers inflammation, and this lowers levels of depression and anxiety.

LIMINAL SPACE BETWEEN LIFE AND DEATH

Many of us lead such soft padded lives that – in the words of Robert Macfarlane from a recent radio interview – discomfort has become its own luxury. Brushing anywhere close to a survival situation makes us feel alive.

In 2019, Hannah Denton, a counselling psychologist based in Brighton, interviewed six outdoor swimmers on land and in the water (attaching a sound recorder to a tow float).[8] Denton's swimmers found that swimming changed their lives – in psychological terms it was transformative, causing changes in mind, body and identity; connecting, enabling a sense of belonging to nature, place and others; and, through the disruption to the sense of time, space and body, re-orientating. The swimmers emerged with alternative and expanded perspectives about themselves and their world.

Denton also recorded twinges of near-death panic. In the words of one swimmer: 'One minute, you are fine, and then literally the next second it is "Shit, I am too cold, I should have got out." And it's literally swim or die.'

In the words of another: 'It's difficult for your mind to wander when your nervous system is yelling at you to GTFO of a frigid-y abyss.'

The point here is that in our complicated, human, overthinking existences, having our bandwidth restricted to survival, and being overwhelmed by our senses, can be a boon. Denton's research was done in summer, showing that it's not necessary to winter swim to experience what, for some people, can be the wow factor of swimming.

COLD WATER: A MEDICAL A TO Z

Your brain is not the only part of your body affected by cold water: from autonomic conflict to urticaria, here are some conditions around cold you may encounter or want to know about.

AUTONOMIC CONFLICT

On entering cold water the cold shock response can cause hyperventilation and tachycardia, a heart rate that is too fast.[9] If the face is submerged at the same time, a diving response called bradycardia might be triggered simultaneously – this is a heart rate that is abnormally slow. This could result in autonomic conflict, which in susceptible individuals can predispose to sudden cardiac death. A high percentage of people who drown in water do so soon after immersion, and autonomic conflict is one possible explanation.

CHILBLAINS

Chilblains are an abnormal reaction to the cold and typically form on toes, but sometimes on other extremities such as finger, heels, ears or nose. Skin becomes red and itchy with small swellings, with symptoms appearing a few hours after you have been cold. Chilblains are caused by warming up fast; blood vessels near the skin's surface narrow in response to cold, then dilate again when warmth returns, but if you warm up too fast the vessels may be unable to handle the flow and blood leaks into surrounding tissue. Chilblains generally get better in a few weeks, during which time avoiding extremes of heat and cold is recommended. Painkillers can ease discomfort and soothing lotions may relieve itching. Wearing neoprene gloves and boots in the water and warming up slowly can help you to avoid chilblains.

HEART ISSUES

Cold water is literally not for the faint-hearted. When you enter cold water your heart rate goes up and blood pressure rises – one study of ice swimmers who were regularly exposed to cold water found that average blood pressures soared from 130/76mmHg (fairly normal) to 175/95mmHg (would need treatment, though unlikely to cause any immediate complications).[10] Simultaneously there is a rise in heart rate – in those people not acclimatised to cold water, this occurs within 2 to 3 seconds and is an increase of around 20 beats/minute. While there is little risk for someone with normal blood pressure or well controlled hypertension, it's something to be aware of, and potentially to talk to your doctor about if you have risk factors.

There have been reports of swimmers with undiagnosed coronary heart disease suffering a fatal heart attack in the water, so it is also worth talking to your doctor about this, as you would if you were starting a gym or other fitness regime.

Counter to the risk, there are also theories that cold water may help fight and manage heart disease.

IMMUNE SYSTEM

Anecdotally, many people say that cold water boosts their immune system and stops them getting so many colds. Science has yet to prove this, however. One study has found that cold and open water swimmers had fewer upper respiratory tract infections than their partners, who were exposed to the same pathogens – but they didn't have fewer infections than people who go indoor swimming.[11]

Small studies have looked at how winter swimming may boost the immune system: one found that cold water boosts white blood cell count,[12] another that five months of winter swimming (4–10 degree river) led to positive changes in the antioxidant system of healthy swimmers, which might increase the readiness of the body to fight stress factors.[13]

NON-FREEZING COLD INJURIES

Extreme cold exposure can lead to non-freezing cold injuries (NFCI). This means the affected body part gets very cold, to the extent that blood flow to the hands or feet is blocked so they look white and numb (but not frozen, as in frostbite or frostnip). Problems start when the swimmer warms back up but sensation does not return. Sometimes the extremity swells or discolours (this is harder to see in darkly pigmented skin), and there is both chronic pain and numb areas (such as fingertips). In the final stage, which may not be apparent until weeks later but can last for years, the affected extremity appears normal, but remains cool, may not regain sensation and may be hypersensitive to cold.

RAYNAUD'S DISEASE

Raynaud's disease causes area of the body – typically fingers and toes – to go white and feel numb in response to cold and stress. My son calls them 'ghost fingers'. Symptoms generally disappear when you warm up, and repeatedly triggering symptoms by outdoor swimming should not make the condition worse. Fitness gains from swimming might even help improve the condition.[14] Swimmers recommend warming up before getting into the water, wearing neoprene gloves (as well as more neoprene generally to keep the core warm) and having hand warmers for afterwards.

ROSACEA

Rosacea is a skin condition where the face becomes red after exposure to many of the good things in life – cold water, coffee, red wine, spices, sun and exercise. It can lead to acne-type spots. There are lots of treatments (prescribed and self-help), which have varying success rates, but the temperature extreme of putting your face in icy water is a strong prompt for a flare-up. Swimming head-up (rather than head-in) breaststroke in winter can help. I suffer mildly and have not found a treatment that works, but for prevention I sometimes use a diving hood, diving mask and training snorkel to train when temperatures are very low – between them they cover most of my face and I think it helps.

SURFER'S EAR

Earplugs are a popular addition to cold water kitbags, and one of the few accessories allowed in the Ice Mile as a safety precaution. Very cold water in the ear canal can lead to dizziness when swimming, and repeated exposure to cold wind or water can also lead to thickening of the bones in the ears. This can compromise hearing and trap infections. Surfers often get it on whichever side of the head the prevailing wind is, or the side that strikes the wave first. In more extreme cases the ear bones need to be operated on.

There are all sorts of earplug options: people have been seen out sporting silicone ones, custom fitted ones, and the kinds you are supposed to be able to hear through (as well as sometimes Blu Tack in the ears). It is one of the rules of nature that when you do need earplugs they are always lost somewhere. Once you do find them, a swim hat or neoprene bonnet will help hold them in place.

URTICARIA

Cold water urticaria is a skin reaction to cold where the skin develops hives (reddish, itchy welts). The hives generally occur in the water but pop up during rewarming, and can last from a few hours to two days. Immersion in cold water is one of the most common causes of urticaria, with symptoms including fever, headache, tiredness, pain in the joints, very low blood pressure, fainting, and whole-body anaphylactic shock. It's something to take seriously: I know of one swimmer who developed it and had to stop swimming for good. If you suspect you have it, place an ice cube on that area of your skin for five minutes and see if a hive appears, then talk to your doctor if it does. In some people it goes away after weeks or perhaps months. There is no cure but antihistamines can relieve mild symptoms.

CHAPTER 7

WINTER & ICE SWIMMING

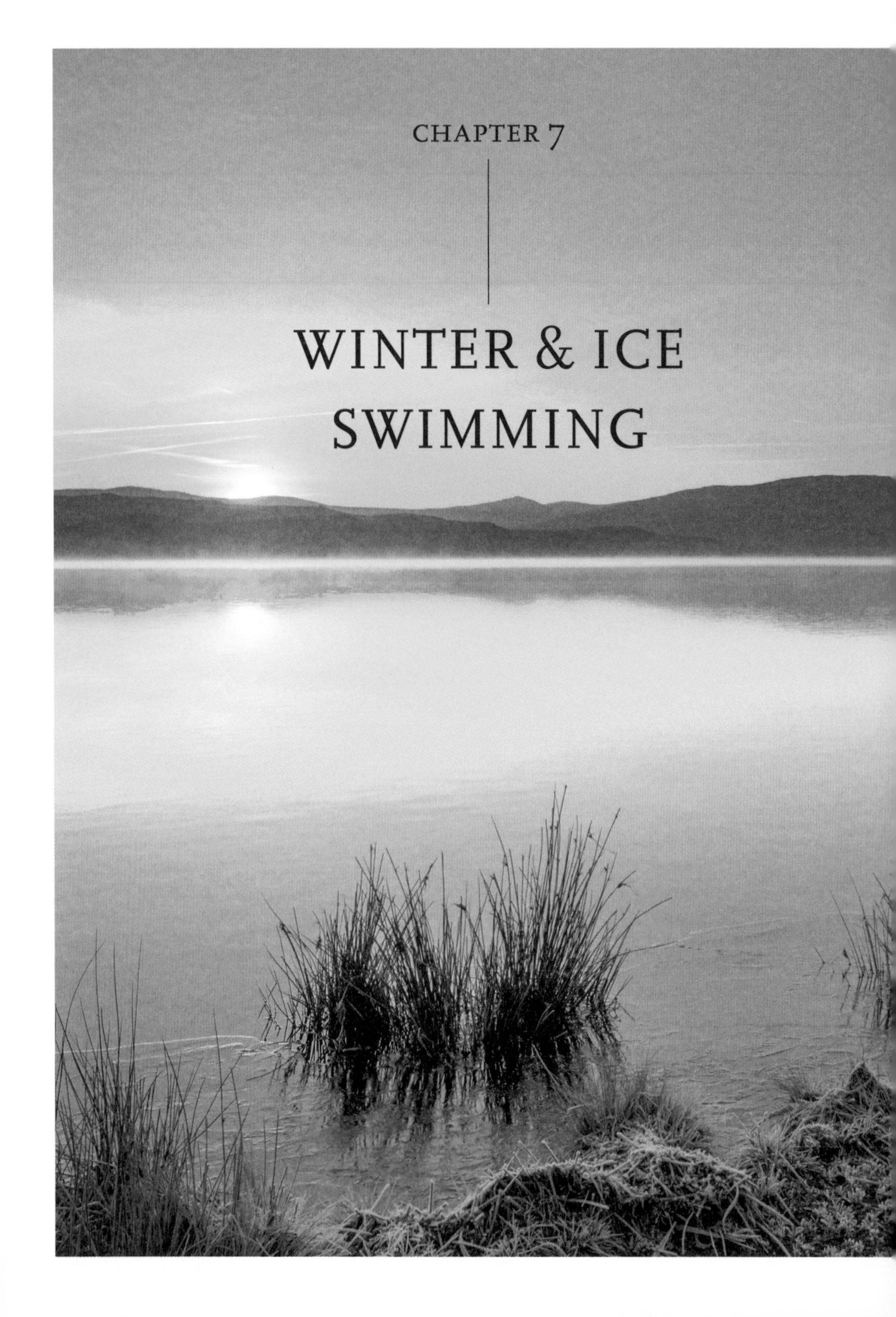

'This plunge into the cold water
of a mountain pool seems for a brief
moment to disintegrate the very self;
it is not to be borne: one is
lost:stricken: annihilated.
Then life pours back'

NAN SHEPHERD,
The Living Mountain

THE BLEAK MIDWINTER OFFERS starkly beautiful experiences. The low sun diffused through leaves on the water's surface. The moon at dawn. Air so cold you can see your breath travel. And the burn of elements on skin. If you struggle to get inside a moment and have it reverberate and expand within you till you believe it is a beautiful world that we are living in, then winter swimming offers a pinhole camera: focus is narrowed down to right here, right now. In that sharpness there is pain but also pleasure; moments and sensations that dilate, with richness and beauty inside of them.

HOW YOU CAN CHERISH IT BEING PERISHING

Where I live, February is the cruellest month for me. By late winter, Somerset can become a symphony of grey-brown damp: sodden earth, dead banks, constant cloud cover. My newest winter swimming accessory is not an axe for the ice but a wooden bath mat to keep my bare feet off the mud. And yet for all the bright white of ascension that I don't have access to – the snow I haven't tramped through, the ice I haven't cracked, the hoar frost that doesn't form, the frosty, steamy fog sunrises at a distant river that I always seem to sleep through (can't we get sluggish in winter?!) – there is always the cold. The shocking, smarting, purifying, enlivening (as in, *I am alive, as it didn't kill me*) cold.

Cold exists on a continuum and to me the point where it stops being swimming and starts being 'winter swimming' is the point where the cold itself becomes the thing – and nature, fitness, landscape, place all recede behind the bodily battle to survive the temperature. At some point – when water temperatures are around 6 or 7 °C, or the season is most definitely winter – people who have worn wetsuits and done front crawl all summer strip off, and start dipping.

That way, they avoid becoming even colder when getting changed.

There is a violence to the low numbers; the experience of swimming below 6 °C is brutal. Water this cold will punch the air out of your lungs, it will bite your hands and feet off. It can cause immediate pain in your buttocks, as if they're in the clench of a giant lobster. It can leave you shaking coffee all over yourself, or sitting on the ground in a car park with a north wind blowing, your clothes in a knot and your hands useless; trapped in your top and close to tears. It can take you out for hours afterwards.

There are different ways of doing winter swimming, and swimmers often vary wildly in approach depending on mood and available company. At one end there are those who plop into picturesque frozen landscapes, serene in the face of suffering, their cold dips an act of observance of the body, of nature, of the seasons; calm and consciously mindful and meditative.

At the other end is the pumped-up wild-eyed hooligan approach, 'like teenagers at a rave' as OSS member Lynne Roper would have said: a fierce, energy-raising, 'Eye of the Tiger'-style social life event with all the shrieks and swears. And afterwards people, hunkered down, huddled together, happy to hug anyone who's open to it: hot drinks, hyper babble, a rainbow of woolly hats, shared shivering, cake. Goose bumps and good times. 'Hysteria takes them in and hypothermia gets them out,' in the words of one Festive Swim organiser.

HOW QUICK IS QUICK?

What most winter swimmers are talking about when they talk about 'swimming' is very short immersions. (It was a revelation to me when a daily lifelong winter swimmer off Battery Rocks in Penzance shared that over winter she counted strokes, not minutes – ten or twenty strokes was her winter challenge (the sea was 6 °C).)

If you are starting out, don't expect to spend very long in the water initially. 0 to 5 °C is, literally, survival territory: a temperature that has been studied since World War Two to try to pin down the period of 'useful consciousness' (this is a medical term, meaning the time people have left when they are hypothermic or hypoxic (lacking oxygen) to perform actions that are useful in saving their lives).

How quick is quick depends on you, air temperature, wind chill and water temperatures. Go gently, build up over time, and understand how your body feels. Kari knows one swimmer who, when the water is under 6 °C, 'waits until the cartilage between her vertebrae feel cold'. Who can imagine what that feels like? Here are some of the things that go on in winter swimming:

- Many people swim or dip for thirty seconds, a minute, or just a few minutes, like our Battery Rock swimmer counting strokes. In Finnish ice holes, the water will be close to freezing and the weather the same – around freezing with cold snaps dropping to –20 °C and sometimes even –50 °C. Here, dips are short – moments, not minutes – and dippers yo-yo between ice hole and sauna five or six times.

- Ice swimming has a long history in areas where winters involve a lot of snow and very little daylight (many Baltic and Nordic countries including Finland, Siberia and Sweden, as well as cold parts of China) and often winter swimming competitions where pools are sometimes cut out of the ice to make lakes. A standard swim distance is 25 metres. Yes! Twenty-five metres, one length of a pool. The culture varies between events and races, with some being all about the silly hats, and others very competitive (head-down front crawl). For context, it's common for organisers to request that swimmers wear safety belts in case they need to be pulled from the water. Winners of a heat are expected to get back in to do another 25 metres, and longer races may be available.

- At the oldest ice swimming club in the world, the Coney Island Polar Bear Club, New York (established 1903), the tradition is to spend ten minutes in the sea (less if there's severe wind chill). In January and February the sea temperature there is between 2.8 and 4.4 °C, while the air temperature averages 3 to 4 °C. The Polar Bears gather on Sundays at 1 p.m., form a circle of up to 100 swimmers, and do some jumping-jacks on the beach accompanied by a chant, 'to establish a cadence,' says president Dennis Thomas. Then it's into the water. Once everyone is in, they form a huge circle again, this time holding hands. Then they swim, for however long feels right. 'We do this for fun,' says Thomas, 'and I tell first-timers to stay in as long as they enjoy it. If it isn't fun, get the hell out and find something that is. This isn't about suffering.'

- At the extreme, painful and dangerous-sport end of the spectrum, Ice Milers train themselves to spend 20 to 40 minutes in water under 5 °C. This feat takes years, is attempted and achieved by very few, and the challenge is controversial because of its dangers, which include acute hypothermia, cardiac arrest and temporary or permanent nerve damage. Many ice milers do not remember finishing because of cold-related amnesia. Below 5 °C the survival rate after 60 minutes of immersion is 50 per cent.

For me, winter swimming remains a high days and holidays sort of thing. Running into the sea on New Year's Day. Joining hundreds of others for a December Dip in a 0.5 °C lido, so cold that when snow fell in it, it floated, like mini icebergs. Striding up a mountain in head torches for a brief naked swim in the dark with my husband, Tim, before Kendal Mountain Festival. Obliterating the bleuughh of winter with a quick plunge in the sea. Coming across a loch or tarn and stripping off. Attempts at endurance often fell me for the day. Right now in my swimming journey, I like it short and sweet.

WHERE TO GO

The sea is generally warmer in winter than lakes and rivers, rarely dropping below 6 degrees. Being a massive body of water, it takes a long time to chill, and only reaches its coldest in February.

Ice swimmers will be looking for lidos, rivers, lakes and ponds during winter, all of which tend to be colder, but once air temperature drops most of us will be happy wherever we have to hand. Places with clubhouses, changing rooms, close car-parking and other people around while you experiment may grow in appeal. Wherever you are, swim along the shore rather than far out.

WHAT TO WEAR

Surprise! Not that much.

As mentioned, far fewer wetsuits are worn in autumn, winter and spring than in summer – for one, the act of putting them on and off in cold air can result in greater overall chilling than wearing less in the water and changing faster. Also, it seems possible that part of the charge that comes from cold water comes from skin contact, and if you reduce that, the experience is less of a high and more like being chilled in a fridge.

Neoprene booties and gloves are effective in reducing pain in the hands and feet in very cold water. Some swimmers like wearing things on their feet to avoid stumbling on hard rocks or cutting their feet without realising (if they are so cold they have lost feeling). Some like gloves, while others think these stop you actually feeling what temperature you are. Some try neoprene swimming costumes as a halfway house.

While the body can achieve a 99 per cent reduction in blood flow to the skin between the extremes of vasodilation (up to 6 litres of blood to skin per minute) and vasoconstriction (blood flow down to 0.02 litres per minute), the only place this does not happen is the head – blood flow to the scalp remains similar across all conditions. Submerged in very cold water in a swimsuit, with wind and rain whipping through your hair, the old wives' tale that 50 per cent of heat is lost through your head is closer than ever to being true. Any kind of hat will help. (See the Gear List table on pages 236–7 for more ideas.)

If you are not swimming because it's winter but in spite of winter, the rules are different. There are a few swimmers who just carry on swimming, because covering miles outside is what they do, and the temperature is just the temperature, the season is an irrelevance or an inconvenience, but not the reason. This athletic subset are more 'whatever it takes' to keep swimming – suits, boots, hoods, thermal wetsuits as required. I once watched one of our water safety guys knock out 10 kilometres before breakfast on 4 January when we were doing a recce for another event. The water was 6 °C – a major hurdle for many of us but for him, an all-season surfer who lives and works in the water, not even a thing.

FASTER ON THE BANKS, SLOWER IN THE WATER

Many swear by warming up as much as possible beforehand in winter: wearing a lot of clothes, exercising gently, a brisk walk, press-ups, a stiff hill climb.

You will develop your own technique for the moment of truth, whether that is the quiet stoic meditative approach (controlled breathing, tree pose in a blizzard, 'the cold is my teacher' style) or the noisy *raaaah!* of an ice squad. Whatever it is, you will want to make the striptease quick and not take too long getting in, as overall immersion time is limited at these temperatures. Before you plunge the key is that you're waiting to be ready, and for breath to be collected, so you can relish the moments that follow.

Expect to swim more slowly during winter and take longer to reach the same landmarks. Ice milers estimate that an Ice Mile typically takes 20 to 30 per cent longer than your time for a mile in the pool because of a reduction of blood flow to limbs, a decrease in nerve conduction, slower muscle contraction in cooled muscle and a fall in aerobic capacity.

Think about your build and your swim speed. Fat and fast is the ideal build for ice swimming – good insulation and good heat generation (in Ice Miles, competitors need at least 20 per cent body fat). Lean and fast also works, as does fatter and slow. What doesn't work so well is lean and slow.

The precipice that many winter swimmers are balanced on is one where they want their core temperature to drop a bit each time so they acclimatise, but not so much that it gets messy or dangerous. Don't mess about once you're out: get dry and changed as fast as you can. By the time afterdrop hits you want to be dry, dressed, with a warm drink inside you.

Being cold reduces mental functioning. In winter it is a valid question to ask whether you or someone you are swimming with is OK to drive. Kari once sat in a car park alone for a few hours waiting for this moment. It can be estranging, pride; or maybe it is that when we are too cold we become quiet and withdrawn. Any which way, she had not wanted to tell anyone how cold she really was, so they all drove off. And there she sat, all alone in her cold car, till she felt right. Always ask swimmers you suspect of being cold twice, and consider getting a non-swimmer to drive.

Walking or cycling to a swim may give the benefit of warming before you get in, and potentially assisting rewarming afterwards.

Just remember the ice swimmer's mantra: the swim is not over until you have recovered, because the lowest deep-body temperatures occur after the swim.

WINTER LUXURIES – NORDIC AND BALTIC RITUALS AND EXTRAS

Nordic and Baltic extras for winter swimming include sheds, shelters and heated tents to change in (to keep warm until the last possible moment), heated carpets to and from the water's edge (otherwise the walkway, once dripped on by emerging swimmers, would become an ice slide), woolly hiking socks to avoid slipping on or sticking to ice, and saunas for afterwards. The advantage of a sauna over a hot tub or bath (yes, this is aspirational talk) is the quality of warming that goes on in them. In a sauna the warm-up is slow, through layers: first the skin, then the superficial layers, then the deep core.

Russian style is often putting hands and feet in lukewarm water while heating your body externally, for example with hot steaming towels. Then when you have warmed up enough you move to the sauna, again putting hands and feet in lukewarm water.

The spartan equivalent? Some carry a Thermos of warm water and a small bucket up hills with them to whatever tarn, loch or lake they are swimming in, and then warm their hands and feet in it afterwards (I kid you not). Another 'treat' is taking a second pair of socks – it's hard to get properly dry when skin is cold, so the first pair will absorb the damp, then you can change them for a dry pair. Who needs a sauna? Basic luxury.

HOW TO CUT A CHANNEL IN ICE (AND GET IN)

There may come a time in the year when lakes – and sometimes (but less often) rivers – freeze over. The swimmer's problem when confronted with this iced-over gloriousness, is how to get in.

First off, decide on which area of water to swim in. Only cut a channel where you have swum in summer, so you know the terrain underneath. Will you go all out for the longest possible, or just a 10- or 20-metre channel close to a shed or some other kind of shelter? You may want to think about factors such as access, where the sun will be at the time of day you will visit, and the view. Somewhere shallow enough to stand up while removing the ice from your swim channel, but deep enough to swim, is ideal. (To be clear, I refer here only to channels, not holes, which require assessing whether ice is strong enough to walk out on, and where swimmers need to be strong enough to lift themselves out.)

Straight channels are popular – less thinking to do as you swim up and down cold. There is an unofficial Russian Orthodox tradition of cutting the shape of a cross in the ice so that swimmers can take a dip to celebrate the Feast of Epiphany, with the cross being cut by chainsaw-wielding priests who then bless the water.[1]

Second, choose your implement with which to break up the ice and prepare a channel. Ice axes are small axes designed for climbing, not channel-creating. Some swimmers choose standard axes or ice saws, and others – less keen on playing with axes with no shoes on – go for heavy and blunt objects, like a hammer, a lump hammer or small sledgehammer.

You may want to clear the snow or a slushy topping out of the way before you set to on the ice: a regular garden shed's worth of shovels and brooms can come into play. If the ice is thin then you may be able to crack it and move it to one side quite easily.

Third, think about getting the ice out of the channel once it's broken. Thin ice is sharp and thick ice is heavy. Broken ice is very sharp so wearing gloves is essential (cold, numb skin is easier to cut). You may want to wear a wetsuit at least on your legs to avoid cuts. You may also want to wear gloves or use a snow shovel to scoop the ice out of the way and create a clear channel.

Finally, recuperate from all that – it can be a huge workout cutting the channel – and then get in for the swim.

FESTIVE SWIMS

If you want to get in for a one-off winter dip, rather than training conscientiously in gently dropping temperatures as suggested in Chapter 6, 'Understanding Cold', observe the following additional cautions:

- Be aware that being hungover, tired or ill (or two or all of the above) will increase pressures on your body and may make you feel bad or worse. Don't plunge after a drink or taking drugs.

- If you're pregnant, be wary – it is not uncommon for winter swimmers to carry on throughout their pregnancy (in the same way as some marathoners carry on running through pregnancy), but a one-off freezing dip makes different demands on the body.

- Be cautious if you have asthma or other respiratory conditions – 'cold shock' makes most dippers hyperventilate as they get in.

- Possibly sit it out if you have a heart condition or poorly controlled hypertension. Cold water immersion greatly increases the danger of heart failure and stroke by causing an instantaneous and massive increase in heart rate and blood pressure.

CHAPTER 8

NIGHT SWIMMING

'The sky opened out above me like an unfurled banner, cascading with stars and blanched by the moon.
The black hulls of barges darkened the water behind me and murky towers and pinnacles rose indistinctly on the other bank. I swam well out... the whole expanse of water was running with light.
It was like swimming in quicksilver'

IRIS MURDOCH,
Under the Net

IRIS MURDOCH WROTE THESE words in 1954, when swimming still happened on the London Thames. It was a 'very still, hot night, burnt with stars and flooded by a moon' and her three characters had just left a party.

Whether it's running off a beach into phosphorescence or swimming down a river at night under a full moon, night swimming is a natural progression – or transgression – for those who love water.

Night swimming is not just a badly lit version of what you do in the day. How many visceral snapshots do we collect as we go through life, moments we can recall so precisely we can reinhabit our physical bodies where we were, decades later? I have many from night swimming. I can remember standing in the frosted ruts of a Cornish field in February, with my back to the sea, startled by the clarity of my moon shadow. I can remember waving my hands around in phosphorescence in Thailand. I remember sitting on the bottom of the Oxford lido looking at the legs of friends underwater after we'd scaled a fence to get in at night. And I can still hear the tinkling of drowned twigs carried by cold water into my ears as I drifted down the Thames on my back in autumn. It is the important experience that is stored, and these times of running around under moonshine make up the recollections of my life.

Night swimming is an elixir of youth: there is an inherent recklessness to being in the water at night, a carefree sense of self such that you could be any age. Some friends and I are making our way through the menopause under the moon at the moment. On land we are losing oestrogen, losing our tempers, losing our hair colour, visibility and status (hey, I didn't make the rules). Who cares about any of it when you're breaststroking through inky black water, picking up a light trail from downy swan feathers?

SUNLIGHT, MOONLIGHT, TWILIGHT AND STARLIGHT

Light and dark do not correspond to sunrise and sunset, and if you plan a dawn swim around the time of sunrise, you may be disappointed to get to the water to find the world already fully discernible around you. Dawn and dusk are not one thing, but a succession.

On the banks the moment when one thing becomes another is never possible to catch, but (measured by angle of the sun to the horizon) there are three stages of twilight and three stages of dawn. The movement from day to night, or night to day, is rapid in countries closer to the equator, and can be lengthy as you move closer to the poles. Dusk and dawn move in faster in the winter months than they do in summer.

DAY TO NIGHT

- **Civil twilight** or 'dusk' is the phase after sunset when the sun dips below the horizon. During this phase you can see objects clearly and the sky is light all over. On overcast days it will grow darker earlier, but at mid-civil twilight you can still read and find swim kit around you. If you're sharing the water with other users (such as boats) you might need to be illuminated for safety, just as you would when walking on a road.

- **Nautical twilight** is the second stage of dusk: the inky-blue gloaming where you can see the horizon, and the silhouettes of objects, but not their details, or things on the ground. During this time, most stars can be easily seen with the naked eye; the term 'nautical twilight' comes from when sailors used these stars to navigate.

This is the phase when head torches are used for most outdoor activities like running or cycling: not just so other people see you, but so you can see.

- **Astronomical twilight** is the last stage before it becomes night. At this stage most celestial objects will be visible, and on a clear night, the moon and stars will be bright.

NIGHT TO DAY

- **Astronomical dawn** is the earliest stage of dawn. This is close to night – you will be able to see the stars, and any light from the moon or light pollution, but not much else.

- **Nautical dawn** is the second stage of dawn, where you can see the horizon, and the silhouettes of objects. How much you can see during nautical dawn depends on the weather – if it's cloudy, it will be darker than if the sky is clear.

- **Civil dawn** is the phase before sunrise, when the sun is below the horizon and starts to colour the sky. During this phase you can see objects clearly and the sky is light all over. On overcast days it will stay darker for longer, but at mid-civil twilight you can read.

In answer to the original dilemma: what time to go out for a sunrise swim? I try to arrive in nautical dawn, so I can see the sky lighten and catch any colours. (For me, this is a better exercise in autumn than summer: around the time of the summer solstice, nautical dawn occurs at around 4 a.m. where I live.) By winter, sunrise is so late you can have something close to a lie-in and still be in the river for a misty pink moment. (All these times are available online.)

My favourite time, though, is not watching the day break but being there when the night falls. I love the gloaming: the hour of the day when colours fall out of the world, day slips into the water, and a rich inky-blue night slides in, bringing with it a stillness, a quietness: hills and trees blacken, winds fall, dew settles, stars rise, and out come the bats.[1]

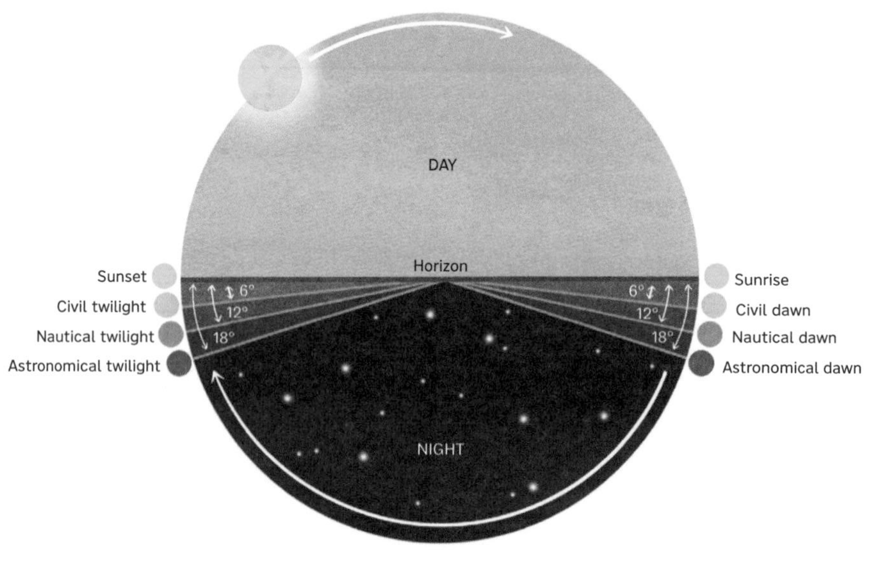

THE STAGES OF TWILIGHT

SIGHT AND OTHER SENSES AT NIGHT

After being exposed to bright artificial light, the eye takes between twenty-five and forty minutes to adapt to the dark, during which time a biochemical reconfiguration of pigments is happening so that an eye that was operating in the equivalent of bright sunlight can operate in starlight (or less).

If you are aiming for a swim in the dark without illumination, you need to stay away from torches, car lights and phone screens for as long as possible before getting in so you have maximum night vision. Absence of colour does not mean absence of sight; there is a change in the way your eyes see and what they pick up: silhouettes of trees, bats swooping above, a sense of the path. In the sea, distinctive characteristics in cliff lines and local buildings can help establish your position: knobs of rocks on cliff lines, church spires, high rises in sand dunes.

Swimming in the dark is best done at a location where you know both the walk in and the swim well; somewhere you have the familiarity to pick out features at night. There is something special about heading out when the rest of the world is heading in. Now you are in the company of animals.

If you are swimming without lights, take extra care to work out how to spot your exit when you come to get back out. I have lost exit points more than once and playing 'would you rather get colder still, or try to climb up a steep bank semi-naked using nettles as handholds?' is not as fun as all that. I now have a couple of familiar places where I swim at night. At one (a river) the exit spot is a ladder roped to the bank; it's silver and therefore manages to reflect just a little more light than the foliage around it, if you've trained yourself where to look. The other is a lake we approach down a wooded path. I am not without fear of the dark; when we do our torch-free walk-in, light behind two hedges forms a shape that resembles, every time, an approaching figure – it is always unnerving, and we bunch together, start holding each other's towels. But doing the whole operation without torches allows us to fully see when we breaststroke out of the skirts of the tree and into the centre of the lake. It is amazing what you can then pick up. Even on cloudy nights it is possible to see a little: I love looking down at my hands, comfortingly visible in the water. I like seeing how a bow wave appears above them, the water like mercury. I have come to know the exit tree and its lighter smaller predecessor well enough to recognise it even on cloudy dark nights – just.

Illuminating an exit point with a small light can be a good idea – just make sure you can see the lantern or its glow from down in the water.

All of this will help set you up for moon-gazey swims, named after moon-gazey hares – calm tranquil nights at known wild places, floating on your back and eating the stars. But some people are out in the dark just because it's winter, and it's always dark before and after work at swim time. Others are out because the dark itself is the challenge. Over a few months in winter 2020, big-wave surfer Al Mennie swam 100 kilometres through the dark on his local surf beach in Ireland, heading out night after night in what he described to me as the 'raging north Atlantic' to do the same stretch. It's rough on the Irish coast during winter: the surf was frantic, breaking with a force that led him to wear an impact vest to help him resurface. He had a land spotter but didn't wear lights, both because they put focus back on sight at a time when it's not that useful and also out of fear that passers-by would think he was in trouble and call out the coastguard.

What he learnt was to stop trying to see, and to use other senses instead. 'The swell lines stand above the horizon just before they break,' he once told me. 'It is not my sight I rely on though. There is much more to observe in the water than what is shown to our eyes. The water is pulled and surged by approaching and passing waves, and it is possible to notice it from movement and sound – the draw of the water can be enough to give you a second or two to prepare for a wave.'

Breathing close to the surface is extremely dangerous in the dark in choppy conditions, so he never swam face-in – to hinder sight is one thing, to hinder sound too much of a risk. He swam 90 per cent head-up crawl, and the rest sidestroke.

This is good advice for any night swimmer: rather than focus on what you can't see, draw on what you can suddenly hear, smell, feel and taste. When your sight powers down, the other senses come to life and, at dusk, a landscape that empties of cars, planes, people and vision starts teeming in other ways. You can pick up the strong smell of earth, the feeling of coldness being dragged across the land to the water where it settles. Wildlife scurries in the undergrowth, nightingales sing, ravens crash-land on their roosts. Dew falls (bag up your clothes), the water tastes oaky and feels like cool ribbons as it runs over your eyelids. In the water your body can feel like it is moving in more dimensions than normal.

A few further practical pointers to night swimming. First, air temperature drops quickly when the sun goes down: night has a way of surprising people, so take more clothes with you than you think you will need. Second, if you do wish to illuminate yourself, the most common way is to put an adventure light or reusable glowstick into a tow float, and pull it behind you like a lantern. Head torches are problematic in groups; they blind other swimmers with their brightness, and make star and moon gazing difficult. And third: it really is useful to have some light for after, so your undies don't add to the summer bankside tally of abandoned pants.

PHOSPHORESCENCE AND BIOLUMINESCENCE

Phosphorescence is the holy grail of night swimming: surf sparkling as it breaks, or lighting up as it laps on the shore. Seeing hands trail through the water, magically throwing off sparks.

Bioluminescence is best seen on dark nights where there is no moon. It is generally found in seawater and is caused by microscopic algae called dinoflagellates. The algae live in the water year-round but breed more in warm water, and warmer, calmer seas allow them to form a mass. The small burst of light they give out as the water moves is thought to be a defence against being eaten.

PREPARING FOR MARATHON SWIMS AT NIGHT

'Even the darkest hour has only sixty minutes.' Legendary Australian marathon swimmer Des Renford, quoting Dr Morris Mandel. Renford swam the English Channel nineteen times.

Marathon swimmers often need to swim into the night to get the job done. Before taking part in a night challenge, prepare yourself mentally for the night-time – practise calming mental disquiet and fear when it is dark and eerie. On a marathon swim you will almost certainly be sighting on a pilot boat rather than landforms. If possible do a training swim of reasonable length in the dark, with your safety crew. 'There is nothing like a night swim to bowl out defects in the organisation,' observed Gerald Forsberg, who shared much valuable practical advice when long-distance swimming was establishing itself in the sixties. 'Light and steering arrangements will rarely be thoroughly effective first time.'[1]

FULL MOON SWIMMING

Swimming under a full moon becomes a ritual for many swimmers. There is the possibility of the night being brightened by the moon, of seeing a glitter path between you and the horizon, but there's also a lot of full moon swimming that takes place under full cloud cover. If swimming in the sea in the spring, remember that a full moon could mean spring tides, which will lead to bigger than average tides and swell. This can introduce more risk and unruliness to a marine night swim.

SEEING THE MOON RISE

Even better than swimming under a full moon is seeing it rise. The moon looks biggest when it is close to the horizon: giant and glowing.

You may be surprised by the number of full moon swims where no moon is showing. Various things will get in the way of seeing the moon rise: daylight, buildings, clouds, trees and looking the wrong way.

The moon rises in the east. If there are large objects between you (sunk down in your waterway as you are) and the horizon, they will block the view of the rising moon and you will not see it until it is higher in the sky, where it appears smaller. I have had my best views of rising moons swimming through wide-open water meadows in September and October, with no objects in the foreground except the odd curious cow.

The moon will only be visible while rising if the sun has set before it begins its ascent. You need astronomical twilight and a clear night for the full effect. Light pollution – an orange haze of distant (or nearby) towns, cars and street lighting – will reduce the moon's luminescence, a dark sky reserve will make it brighter. Supermoons are when the moon appears larger as it is closer to the Earth. On autumn full moons, it appears equally large: a combination of warmer water, the residue of summer acclimatisation and earlier sunsets make September a fantastic month for a full moon swim.

MOON BATHING RITUALS

So the moon has drawn you out, and you're stumbling around in the dark, courting borderline hypothermia, pouring hot drinks on each other as you can't see the cups. Are there any more layers to add to this full moon swimming thing?

The key part of the moon in neopagan and Wiccan tradition is that it has cleansing powers and is a time for drawing the last month to a close, letting it go, and setting intentions for the next. Some white witches 'charge' their silver, others 'moon bathe' and charge their bodies. Lune, lunar, lunatic: whether you embrace this or think it is a bit woo-woo, it might still inspire you to swim in nothing but some silver jewellery.

Extras like Thermoses, chairs (the ground gets damp) and open fires afterwards are a bonus. One swim group takes a small fire-bowl and wood in a wheelbarrow so they can have the warmth of a fire while leaving no trace.

MOON BREATHING

When I moon swim with a yogini friend, she has us do some alternate nostril breathing (*Nadi Shodhana pranayama*) to balance our energy (*prana*) and then a couple of rounds of 'moon breathing' (*Chandra Bhedana pranayama*). To do this, sit upright or lie down, whichever is more comfortable. Close your eyes or lower your gaze. Close your right nostril with your right thumb, resting the second and third fingers of your right hand in your palm or on your third eye (forehead) and extending your fourth and fifth fingers. Breathe in through your left nostril and then close it with the fourth finger of your right hand, while releasing your thumb from your left nostril and breathing out through your right nostril. Regulate your breath and keep repeating this action, breathing in through the left nostril and out through the right, for a few rounds or a couple of minutes until your breathing is slow and you feel more relaxed. Now you are ready. In traditional Indian medicine the left side of the body is 'Ida' or moon energy, which is female, cooling and calming, so moon breathing connects with our calming, compassionate, creative and feminine side.

THE FULL MOON CALENDAR

Swimmers are just the latest in a long line of peoples to use full moons to keep track of the passing seasons. The folk names included here are drawn from Celtic, Medieval, Chinese and Native American traditions.[2] With thirteen full moons a year now squished into twelve Gregorian months, whose names have been passed around through word of mouth for centuries, this is not intended to be a definitive list. Rather, it is there to inspire us to look up and get out there, and adopt our own.

January: Wolf Moon

Also referred to 'Sun Has Not Strength to Thaw' moon by the Algonquin people of Eastern Canada and 'When Snow Blows Like Spirits in the Wind' moon by the Arapaho (who lived historically on the plains of Colorado and Wyoming), the term

Wolf Moon originates from hungry wolves howling outside villages late at night at this time of year. By now the nights are drawing out, but it is severe time of year.

February: Snow Moon
Named Snow Moon as February is one of the most common months for snowfall in the northern hemisphere; and for swimmers this is the hardest time of year. Northern American Indigenous Peoples also name it the Hunger Moon, when food sources are scarce and the hunting conditions are difficult.

March: Sap Moon
Can you feel your sap rising, or not quite yet? The arrival of spring with the March full moon has generated different names across the world, among them: the Storm Moon, Worm Moon, Chaste Moon (as it symbolises the purity of early spring), Crow Moon, Warming Moon and Moon When the Leaves Break Forth.

April: Budding Moon
May is when the outdoor swimming summer starts in earnest in the northern hemisphere, but the bright days of April are when many start thinking about it, so one little full moon swim may germinate and bud. Also called the Full Pink Moon, Full Melting Moon, Moon Where Ice Breaks in the River (by the Arapaho) and Fish Moon (as fish begin to swim upstream).

May: Blossom Moon
May's full moon signifies the month when things grow warm again, leaves and blossom burst into life, corn is ready for planting and swimmers return to the water in droves. Also called the Big Leaf Moon, Full Flower Moon and Hare Moon – and wouldn't you like to see one of those animals gazing up at the moon too?

June: Strawberry Moon

June is prime time for strawberries (remember to pack a punnet), and is when the moon follows its lowest arc across the sky, which gives it a glowing yellow hue. Also known as the Hay Moon, Hot Moon and Honey Moon.

July: Thunder Moon

Also known as the Buck Moon; this is the season for thunderstorms and when new antlers emerge from bucks' foreheads.

August: Grain Moon

Expect to hear crickets. Also known as the Sturgeon Moon, as Native American peoples knew this was when sturgeon were at their most abundant in the Great Lakes.

September: Big Moon

September's full moon is often the closest to the autumn equinox and has a tendency to look brighter and bigger than others, its luminosity and brilliance earning it the name Big Moon among the Tlingit peoples in Alaska as well as swimmers in the UK. Other names include Full Corn Moon and Harvest Moon – a time to listen out for combine harvesters, which often work at night.

October: Blood Moon

Like September's moon, the Blood Moon rises early in the evening, which means you are more likely to see it near the horizon. This creates the illusion of it being bigger. It also scatters more blue light, letting more red light reach your eyes, hence the name.

November: Reed Moon

Nature becomes a bit more introspective at this time of year, with energy sinking down into the plant roots, and life dying right back on the banks, leaving you among cold, swaying monochrome reeds. In Celtic tradition the time between this moon – which is the closest to Halloween, a time of year when festivals around the world honour the dead – and winter solstice is also used as a pause, a chance to withdraw from the world, look into yourself, release the old year and dream (but not start) what lies ahead. Pagans call it the Mourning Moon and after a full year of accumulating possessions (physical and otherwise), some use the Mourning Moon to let go of old, unnecessary things and mourn their passing. In North America, it has been known as 'The Moon When Rivers Start to Freeze' by the Arapho tribe and Cree indigenous people: the temperature will have dropped again since October.

December: Cold Moon

The Cold Moon (a name attributed to Christian settlers in America that is an easy fit) occurs near the winter solstice and is the last full moon before Christmas. Nights are the longest of the year: if you are lucky you may get to tramp to the water's edge over frosted grass. There are Native American references to the names Full Long Night's Moon and Oak Moon as the oak is a symbol of strength – to survive a December full moon swim you will need it.

CHAPTER 9

PLANNING A SWIM

'I was using the map, in fact, not to find my way but to get lost; to lose myself in the landscape'

ROGER DEAKIN,
Waterlog

IN SWIMMING AS IN life: there are planners and passengers. However the inspirational, logistical and emotional work of a swim journey is divvied up, many of us like taking our swim adventures with someone. Swim plans need leaders as much as they need followers.

Just like any relationship, you learn lessons from everyone who you swim with. You can learn all sorts of things: to push yourself, duck waves, have patience, read a map. How to identify a moorhen, press seaweed or feel a storm coming.

One of the riches of The Outdoor Swimming Society journey is the chance it's given everybody to meet everybody: the poets meet the Channel swimmers and learn how to do front crawl, which broadens the type of swims open to them. And the Channel swimmers meet the poets and discover that it's completely possible – sometimes preferable – to stop in the middle of a swim, look around and notice the moment. There's always more than one way to do something. In the early days Kari and I were invited to cross the Corryvreckan with some locals as our hosts. 'We never saw anyone swim like you,' said Alistair. 'Ones who stop midstream for a chat.' The swimming world is crawling with people who don't swim like you. Some don't even swim: they sit under waterfalls in the woods or float about in rivers meditating. The variety is what makes the community.

Whether you are going to be the planner or the passenger in any scenario, being able to assess the risks of any swim is non-negotiable. If you don't know whether you can make it home you shouldn't set out. With the right to swim freely, without lifeguard or cost, comes the responsibility to do it safely. Swimmers call this 'doing their own risk assessment before they get in' – a process that involves thinking about what factors in a swim might lead to peril, and putting measures in place to reduce them. On a simple plunge the risk factor might be not being able to get out where you jumped in. On an epic adventure the risk factors (cold incapacitation, boat traffic, weather) could run to pages.

Whatever the swim (crossing an ocean, taking children to the beach, organising a swim for 6,000), the planning process is the same: find something you want to do, identify the risks and how to moderate them, and then work out how to do it. Planning a swim is not about eradicating risk, it is about managing it. There is no such thing as a safe swim, there are only safe swimmers – ones who can choose swims within their capability. A still pool deeper than you are tall is dangerous if you can't swim, while at the other end of the spectrum there is a swimmer (Kalani Lattanzi) who feels 'safe' enough to swim into one of the biggest surf breaks in the world at Nazaré, Portugal, where waves are up to 100 feet tall. There are swimmers who cross oceans with and without shark tanks, who cross continents via 1,000-km rivers and complete endurance swims in cold that would kill most of us. Out there, swimmers are training their bodies and wits to all sorts of feats, and choosing different levels of risk to live with. 'Safe' is a relative term.

Whatever type of swim plan you have, it begins with the best bit: where are you going?

FINDING A SWIM

Finding a swim is the fun part, where it all starts. I often begin with having seen a place or a picture of a place and just wanting to swim there. I once took my whole family to the Eastern Sierras in California to swim in its meandering hot river and dip in its hot pots, based on images that popped up on Instagram. It was more dipping than swimming and perfect for our sons' age at the time: a Sunday afternoon we spent chatting to locals in pools on a ridge I will never forget, a shared experience found via a mutual love of water.

We always peer out over bridges as we drive about, and look out of train windows, studying and naming the rivers below.

Desk research can involve Google, Instagram, books (guidebooks, autobiographies, other non-fiction and fiction – swimming pops up everywhere), articles, features and maps. Information about where other people have swum is widely and freely available now, and knowing someone else has swum there gives us a feeling of permission – we can too. But there is a huge amount of pleasure to be drawn from looking around where you are or searching for blue spaces on maps, and working it out for yourself. Guided swims are one thing, but being able to make it up is a whole different vehicle.

Talk to people, and let one thing lead to another. Swim plans take us off the beaten path and incidental conversations often lead to the next discovery or the next angle on your swimming. You will likely develop a sixth sense for people who share this love of water – swimmers are everywhere and all ages, they're in boats, at lifeguard stations, in waterfront cafés, and barefoot trailing damp towels behind them on a hot summer's day. Start seeing rather than overlooking teenagers – with time on their hands, an appetite for fun and no cars, they have often done a lot of legwork finding swim spots in an area.

A primary driving force for new inventions is need ('necessity is the mother of invention') and adding a framework to our swimming can force us (in a good way) to be creative and make new discoveries. Frameworks come in all shapes and sizes. Perhaps we want to swim a stretch of coast one bay at a time, or the length of a local river, or all the tarns in the Lake District. Perhaps we want to try a source-to-sea journey, or a swim across the seasons via every full moon. Experiences can be the driving force – the desire to swim by a frosty riverbank at daybreak. So can practicalities – where can we swim on the way to or from work, or what swims lie most conveniently between us and a swim buddy?

Sometimes frameworks are epic and sporting: being the first, going the furthest, doing something no one else has. The current Queen of the Channel is Chloë McCardel with forty-four crossings – she also holds the record for the longest unassisted ocean swim, 124.4 kilometres from South Eleuthera Island to Nassau in the Bahamas in 41 hours 21 minutes. Make up your framework: in 2014, aquatic ecologist Peter Hancock in Australia swam in 333 different locations, a response to reading *Pondlife* by Al Alvarez, and it has turned into a continuous swimming journey – he has currently swum on 2,682 consecutive days (as at 1 January 2022) and thinks the challenge may stretch as far as ten years.

I met Kari, my 'swim twin', in the Thames in 2005. We live 100 miles apart so what we have been doing, ever since we first met, is planning: first our own adventures, then social swims, and then swims for hundreds of people through mass participation swim events. In the early days we were planning to swim in particular places, but almost anything can form the hinge of a plan – fitness, technique, convenience, art work, book work, the hunt for particular experiences (swimming over kelp forests, for example, or into a rock chasm). In 2018 we made the 'peak experience' of swimming itself the framework, filming *Chasing The Sublime*, which sought to explain why we (jointly, as human beings) put ourselves in the path of discomfort and risk, and what drives us to get too cold and too tired and to battle with fear in the name of adventure.

There is always newness to be found. Some people don't even change their swim location – they just show up at their spot and experience whatever nature has in store for them that day. One thing to be sure of: you could swim every day for the rest of your life, and always have a different experience.

THE DIY RISK ASSESSMENT

The first thing to do in creating a plan is step back and look at the swim itself as a journey. Some of this is positive: where is the best swim experience to be had, with whom and with what extras? But a good deal of planning is casting your mind over what might go wrong and putting 'control measures' in place to make sure that none of them happen, or that you are prepared when they do. You are not looking to remove risk – it wouldn't be an adventure if there was no risk – but you are seeking to name the risks and manage them.

Where possible, do recces of swims before you get in, looking at the swim route from the bank or on the water. Google Earth and other satellite photo programs can be a great way to scope out swimming spots, especially if you're visiting new locations and wanting to find possible swims before you arrive; the level of detail can be fantastic and you can also use it to measure distances along a lake, or from one bridge to another.

If you are a part of one, local swim groups provide excellent bush telegraph services to each other about anything – kingfishers, water levels, the times of motocross or fishing competitions.

THE DIY RISK ASSESSMENT

ELEMENTS OF A PLAN	RISKS, PROBABILITY AND HANDLING MECHANISMS
Distance and route	How long is the swim? Are you fit for this distance or is there training to do? Where can you get out early if it feels too long on the day? If you are doing an A to B swim, you will need to work out how you can get required gear/transport to the finish. Are there any obstacles (such as weirs) in the way?
Water conditions	Is there a current? How strong? What is the water quality? Do you need to delay for a few days while storm water washes through?
Duration	How long will it take? Look at best - and worst - case scenarios, allowing (for example) for swimmer speed in this type of water, current or tidal assistance, wind resistance and chop.
Location	Where will you get in and out, where will you park and meet? Will it be busy or quiet, or affected by other activities in the area? How can you identify in and out spots, or the route from the water? Are there other water users to be aware of?
Timings	Are there any best times to do the swim? Identify any restrictions on the time you can swim, such as daylight hours, use of the water by rowing clubs, or tides.
Temperature	Look up (or measure) water temperature and air temperature. Are you sufficiently acclimatised? If no, what precautions can you take: can you wear more neoprene, do more training, get out early if you get too cold or wait till the water warms up?

ELEMENTS OF A PLAN	RISKS, PROBABILITY AND HANDLING MECHANISMS
Weather	What is the ideal weather, likely weather and no-go weather? Identify conditions that might make it easy, difficult, dangerous or impossible, such as wind speed and direction. Closer to the day: what is the weather going to be during the swim? What has the weather been like recently – has it rained or been stormy?
Swimmer ability, mobility and disability	Who, if anyone, is coming? Are there any differing abilities or unknown entities? Are there age, mobility or disabilities to work around in the water or on land? If one of you is 'not sure if I can make it', can that person get out early and look after themselves while the others complete the swim, or will someone go back with them? Will you be able to swim in pods, based on speed, or are there loners at either end of the spectrum? Fast swimmers can swim back to join a main group, keeping warm and moving without the group spreading too far apart. A solitary slower swimmer does not have that option. Factor in confidence and open water experience: a physically strong pool swimmer may feel 'out of their depth' and struggle with fear and panic in big swell.
Specific hazards	What is unique to this swim that may cause a hazard and what can you do to reduce these risks? You are looking at anything here: boat traffic, water flow and force, water quality and more. Any dangerous biota? Blue-green algae, jellyfish, sharp oysters on rocks at entry or exit. Solutions are as various as problems, whether that is wearing a bright hat and tow float to make yourself visible, going super-early before anyone else is out, applying anti-jellyfish suncream in the hope of deterring duck fleas, or packing dive flippers in a tow float to deal with unknown strength of tide.
Gear	What will be useful? A mat to stand on when the ground is chilled, a torch to get back to the car when it is dark, an extra layer (always)?
Responsible use	Can you do this swim without negative impact? Think broadly here: this may mean not disturbing gravel where fish lay eggs, not parking in farmers' lay-bys, avoiding crowded 'honeypots' and going elsewhere, and leaving a location in better shape than you found it by taking debris bags for litter. Has gear been washed, checked and dried since your last swim, to avoid spreading invasive weeds? See 'Swimming Without a Trace', page 257.
Extras	Who doesn't love the person who remembers suncream, has a spare pair of goggles, brought emergency sandwiches or worked out that if you walk up the footpath behind the car park, you can see the entire stretch of river you have just swum? Again, think broadly: what will enhance the day? Snorkels, a notebook, an underwater camera?

GETTING IN AND OUT

Breaking news: you cannot always get out where you got in. For example, it is more difficult to get out where the water is deep than it is to get in when gravity is on your side. A muddy or steep bank may be easy to slip down but hard to ascend. A current may take you away from your get-in spot. The sea can also retreat or advance and make things difficult. There are all sorts of ways to end up stranded in the water. When I was on an early trip with Tim, we spontaneously stripped off and jumped in from some limestone rocks on a remote coastline and returned not that much later to find the tide had dropped exposing an overhang. There were tall cliffs in either direction, no one around, and no other way out. We were marooned. How happy I was to be with a climber with sufficient tolerance to fingertip pain to both cling on to the pocked rock with one hand and push me over the overhang with the other. Also, how happy I was not to have discarded my pants.

Climbing out can also be made more difficult by becoming cold, and losing dexterity – you may lose the ability to grip and to pull yourself out.

On rivers with flow it's a good idea to look for more than one downstream exit point in case you miss the intended one.

Issues with not being able to find the in/out spot again are more common than you might think. Floating down a small river into a small lake, a friend and I swam through a reed bed and out into the lake, around an island and back... Only to realise the path through the reed bed was not at all easy to spot coming the other way. When you are 20 metres from shore, turn around and have a good look at where you started and pick out some landmarks so you can find your way back again.

VISIBILITY AND STEALTH SWIMMING

Most swimmers plan on being visible – as a swimmer you're lowest down the 'food chain' because you're low in the water and small, so being bright helps your chances of avoiding collisions with kayakers, jet skiers and people in boats of all sizes.

Ways to make yourself visible: first, wear a bright hat in a colour not found in nature like red, yellow or orange, or neon. A lot of colours camouflage with the water or with light bouncing off it: green, blue, black, silver, gold and white are not good colours for swim hats. There is always the risk of swim hats being mistaken for buoys even if they're good colours. Open water wetsuits increasingly come with brightly coloured arms, legs and sometimes backs.

Tow floats give another strand to your visibility (see page 229). In tests in marine environments bright yellow/green (such as safety yellow) has been shown to be the most conspicuous colour for floating objects, and visible from a greater distance than other colours. Tow floats with reflective strips will increase swimmer visibility in low and poor light.

All these things will help people see you, if you have spotters on the bank or in the event of needing to be rescued. Having just finished a swim in Devon one day, we spotted a kayaker who appeared to be in trouble, bobbing offshore. A friend in a bright orange neoprene bonnet swam out and waited with the kayaker while the coastguard was called. The light was 'dimpsy', as they say around those parts, and later the RNLI reported that it was the orange bonnet they had tracked when looking for the pair – one bright orange hat was more visible at dusk than an entire man and his kayak. Reusable glowsticks attached to wetsuit zips or goggles, and torches placed inside tow floats to work as floating lanterns are good for choppy, darker and mistier conditions.

However bright you are you need to stay alert to other water users as much as they need to be alert to you, particularly in areas where swimmers may not be expected.

There are times when visibility is not always wanted or required – en masse, a group of swimmers bedecked with neon can look like so much marine trash bobbing along, a plastic vortex you've created yourself at a river or lake near you. For 'stealth swims' you can choose a dark hat or no hat, and if there is any need to tow gear, use a drybag that's brown or black.

TOW FLOATS AND THEIR USES

A tow float is an inflatable bag which is attached to a swimmer by a leash, which then buckles up around the waist. Tow floats carry things you may find useful on your swim, with minimum drag.

Tow floats may tap your toe lightly as you swim, and in windy or choppy conditions they can interfere with your swimming. Some swimmers swap the waist strap with a surf leash and attach that to their ankles. Various shapes and sizes are available – even up to raft-like ones that carry 30-litre rucksacks. They are not buoyancy devices but have various uses:

- For visibility. Some harbourmasters are beginning to lend tow floats to swimmers for this reason, and swimmers in water chock-full of boats and ferries often say they would not swim where they do without one.

- For storage, as a floating kitbag where there are no locker rooms.
    - For car keys and valuables (double-bagging things like phones, notebooks and electric car keys in a smaller drybag is popular, and so is wrapping sharp items such as car keys in something to protect the bag).
    - On a longer swim you may wish to carry food, drink, or inhalers.

- On A to B swims you may wish to put in clothes, towels, flip-flops or changing robes (a 20-litre bag can hold these if they are small enough).

• For children who are starting out on their open water journey, anything that floats can increase their confidence in the water. Paddleboards, life jackets and buoyancy aids fulfil the same function – providing a handy bodyweight support and giving them a rest. (Health and safety reminder: nothing is a replacement for one-to-one adult supervision in the water.)

• Ottering refers to the practice of drifting downstream, lying on your back, wrapping your arms around the float and quietly enjoying the nature around you. You can also try this with the float under your head, as a pillow.

BOATS AND OTHER WATER USERS

Just because you have the right to swim somewhere doesn't mean you should. The Outdoor Swimming Society has a code of good conduct which stresses the importance of being considerate to other water users, but it's not just about putting on a show of good manners; it's an important part of swimming safely.

AVOIDING COLLISIONS

Being hit by a boat is a nightmare fear for a swimmer, so find out where they are and take all reasonable steps to avoid collisions. Defences include swimming in a different area to boat traffic, making yourself highly visible, and sighting regularly.

Where lakes and reservoirs have sailing clubs there may be a specific area of the lake allocated for their use, which can be duly avoided. Swimming at the edges of lakes where water is shallower can also put you in a different zone to bigger boats. If your swim spot has a lot of holiday leisure boats over the summer, you may wish to swim early in the morning while holidaymakers are having their breakfasts, before the water gets busy.

On rivers in the UK boats drive on the right (the opposite of a car on the road); however, if the river is narrow or shallow, they may be in the middle. Where this puts you as a swimmer depends on the waterway – sometimes it may seem safest to be on the same side as boats, other times being on the left may feel safer, so you can see traffic coming.

Training hours for rowing clubs can be looked up and should be avoided: rowers row backwards, and have no chance of seeing you. Jet ski and waterski clubs similarly.

If it's anglers not boats you are avoiding, flank the opposite bank.

SWIMMING IN BOW WAVES

A swimmer swimming front crawl with enough speed, with their head tucked down, will produce a small bow wave – the trough of which is near our mouths, making it easier to breathe with just a small rotation. A boat will produce a much bigger bow wave, and more of them, as they pass. Boat speeds are regulated on many waterways to reduce the bow waves that hit the banks, disturbing wildlife – this is also a bonus for us swimmers.

Being hit by a bow wave can be the first sign that there is a boat in the water with you, and can cause you to wobble about, interrupt your breathing pattern and inhale water. Bow waves don't always come from the expected direction. If you do inhale water stop, lie on your back and get your breath back, then once the wave has gone you can carry on.

SNACKS: BEFORE, AFTER AND DURING

Very brief common-sense advice here: warmth and nutrition are related, so don't swim hungry, and consider rounding out a swim plan with a hot drink and a snack for afterwards even if it's not a regular mealtime, as both will help with warmth.

On longer swims you may wish to 'feed' during the swim. (This is marathon swimmer speak; they don't eat food, they 'feed' at regular intervals.) How often is up to you. I am prone to cold and low blood sugar and have found on longer swims that if I swim for 60–90 minutes and then start taking an energy gel or equivalent every 30 minutes it helps me stay warm. For the Channel many swimmers use warm energy drink, and feed every hour for the first 2–3 hours, and then every 30 minutes until the end of the swim. Some people prefer to eat real food on a swim – flapjacks and bananas are popular. Dairy produce is not recommended in salt water as it's likely to make you sick. Kari doesn't share my snacks but might take an egg mayonnaise sandwich on a long swim.

If wearing a wetsuit, energy gels can be popped inside a leg or arm (just make sure the litter doesn't float away afterwards). Sealable containers holding jelly babies (for example) can give you the same amount of energy with less waste, and can be added to a waistband or tow float. If you are in freshwater, a nifty way to drink is to carry a personal lifestraw – literally a fat straw that filters fresh water so you can drink the river or lake as you swim.

Refine what works for you through practice. If you are training for a big swim it's worth making sure whatever you practise with can be delivered on the day. 'What's on the feeding station?' is a common Dart 10k concern, but alongside 'What do you mean I can't get out halfway?' my favourite tale of indignation at the event (possibly tweaked by the teller) remains 'What do you mean I can't put my beetroot juice and lapsang souchong on the feeding station? I *always* have them.'

YOUR HEALTH AND READINESS

Pay attention to yourself in any swim plan: how are you in yourself, where is your head at?

Outdoors, 'swimming within your limits' is an equation, and looks a little like this:

Swimming within your limits = **swimming ability**
(fitness, speed, endurance)
x acclimatisation
x understanding of the water conditions
x understanding of weather
x open water skills and experience
x learned confidence and calm in dynamic outdoor adventure situations
x form on the day

A strong pool swimmer can be a weak outdoor swimmer and vice versa. Never judge a swimmer on the banks; unlike with other sports, where body size and shape often signpost athleticism, with swimming appearance tells you very little about the swimmer. Those with body shapes we tend to associate with athleticism – low body fat, high muscle – may even suffer in the water, finding it harder to float and stay warm than those with softer physiques.

Sleep, stress levels, general health and recent diet will all affect you in the water. Don't drink or take drugs before swimming, even in small quantities; alcohol and drugs impair judgement, swimming ability and body temperature. Don't take part in one-off winter swims if you have a fever or chest infection. Do be cautious entering cold water if you have asthma, other respiratory conditions or heart conditions or poorly controlled hypertension. Go gently if you are pregnant.

PLANNING FOR ABILITY AND DISABILITY

Creating an enjoyable swim that can accommodate ability and disability on land and in the water all comes down to planning.

In 2009 Wayne Ridden, operational director of the biggest swim in the world, reached out over the African continent and invited Colin Hill and me to attend the Midmar Mile swim event in Pietermaritzburg, South Africa. Hill and I had started the first mass swim events in the UK, in 2008 and 2006 respectively, and Ridden wanted to meet and share what he had done in his corner of the world.

The Midmar Dam was full from a week of rain, and 19,000 swimmers were getting ready to cross it in a 1-mile swim. Barefoot on springy African grass, we made our way past the standard No Swimming and Submerged Obstructions: Do Not Enter Water signs, and entered in waves of 600. Like huge migrations in the water, but of red hats and yellow hats, rather than wildebeest.

Among the swimmers were 5-year-olds (who crossed with their parents), 85-year-olds, blind swimmers (who crossed with partner swimmers, all of whom had had to work out a system for how to lead and how to follow), deaf swimmers and swimmers who wheeled themselves to the water's edge in wheelchairs and on chest trays. Swimmers over the age of 31 swam with those under age 13 as their speed tends to synch; 14–30 years old was the other category. Among the prize categories were 'mentally challenged' and 'physically challenged' (not my labels).

There were swimmers with cystic fibrosis, cerebral palsy and injuries from accidents. A swimmer with no arms, one leg, and one prosthesis, which she removed for the swim, won her category for the third time, and nominated a guy with no legs on a chest tray for the Courage Award. 'Could the lifeguard that has the leg from the start please bring it to the slipway?' was a regular PA shout-out.

What Ridden and his town have created is a swim for everybody that shows how water can be accessible to all. Difficulties moving or integrating on land often free up in the water, where peace, fluidity and balance are found. The biggest issues are often encountered getting to swim spots, not in the water. Where there are barriers to entry there are no cookie-cutter solutions, but plenty of individual ones waiting to be invented during planning.

A longstanding OSS team member is an ambulant wheelchair user (which means she uses sticks and mobility aids as well as wheelchairs). Her swim plans involve looking for easy access to the water – a sloped entry like a boat ramp or densely packed sand. She does not feel able to swim against any level of current, so she chooses relatively shallow millpond beaches where the water is calm and there are no rip tides, and does widths between groynes. As extra security she takes a land spotter. With these measures in place she finds more dignity in wild swimming than the pool, where she cannot manage steps and dislikes the 'sack of potatoes' feeling of a pool hoist.

A registered blind OSS swimmer once shared how, over time, he learnt to swim around his local lake without a guide. He describes himself as having enough sight to avoid walking into lamp-posts, but not enough to see buoys, so he started off following his wife round the lake but came to know when to swim towards the sun and when to look out for the shadow of the trees as he breathed, until he could do it by himself. (He also told a tale of a friend with similar vision being lost in the Mediterranean as he couldn't see the shore, and stumbling onto some rocks eight hours later, worn out and delusional from sunstroke; so no one is saying this is easy.)

It is increasingly possible to find open water venues accessible to wheelchair users, and to find other swimmers and open water coaches with relevant experience. With thought and preparation, it can be more accessible than you might first imagine: there are difficulties, but also opportunities. There are some aspects of open water that may be more accessible than pools: for example, some swimmers with autism have shared how the natural world has been a relief from the bright lights and disorientating noise of overcrowded swimming pools.

ALL THE GEAR

I used to think the best thing about swimming was that you could do it anywhere without anything. How the mighty fall. My years of travelling around with a tiny swim bag (bikini, goggles and pack towel) ready at all times are long gone. Now that bag lives in the boot of my car, and we have a whole kit room.

I generally forget something, so have created a pack list with some ideas. In the list that follows, items are ticked if they might prove useful in certain situations; however, you might equally not use them (if you never use a wetsuit, for example). There are also spaces to list things peculiar to you. Some of the best solutions are personal: a 2-litre bottle of water left in the car in summer to heat, providing a

GEAR LIST

- Swim costume/trunks
- Second costume/ trunks
- Swim wetsuit
- Second wetsuit (even if you don't need it, someone else might have a malfunction)
- Neoprene boots & gloves
- Other neoprene – costume, vests, jammers
- Goggles x 2 (1 clear, 1 dark)
- Goggle spray
- Bright swim hat
- Neoprene bonnet
- Tow float
- Towel – lightweight or hammam
- Second towel
- Changing robe
- Changing mat (wooden bath tray or a square of carpet also work)
- Aqua shoes or flip-flops
- Waterproof bag(s) and rucksacks – to carry and separate dry and wet stuff
- Phone/gopro/notebook
- Drybag for valuables and car keys
- Info – piece of paper/ tide timetable/ postcodes/ forecasts/event info/accom info (bonus points for reading event information before you set off)
- Map/guidebook/ this book/ field guides
- Reef-friendly suncream
- Anti-rub cream
- First aid including antibacterial hand gel, waterproof plasters, sudocrem
- Warm things for after (woolly hat, insulated jacket, thermals, big changing robes)
- Snacks, warm drinks
- Snorkel & dive mask , maybe weight belt and fins
- GPS watch
- Bag or flexi tub for rinsing gear
- Adventure light/reusable glowstick

DIP (NO WETSUIT)	WETSUIT SWIM	SWIM SAFARI (MULTIPLE SWIMS IN ONE DAY)	WINTER SWIM	LONG SWIM/ EVENT SWIM	SWIM HOLIDAY (DIY OR GUIDED)	SNORKEL SWIM
X	X	X	X	X	X	X
		X			X	X
	X	X	X	X	X	X
		X		X	X	X
	X		X			X
	X	X	X	X		X
X	X	X		X	X	X
	X	X		X	X	X
X	X	X		X	X	X
	X		X	X		X
X	X	X	X	X		X
X	X	X	X	X	X	X
		X	X		X	X
X	X	X	X	X	X	X
	X		X			X
X		X			X	X
X	X	X	X	X	X	X
X	X	X	X	X	X	X
X	X	X	X	X		X
X	X	X		X	X	
	X	X			X	X
X	X	X		X	X	X
				X	X	
X	X	X	X	X	X	X
X	X	X	X	X	X	X
	X	X	X	X	X	X
						X
	X	X		X	X	X
		X				
					X	

quick post-sea shower, for example. Or octopus coat hangers to dry neoprene accessories on swim camps.

By 'changing robe' (see below), I mean something you can change in quickly and easily without flashing – this could include microfibre or towelling robes, or two towels sewn together. I count big fleecy long robes to wear over clothes as 'more warm things'.

All suncream ends up in the water, whether you swim in it or shower it off at home, so consider using reef-friendly suncream and increasing the role of rash vests, hats and clothes in your defence against UV rays. (See pages 240–41.)

SUPPORT CREW: PEOPLE AND BOATS

For some challenge swims and crossings you may wish to have a support crew, who perform various functions such as protecting you from other boat traffic by making you more visible, helping you navigate the best swim route, carrying food supplies and spare goggles, and offering you a ride home if you get too cold or run out of steam, or if conditions become difficult. Having someone there with a smile ready to hand you a drink can make a huge difference to your energy levels. On long-distance swims feelings can fluctuate between feeling amazing and wondering why you ever wanted to do this stupid swim; the support crew are there to keep positive and have everything you need to hand. You can take so much from your team – it really can't be underestimated; so if you get a chance to support a swimmer on a long swim I'd say jump at it, and be positive and organised.

In terms of the actual craft the support crew are in, I have acquired the knowledge I have via mild misadventure. I recall my friend Michael and I having to tie two blow-up canoes to ourselves and swim-tow our support crew back across Derwentwater as they couldn't make progress into the headwind stays in my mind (key learnings: look at the weather forecast and don't use inflatable safety cover). But so does swimming between islands in the Isles of Scilly only to find ourselves suddenly befogged; if we hadn't – by chance – been joined by a friendly paddler we'd met the night before,

Dominick Tyler and I might have died looking for Bryher. Once the fog descended we couldn't see anything.

Support crew who can actually carry you home should you need it really expands the types of swims you can do – A to B swims that are logistically difficult come within range when you have a boat, as do more adventurous challenges (not sure if you can make a swim? No matter; you can try, knowing that you can always retire to the boat). The marathon community has appointed 'pilots' (boat support) on recognised swim routes, which must be used for the swim to be officially recognised, but can cost Monopoly-level money. If self-organising self-created challenges, the best and only way to find boat support is to ask around. Be aware that there isn't much a kayak can do if something serious happens; with a paddleboard or boat a swimmer can climb on and be paddled to shore more easily.

My chief observation from doing this casually over the years is that having an RYA2, or whatever certificate is appropriate to the craft at hand, is no guarantee of being able to help swimmers in the water. It takes time and mutual learning to become a team, and things that seem obvious from a swimmer's perspective often aren't to a person in a boat (and vice versa), so some practice together is recommended before a big swim. Kayakers who can't read currents, can't right their boats, who eat ALL the snacks ('What? I was bored') – we have met them all. Many a paddleboard and kayak will drift out of a position where you can sight on them, and need to be trained about where your sightline is, and how close you want them (if there are seals or boats in the water, for example). We're all always learning.

Wind can make it difficult to safely stay close to a swimmer: you need momentum in a boat to stay on course, and keeping at swimmer pace may mean the boat is blown around by the wind. Paddleboarders are great to sight on as they are so tall, but (like blow-up canoes) they will struggle in chop and wind. Electric boats are available on some lakes and travel at just the right speed for a swimmer, without polluting the water.

If you are using a boat, you will normally come across fuel in the water; only a drop or two of fuel needs to leak for you to be able to taste it, as fuel doesn't break down and spreads quickly. Marathon swimmers can end up sick from the fuel leaking from their boats. On Channel crossings, support boats go downwind of swimmers for this reason, but when it's rough there can be a double whammy: exhaust fumes may swirl around the swimmer, accentuating sea sicknesses.

WEIL'S DISEASE AND OTHER SICKNESSES

Most freshwater swimmers will, at some point, hear about Weil's disease. It is not actually a disease, but the development of a water-borne bacterial infection called leptospirosis. There are many myths around it, and a cynic might think that it has been used in the past to provoke fear and deter people from swimming.

Leptospirosis is no more common in urban than rural water-courses, and doesn't correlate with water purity generally. You can find it in crystal-clear and clean salmon and trout streams as well as in urban docks or Camden Lock. While rats are very prevalent in all literature about Weil's, this does not reflect their importance as a source. The bacteria is actually harboured in the kidneys of a wide variety of animals – cattle, deer, pigs, sheep, horses, dogs and many other rodents. Pee from any of these animals, carried into water, could carry the bacteria.

There is less than a 1 in 10 million chance of contracting Weil's, and it is mostly an occupational disease, affecting animal handlers, livestock farmers, people who work in the waste management and fishing industries, and anyone who works around the back end of a cow. Most cases are successfully treated with antibiotics.

It can however affect rowers, swimmers and water users. The most common route of infection is through a cut or abrasion, although the mucous membranes in the eyes or mouth can also provide an entry point, particularly if there are cuts, bleeding gums, or de-roofed blisters. Swallowing water is not thought to be a common route of transmission, and the bacteria does not survive salt water, so you cannot be infected in the sea.

Advice is to apply waterproof plasters to cuts and abrasions before you get in, and be aware of the symptoms so that if you feel at all unwell after being in water you will seek medical treatment promptly. This is important because while the condition it is not common, it can be severe when it does hit. If you cut your feet in the water, clean the wound thoroughly, use an antiseptic, cover with a plaster or bandage and check it regularly for infection (redness and swelling).

Symptoms of leptospirosis usually develop within seven to fourteen days after contact with infection, but can take as little as three, or as many as thirty. The initial symptoms are like common flu: fever, severe joint pain particularly in joint muscles, headache and chill (and, less commonly, nausea and vomiting), so telling a doctor that you have been in contact with water in some capacity and getting a blood test are key.

Symptoms generally pass within four to nine days, without treatment. But in around 10 per cent of people, a second more serious phase occurs, and it is not fully understood why. This is the result of the bacteria infecting organs such as the brain, kidneys, liver, eyes and lungs. It is treated with antibiotics, and the earlier the better as it can lead to fatal complications such as liver, lung or kidney failure.

Always wash your hands or shower after a swim, particularly if you have cuts and abrasions, which should be cleared of bacterial crud.

LEVELS OF ADVENTURE

How touch-and-go do you want it? Everyone's definition of an adventure is different, so when planning a swim it is useful to locate yours, using the concepts of flow and peak adventure.

FLOW

'Flow' is a psychological state that seems particularly easy to tip over into when swimming. First popularised by the positive psychologist Mihaly Csikszentmihalyi,[1] flow is characterised by those moments when we are fully absorbed in what we are doing, and nothing else seems to matter.

To access the flow state, seek a balance in your plans between challenge and skills. Struggling and flow don't go together, but neither does passivity; things are fulfilling when there is some difficulty. In training for an event or challenge, your ambition might be not just to be able to do a swim, but to do it comfortably, so you have something in the tank if things get tricky on the day.

Second, be honest with yourself. Crucial to the flow state is that we are intrinsically motivated and enjoy the experience, and are not doing it for a secondary benefit (prestige, health benefits, because everyone else is). If you really don't enjoy winter swimming, distance swimming, or swimming without your wetsuit: who cares? Maybe you will next year. Maybe you won't. Many swimmers before you have found something else they enjoy and flowed into that instead – wild synchronised swimming, high-diving and chasing octopuses with a snorkel being some of the paths less travelled.

PEAK EXPERIENCE AND FRONTIER ADVENTURE

My friend Michael has masterminded many a great group adventure – a lake to lake 10k down a swollen river and the Seven Sisters swim being two of the most memorable. A natural maverick, the edge he is always looking for is where 'things get a bit dicey, and then we all make it home in time for tea'. It's daring but not reckless: swims may teeter around peril – people getting cold, tides being unswimmable, conditions rougher than anticipated – but none have tipped over into jeopardy.

What Michael it pitching for by pushing things a bit is 'peak experience', also defined as 'transcendent moments of pure joy and elation' or an 'oceanic feeling' of being at one with the world. It's similar to but more intense than flow, and you can only access it by taking risks. Colin Mortlock encapsulated this in his 'Theory of Adventure Paradigm', which outlines four adventure states.[2]

- **Stage one is play**, where we experience little emotion through relatively easy participation in activities below our skill level.

- **Stage two is adventure**, where we're both enjoying ourselves and excited, using our capabilities more fully. Nearly all the brain's available inputs are occupied, discomfort is at an unnoticeable level, and stray negative thoughts don't enter the mind (this could also be called flow).

- **Stage three is frontier adventure** and is characterised by peak experience: adventurous challenges very close to our limits.

- **Stage four is misadventure**, which occurs when a person chooses or ends up in a challenge beyond their ability. Misadventure can happen when we have chosen – or been pressured into participating – challenges beyond our abilities, leading to fear, anxiety and possibly getting into trouble.

The theory underlines the individuality of swimming; what is adventurous for one person could be too easy for another and harmful to a third. Perceived risk and actual risk are not the same. Risk is something to be managed, but you can't have a good adventure without it.

SWIMMING ALONE AND TOGETHER

Swim buddies can radically alter the shape of your life. Whether your swim buddy is one person, a group of people, or a virtual community, they are likely to become high-status players in your social circle.

Meeting Kari in a river was an encounter that, for me, has changed the direction of everything. Many of the things I'm most pleased to have created, shared and experienced in life so far have happened with her insight, support and renegade 'who says you can't?' attitude, which have been amusing me ever since. I lay all that co-creative life-wealth at the muddy gritty feet and exposing honesty of outdoor swimming: one minute chasing the sublime, the next feeling a bit desperate.

So what are you looking for in your swim buddy, and how do you find them? Some qualities I'd really recommend:

- **Reliability** – for one thing, you are taking your life in your hands together. For another, who doesn't want to spend more time swimming than arranging to go swimming?

- **Shared abilities and bravery** – the comfort and discomfort zones. It's the middle of a swim: do you want to go this way or that? Should you duck out, or press ahead? It's hard to swim at a different pace to the one that is natural to you (for a start, you'll get cold, or tired), it's hard to enjoy a different stroke or distance journey to the one you want to do (to have an adventure you need to get close to the 'edge'), it's hard to be less or more adventurous than you naturally are. You may end up with different swim friends for different swims – distance, winter, wild, night. But sharing a basic bandwidth of swimming speed and concept of what makes a swim fun is required.

- **Shared goals and dreams** – where will swimming take you? When we wake up in some horrible hotel room eating dry cereal out of a box Kari and I are sharing a lot of things, including a sense of how comically ridiculous we are moaning about our conditions (we're not bivvying in a snowdrift here, what is the problem?!). We are somewhere on a spectrum between people who can spend days with frostbite without moaning, and people who would never spend a night in a room with dodgy hygiene and flickering electrics in the first place. So, to enjoy your journey: shared expectations are key.

- **Time together.** Any form of communication in 'exciting' situations is, in my experience, difficult and often flawed. But if you understand when the other is hungry, too cold or too intimidated without having to say a word, that's a solid start.

A bit like with love, you can't go looking for this, but swimming with people you do sometimes find a deep unspoken understanding. Both Kari and I are prone to expressing regret before getting in: it's cold, we're not fit enough, our clothes are cosy. The other understands that this 'Eeyore moment' is just a dance that is done, not an opening gambit that means 'cancel the swimming!' Many swim buddies would find that off-message and irritating; it's good to have one who understands that it's just part of your process.

A question that often comes up is: 'For safety, do I need to swim with someone?' I would say no, not necessarily. Why swim with someone? What do you think is going to happen to you exactly, and what are they going to do about it? Maybe they can help you, maybe they can't – but look at the information, interrogate the facts. The type of help someone might be able to give you if you 'get into trouble' will depend very much on which type of trouble you are forecasting, and the skills or risks of your 'someone'. Other human beings are useful for:

- Mobility or sight issues – another person may be able to help you physically get in and out of the water, or to a swim location.

- Learning! Apparently we may need to hear something seven times to remember it. Reading this book once is unlikely to be enough. Hang out with other swimmers and it will all go in gradually.

- Confidence issues or fear – you can help each other grow as swimmers, and someone else being there can drastically reduce random fears.

- Fun.

- Sharing observations and noticing things.

- Visibility – two swimmers are more visible than one if there are other water users.

- Discussion and reduction of specific risks. Does the other person have more knowledge than you of the tides or currents, does discussing things with someone clarify things for you, make you pay attention to risks?

- Physical assistance if something like a heart attack, panic attack, asthma attack or hypothermia overcomes you in the water. The risks of these things happening may be extremely slight, and physical assistance is the hardest thing of all to give, unless they're a trained beach lifeguard or in or on something like a paddleboard or boat.

- Ability to call emergency services – do they have reception and a working phone?

But if you don't need or want a swim buddy for any of those reasons, then why not swim alone? Sharing swim adventures is special, but so is solitude. Space to be, space to hear, freedom from any need to verbalise or empathise. I love slipping out by myself and becoming part of nature for a while, particularly when things are busy; the ego dissolves faster alone. I have friends who do a lot of solo-ing on lakes: picking their own line down the lake, carrying their own stuff (including a phone, socks in case they need to walk out, gels, a top, lifestraw and hat), fitting it in when they can – it's made them fall in love with long-distance swimming again.

If you are swimming in a group, be aware that people are the most unpredictable link in any plan. Any very focused or extreme adventurer will also tell you that they limit the number of people in their plans for that very reason.

There is a huge plus side to social swimming, but in a group it's easy to start being a passenger, to forget to take responsibility for yourself, to rely on others and to assume they know what they are doing. Beware the unconscious incompetent: the person who does not know what they do not know, but leads anyway. All of human life is here on the bank, and if you're used to a cosy social nook with other people whose idea of rationality matches yours, getting in the water with total strangers will remind you that other people's minds can be staggeringly different to yours. There is no rule to say that they make you safer than when you are alone.

SOCIAL SWIMS AND THE SWIM RESPONSIBILITY STATEMENT

'Social swims' are those where people go on to social media and post swim plans, and see who else wants to join them. If you are going to do this without accepting legal and moral responsibility for others, it is important that make you clear it through your language. In the OSS we use the 'Swim Responsibility Statement', mentioned briefly earlier, which was created by OSS member and lawyer Nathan Willmott in 2007.[3] It was a game-changer, enabling a culture and community of free swimming to mushroom, in the UK and beyond.

The key to social swims is that you:

- Make it clear that the swim is peer-to-peer and all

swimmers must be solely responsible for making their own assessment as to the risks involved in any particular swim. Avoid language that positions one person as a leader or organiser.

• Make it clear the decision to participate in any swim must be taken individually, and swimmers must not rely (in whole or in part) on views or information provided by any member of the group of which they are a part. Swimmers may be advised that if they are in any doubt about the safety of a swim or their ability to complete it, they should not take part.

• Do not take any money (which heightens the risk of legal responsibility, even if the money is collected for charity).

• Do not advertise (which risks conveying that you have assessed the swim as safe and therefore are assuming legal responsibility for others).

If you do take money, organise and advertise, the swim transitions from being a 'social swim' to being an event, where you are legally required to be qualified and/or competent to take responsibility for people: this involves risk assessments, safety plans, insurance and possibly safety cover.

ON THE DAY

Like motorists who can't do a U-turn, many of us find it hard to alter a swim plan that has momentum. The earlier I've made a plan and the further I've gone to enact it, the harder it is to change it on the day. Drive 160 miles to swim into a cliff on a neap tide, pull off the magic trick of having someone take your children for a few hours, then arrive at the shore to find the sea more than a bit surgy – do you want to stop before you get in, and have it all come to nothing? No, you don't. You want to keep going. Tim and I did get in on that particular occasion. I took the (frankly inadequate) precaution of putting my trainers on so I could fend off rocks, timed the entry between waves and set off in a 'maybe it'll be quieter round the headland' kind of way. It was not quieter round the headland, of course it wasn't; it was raging. We got out minutes later, battered, hair splattered, hearts pumping, to find a stranger had been moved to video the entire escapade (what were the plans for that footage?). I have had to train myself to move to plan Bs earlier rather than later.

A PIECE OF PAPER IN A POCKET

The first on-the-day issue is remembering what the plan actually is so you can follow it. I advocate carrying a piece of paper in your pocket, on which you have written down any key logistical information you need on the day – tide times, parking and meeting postcodes, name of accommodation, that kind of thing. Then put phones away and on silent and focus on the day at hand. This not only keeps your mind clear for the swim, it means that as a group you can operate without reception. Plus, everyone is punctual, everyone retains information and takes responsibility for themselves on the start, and there's a lot more 'being there'.

We have also taken to writing crucial get-in times on the backs of our hands with a Sharpie. We do a lot of planning in camping chairs with a glass of wine, which often goes something like this: if HT is 8 a.m., we want to get in around 7.15 a.m. while it's still slack, it's around a 20-minute walk ... Cue alarm goes off who knows when, we can't remember when we're supposed to be eating/walking/faffing/swimming, and we invariably plunge in at a completely different time to the one required and wonder why the tide is not doing what we thought it would be.

TALKING TO WATER USERS AND ON-THE-DAY RECCES

Tap into local knowledge: if a new rip current has appeared, a sandbar has moved or there's a mass stranding of jellyfish, someone locally will know about it. If we can show up to our swim locations calm and clear-headed then, as we walk about doing an on-the-day recce, there is more chance of relevant information finding its way to us. Dog walkers, anglers, coastguards, helms, walkers – it's always worth saying hello. If you are on a beach, tell the lifeguards what you are doing and tell them when you are due back – they may get calls about you and they may have advice to give.

When you get to the location, enjoy the moment of hesitation that often comes with entering unknown waters. Look at conditions – what can you see in front of you and feel in the air? Do your calculations about weather and tides match what you see? No matter how familiar a swim is to you, it's fresh every time depending upon water conditions. Look into yourself: sometimes, when we're not feeling it, we need to (wo)man up and get on. But always be open to moderating and swimming a plan B. Just because you've made the effort to get to a certain point, you're not tied to carrying on.

TALK THROUGH PLANS AND PLAN BS WHILE STILL ON LAND

With your swimmers or support crew, run through your planning on land – it is surprisingly hard to reach group decisions in the water. In anything close to a survival situation – times when stormy weather, cold, swell, chop or difficulty are strong to overwhelming – it becomes harder still. Things you might want to get clear about is who is swimming with who, and backup plans – whatever risks you've perceived, know your handling mechanisms for them.

IN THE WATER

Discuss what you are sighting on with your swim buddy, swim side by side, check in with each other. Stay vigilant for other water users with regular sighting – it is your responsibility to see them as much as their responsibility to see you. Always consider going back, or stopping, as an option.

THE INCIDENT PIT

Forgive me for all of this, especially if you're Lisa.

It is just after Christmas 2006 and my sister Lisa is over from Montana. She lives in a land of fairly extreme sport and is way fitter and tougher than me. The last time I saw her we were skiing off-piste when my brother-in-law said, 'Don't fall here Kate, it's a no-fall zone.' A no-fall zone, it transpired, is one where if you do fall you will likely carry on falling, until you die. Good to know, although perhaps something to have mentioned before I pushed myself out on to the precipice and past the point of choice. Anyway, what happens next is in no way payback for that.

Having become freshly passionate about swimming (it was something my siblings and I did together when small), I made a plan to take Lisa swimming around Burgh Island in Devon with Michael and Kari. It's about a mile round, and a novel adventure. Backs of islands are always wild places: tall cliffs and scattered rocks that belong to seabirds and seals, with swell that feels a little hostile for people.

As we reached the first corner of the island the swell was huge – with one of us on the crest of a wave and another lost in the troughs, it was hard to catch sight of each other, or group together. We were approaching a rocky chasm dubbed 'Death Valley' by Kari, because it amused her (no one has actually died there) and stopped for a little discussion – should we go through or not?

I thought we'd agreed not to. But the next thing I knew Michael and Kari had shot off towards Death Valley, and Lisa and I were bobbing towards the far corner of the island on our own. I shouted after them but they were gone – ears submerged, surf too noisy, my voice lost. It's incredibly hard to communicate when you're in chaotic water, and when you're cold – on one level you're having a fun day out, a mini micro adventure, but on another it's a bit 'every man for himself' territory. Everyone needs to push on. Decisions and communication that are easy on land just don't process.

We reached the far corner. Stopping to talk, I realised Lisa's lips were blue. It occurred to me then that my sister was really, properly cold; the wetsuit we'd borrowed for her had holes and didn't fit her properly, the December sea was sluicing in and out. It also became apparent that, while she was fit as a flea, she wasn't a powerful swimmer, and the tide was against us (which hadn't been supposed to happen). I was shouting 'Push for ten' but she just couldn't make progress. There were no lifeguards, no one on shore was looking for us and towing her wasn't an option – I wasn't making much progress against the tide doing full front crawl myself; there was no way I would be taking one arm out of the process. So we were left with 'Swim Lisa, swim!', and putting our heads down.

When I asked Kari afterwards what she remembered, she said, 'We weren't worried about you... you swam off in a different direction, which was irritating, but we knew Lisa was athletic; it never occurred to us that she was having a difficult time.'

Somehow, eventually, we managed to get past the corner currents – I think we went wide, where the currents were less, and then back in again – and clamber on to some rock. We made it back to the beach by a mixture of clambering on barnacled rocks, getting quite cut up, hugging for warmth and swimming through the calmer areas.

This, basically, is an incident pit, a term used by divers (as well as engineers and medics) to describe how things can go from bad to a lot worse, with sometimes fatal consequences, without any of the incidents in themselves being high-risk. An incident pit is a conceptual pit, with sides that become steeper over time with each new incident until a point of no return is reached.

The things that pushed us into the incident pit are obvious in retrospect. We were excited for the swim and cavalier about the details (wetsuit, acclimatisation, swimming ability). We hadn't seen each other for a long time, were busy catching up pre-Christmas and took the swim for granted (did someone say 'Have you checked the tide times?' Perhaps not...). New people bring new chaos to a group – the time when we might otherwise subconsciously have picked up on weather or conditions was taken up with small talk. The 'safety in numbers' sense groups give was false – I would have been much more cautious, it would have felt more intimidating, if it was just the two of us.

So, a cautionary tale. Disasters are rarely a single event, and instead often a progression of minor mistakes. If you start sliding into one of these, notice it and slow things down.

ACCESS: IS IT LEGAL?

There are some grey areas concerning legal rights of access to water in England and Wales at the moment. Swimmers face two legal obstacles – firstly, whether it is lawful to cross land to get to the water's edge, and secondly, whether it is lawful to swim in the water. In practice, given some of the legal uncertainties in both areas, whether you swim somewhere sometimes comes down to the interpretation of both landowner and swimmer – does one tolerate it, and does the other think they are within their rights? At one end of the spectrum there are swimmers who would not dream of passing a No Swimming sign; at the other are people who pass all of them and stick a sign on the gate saying Trespassers Welcome. There is currently a feeling that better access rights need to happen and will happen, and clarity will be achieved, and it's just about how long the complicated negotiations will take. Until then access is, in places, open to interpretation.

In Scotland the right to roam is included as part of the public's right to responsible access to outdoor spaces, providing swimmers with much broader rights to swim in rivers and lakes as long as they observe the Scottish Outdoor Access Code,[4] which requires us to take responsibility for our own actions, take care of the environment, and respect other people's interests. As long as we meet these overriding principles, landowners must respect the public's right to access outdoor spaces, including open water and the land adjoining water.

If you're going further afield it is worth looking up access for the country you're visiting – Norway, Sweden and Estonia are the only other countries that currently have a right to roam.

THE CROW ACT, MOUNTAINOUS AREAS AND NATIONAL PARKS

In mountainous areas in England and Wales it is increasingly the case that we have the right to roam – especially if the National Trust manages the area, as they are making as much land open access as possible. This right is enshrined in the Countryside and Rights of Way Act 2000 (CRoW),[5] giving ramblers the right to walk over mountains, moorland, heath, downland and common land, without having to stay on paths. It does not explicitly give the right to swim, but does give you access to the shores of all sorts of water in those areas (there are campaign groups working to have the CRoW Act extended to explicitly cover swimming).

SEA AND TIDAL WATER SWIMMING

In Britain, the right to swim in the sea is clear and not disputed. Beaches in England and Wales are often privately owned, but access to the sea from them is rarely restricted. The Crown Estate, the Duchy of Lancaster and the Duchy of Cornwall own 55 per cent of the foreshore in Britain, and the entire seabed between low water and twelve nautical miles.[6] (The foreshore is the land between low and high tides.)

There is a common-law right to swim in tidal waters (estuaries). This may, however, be overturned by local laws. For example, in the tidal Thames the Port of London Authority was given the power in 2012 to control access, and swimming in the area between Putney Bridge and Crossness in Thamesmead is only allowed with special permission of the Authority.[7]

NAVIGABLE RIVERS

In broad brushstrokes, if a waterway is deep, wide and calm enough for a water vessel (e.g. boats) to pass safely, then it is considered a 'navigable' river and anyone can take a boat to it without permission. Although the position is not entirely clear, detailed studies of historical court decisions have asserted that swimmers have a right to swim in any such navigable waters in England and Wales.

NON-NAVIGABLE RIVERS AND FOOTPATHS

What about smaller, non-navigable rivers? Riparian means 'relating to or situated on the banks of a river' and, according to English riparian law, it is the bank that is owned, not the water; so if there is a footpath or bridleway along a riverbank that you can use for get-in and get-out spots, many people assume that this gives you legal access.

A to B swims that wander beyond footpaths can be contentious. Some swimmers, paddlers and landowners understand the law as meaning that as long as we don't touch private land we can travel through it in the water. But some anglers and landowners think differently, and you may experience people waving their fists. I have come across barbed wire strung across a river – a fallen-in fence, cattle control, or deliberate deterrent? Regardless of whether you are right or wrong, there are places where swimming is accepted, and others where it leads to confrontations, which are generally best avoided.

PICNICS AND GATHERINGS

Leaving a footpath (for example, to create a changing area for a wild swim group), obstructing a footpath and picnicking are not within footpath rights – footpaths were made for walking, and while a hiker may sit on a rock for a cheese sandwich and a swig from a water bottle, this is not the same as leaving gear all over a meadow, flattening grazing pasture, sunbathing and settling in for a picnic. Be aware of this before you take liberties at a swim spot.

RESERVOIRS

Reservoirs are privately owned by water authorities or local councils, who in England and Wales generally go to some efforts to make it clear that swimming is not permitted. In contrast, in Scotland and other countries reservoir swimming is allowed and lawful.

'TRESPASSERS WILL BE PROSECUTED'

'Trespassers will be prosecuted', say the signs. 'Statutory Fine £1000. NO SWIMMING.' Ahem, will they? Actually? Is this going to be the most expensive swim in history? Probably not. Damaging property, actively disrupting someone else's use of the land as a trespasser or causing a nuisance can constitute criminal offences, but simply being on someone else's land as a trespasser does not, although it may constitute a civil wrong. As such, 'trespassers will be prosecuted' is a hollow and inaccurate piece of signage.

What could happen where you are on private land as a trespasser, is that the landowner may ask you to leave, and if you don't they are permitted to use 'reasonable force' to remove you. And in theory you could have a civil claim brought against you for having committed the tort of trespass to land (but civil suits have plaintiffs and claimants, they are not 'prosecutions'). Here the potential damages awarded would typically be limited to the amount that you and the landowner would, hypothetically, have agreed for the right to use the land for the period it was used for. For individuals travelling across land to go for a swim, any such damages are likely to be very small. And no 'fine' would be permitted to be levied by the landowner. But if the trespass is by a commercial entity accessing land without permission (holiday companies, guides, coaches, events) then it could be more susceptible to trespass claims as the value would be both quantifiable and materially higher.

SWIMMING WITHOUT A TRACE

The Outdoor Swimmers' Society Code of Conduct states that: 'With the right to swim freely comes the responsibility to respect and protect the environment we love.' This means everything from taking litter home to be disposed of responsibly, to ensuring that we don't inadvertently pollute the environment by virtue of our presence.

BIOSECURITY: CLEAN, CHECK, DRY

As wandering swimmers we need to take care that we do not take invasive species with us on our travels: anything that reaches a lake, stays in a lake – and anything that reaches a river will get to a lake or sea one day too.

Non-native invasive species can harm ecosystems as they have fewer natural predators or may outcompete native species. In the UK swimmers can come across a number of invasive species – pink Himalayan balsam exploding on the banks at the end of summer, floating pennywort taking over streams (it floats like watercress but the leaves look a little like four-leaf clovers), New Zealand pygmyweed choking out other plants as well as wildlife in some lakes.

Kit that looks clean can still hold small pieces of plants, microscopic organisms and invertebrates that travel with you and are able to propagate in the next place you swim. There are three simple yet highly effective ways whereby you can avoid this:

- CHECK your equipment, clothing and yourself for living organisms and pieces of plants. Pay particular attention to damp or hard-to-inspect areas (seams, folds).

- CLEAN and wash all equipment, footwear and clothes thoroughly at an outside tap to get rid of what you can't see. If you do come across any organisms, leave them at the water body where you found them, or on a hard surface to die out. Don't wash kit in nearby water bodies (streams and ponds) as this may contaminate it.

- DRY all equipment and clothing before you use them again. Some species can live for many days in damp conditions.

If you are intending on doing a swim run or swim safari, where you swim in multiple water bodies, it is extremely important to hose down and change costumes between swims, and possibly opt not to do them in areas where pygmyweed is present.

SWIMMING IN NATURE RESERVES AND SSSIS

A Site of Special Scientific Interest (SSSI) is a conservation designation awarded by Natural England. Usually the area is of particular interest to science due to the rare species of fauna or flora it contains, but the designation can also come from geology or landforms. If you want to swim in an SSSI then look into the designation online to see if you can do so without disturbing a habitat; people and nature can often thrive side by side but there may be areas or times of years to avoid.

Nature reserves are usually privately owned and managed specifically for wildlife, so swimming may be out of bounds. If the reserve is designated for heathland, grassland, fen or marshland, rather than any aspect of its rivers and water bodies, water sports may be allowed.

TREADING LIGHTLY AROUND PLANTS, FISH AND FOWL

Wildlife is part of the joy of swimming – what is out there, and how do you avoid causing it harm? The short answer is to get to your swim spot and into the water with minimum disturbance to anything – drystone wall, path (stay on it, don't widen it), riverbed (float over it, don't kick it up), aquatic plant. Keep away from plants, avoid stirring up excess sediment or kicking over rocks, avoid touching spawn (March to June), take care during bird breeding season (March to August) to give birds space and don't get between animals or birds and their offspring. Conservationists advise that we do not seek out seals to swim with but, if they interact with you, engage on their terms. Seals have sharp teeth, move fast and are big, so they can be intimidating. They also have the intelligence of a dog and seem quite good at reading body language and intent; remain calm to avoid frightening them, and (as with all wild animals) never get between them and an escape route.

CHAPTER 10

SWIM BETTER

'The day was beautiful, and it seemed to him that a long swim might enlarge and celebrate its beauty'

JOHN CHEEVER
'The Swimmer'

The physicality and athleticism of swimming is a huge part of its appeal to me: working on the actual stroke that I am performing, over and over again. Great technique requires fitness, strength, flexibility, stamina and coordination, but applying that to open water requires lots more: courage, experience, the ability to sight, the ability to respond to choppy conditions ... the list can go on. Swimming is not one thing, it is many.

People come into the 'sport' of outdoor swimming from multiple angles – from the pool (with great technical ability but maybe not good outdoors sense), from the outdoor life (maybe good outdoors sense but weak swimming ability), and from childhood, with no particular skills but enough passion for doorstep adventures to achieve a myriad things.

Whatever you do, enjoy it. Happiness is at the core of this thing: if it becomes loathsome work in any way, slack off, vary it and treat yourself to something new. Swimming involves a set of skills that you can be a student of for the rest of your life.

A GOOD FRONT CRAWL

The best way to be a safer swimmer is to be a stronger swimmer, and for most of us that means having a good front crawl. Front crawl is an energy-efficient stroke that can do the distance and also offers speed when you need it (against a tide, out of an eddy, to raise the tempo and get home before you're too cold). Practised as a long-distance stroke it doesn't *exactly* become like walking, something you can carry on doing for a long time, but it does a bit. Front crawl also uses all the major muscle groups, and is an excellent way to build fitness and endurance.

A good technique is freeing. The athleticism of a well-executed, regularly practised, consistent front crawl is a joy and being able to move effortlessly and fluidly through water never gets tired. I remember a solo swim of a small warm lake in the Lake District during a summer of endless swimming and thinking that's it, I've done it, I am now articulated like a fish: not so much bone as muscle, flexing through the water. The water was moving past me like ribbons peeling down the side of my body, the sound of my own breath an echo-beat in my ears.

THE LONG-DISTANCE MINDSET

The truth is you never finish practising: for its mental liberation swimming fits into the same category as many other repetitive, solo forms of exercise like running, cycling, yoga and rowing. By repeating the same action over and over, and controlling your breathing, your mind becomes free. I learnt how pedestrian this process is on one of the first SwimTrek trips to Greece. This was the furthest I had swum offshore and I had been expecting to have big thoughts, deep as the sea.

The trip was led by Simon Murie, the pioneer of what is now a huge swim holiday industry. We were midway between islands in the Cyclades and Simon was throwing bottles of warm glucose drinks to us over the side of the boat. 'Awl-ryt guys?' he drawled in his Aussie accent. We shouted up between gulps of warm fruity drinks. 'Simon! Simon! We're not having any big thoughts! What do you think about when you are swimming?' Simon paused. This is a man who has swum the Channel. A man whose new venture was inspired by Byron and Greek mythology. We were expecting something big. 'I just think arm, arm, breath,' he said, 'or it all goes to shit.'

And that really is the mystery about longer-distance swimming in a nutshell: most long-distance swimmers rest their thoughts on technique. And put their attention firmly on doing the same thing over and over again, but better.

So, the question is: if you want to rest your thoughts on technique, what do you think about, and where do you learn it so you can think about it? There is a massive industry of support: coached weekends, adult open water lessons, clubs, coached fitness sessions, long hours of watching good technique in others and happy practice are all part of developing a strong front crawl. One-to-one observation by a coach, perhaps even one who can film you so you can see what you are doing (it's not always at all what you think), is priceless. But you can even teach yourself by doing drills or in a tri group.

BETTER FRONT CRAWL

Good technique is not just about where your arms and legs go, it is also about the more esoteric skill of relaxing in the water, having awareness of your body in space, and learning to float. This side of swimming can be picked up over time with experience and patience, but here are some physical tips on effortless front crawl that might start something for you:

1. Look down, into the bottom of the pool that's not there. Your neck should be long and extended. When your head tips down, your feet bob up, creating a much more efficient body position in the water. If you suffer from wetsuit chafing on a long swim, it's a sign that your head position is high. If the depths freak you out, just shorten your field of vision. Kari leads floating sessions where we all try to learn how to tip our heads down, so our feet and legs come up. It feels like swimming downhill.

2. Breathe out underwater. Getting a handle on easy breathing is when things really start to come together, but one of the most common mistakes people make is not breathing out underwater – so when they turn their head to breathe, they are trying to breathe out and in in one go, leading to lack of air. Breathe out long and slow, then when you turn to breathe keep your neck long, and your cheek in the water.

3. Climb the ladder. When your hand enters the water it should be in a line with your shoulder, and not cross or drift towards the centre line of your body. Kari calls this 'climbing the ladder', and this is how it might look from above. If you have a long history of bringing your hands in to the centre line, exaggerate

so it feels like you are swimming with your hands at ten to two. Front crawl is all about rotation – with your arm out as one strut of the ladder, and your hand a flat hold on the water, this is the position from which you can rotate fully and which sends your arm out further. The longer the rotation, the faster and further each stroke. This is an easy one to try on land, with your arm above your head. You will see that if your arm crosses over your head, you cannot get the same length of rotation as if it is straight up from your shoulder.

4. Aim for a flattish, wide hand entry. Keep your hand relaxed and your fingers slightly apart. The hand goes into the water slightly downhill (not along the surface) – as if you were aiming for the bottom corner of a pool. Rotate the body as the hand enters to provide length in the stroke but keep arms shoulder width apart (see point 3 above). The downward-angled hand entry and shoulder width climbing the ladder both lessen the risk of shoulder impingement and rotator cuff injuries.

5. Practise high elbows. High elbows are the foundation for a strong catch, and a higher arm recovery also sets you up for choppier conditions. Your elbow should be the first part of your arm out of the water and the last part to be submerged. You can also use your arm recovery to wriggle your fingers, to relax your arms and increase blood flow. If it's too low your hand could enter the water too early, or be hit by a wave, causing you to lose balance.

6. Develop a lazy kick. The kick uses up a lot of energy for little addition to speed, so in longer-distance front crawl, swimmers develop a lazy kick – just enough to keep the legs up and position streamlined in the water, horizontal, not like a slide with the heavy feet down. One situation in which to break this rule and kick more is if you are getting cold, when burning up more energy could be just what you need.

7. The timing of a stroke is crucial – your arms should not move like a windmill, constantly opposed to each other; there should be a point in each stroke where the front hand is outstretched and the second arm is forward of your head. Then you start the catch.

A final top tip for from Queenie Martin, who has swum the Dart 10k more times than most: do ten strokes of breaststroke every ten minutes at least. Why? So you can see what's around.

BILATERAL AND IRREGULAR BREATHING

Being comfortable breathing on either side (bilateral breathing) is a crucial skill for open water. Bilateral breathing balances out your stroke so you have a symmetrical pull and enables you to favour either side depending on conditions – allowing you to sight a support boat, for example, or breathe away from wind and chop, so you don't inhale water.

It is common for bilateral breathers to do all their training breathing every third stroke, but to fully weatherproof your stroke, practise breathing every second or fourth stroke, every fifth, seventh, ninth or eleventh stroke, and practise breathing at irregular intervals. This will make you ready for anything: regular deep breathing is (consciously or not) what many of us are mentally soothed by in swimming and when it is taken away by conditions it can be very disturbing. If we practise different breath patterns we are likely to do better – for example – in mosh-pit starts at open water events, in rough weather, and long-distance challenges. On longer marathon swims some swimmers opt to breathe every two strokes so they can get plenty of air in and do not stray far from support boats.

THE SKILL OF SIGHTING

Sighting – the ability to look up from your stroke, identify your surroundings and set a direction to swim in – is a key skill for open water. On longer swims you will often meet the tortoise and the hare: a faster swimmer who finishes second as they cannot sight and end up swimming a longer course, and a slower swimmer who comes in before them. The ability to sight is equally important for recreational swimmers, who need to both keep a course and identify hazards (fallen trees, and other water users).

The greater the distance you are covering, the more important sighting is – once you reach 5 kilometres plus, effective sighting will be up there with overall stroke efficiency and fitness as a determinant of how long a swim takes you.

Change how often you sight based on conditions. When waves pick up, attempt to sight at the top of the wave so that you'll have the widest view of what is ahead of you and avoid getting a face full of water. When there is increased chop or swell moving you around, increase the frequency of sightings, as the moving water will push you about more.

CHOOSING YOUR LANDMARK

Choosing your landmark to sight on is a key part of the skill – you need an easily and instantly identifiable marker to sight against, something you can see in a split second above any waves – something taller than a person and visible in different lights. Favourite swim routes develop favourite landmarks: the cormorant tree, the white rock, the green field (not as tautologous as it sounds). Pod swimmers share landmarks as they travel (e.g. 'sight on the giant's nose').

Pick something near to where you are attempting to finish (or swim next) and direct your swim towards this. Make sure to sight frequently so you don't lose direction, but don't feel tied to having to sight after a certain number of pulls; have the flexibility to adapt to your conditions. Change your marker as your surroundings change.

HOW TO SIGHT

Poor sighting technique can lead to problems such as stiff and sore necks and cause hips to drop in the water, which affects swimming speed. You need to be able to incorporate sighting into your stroke rather than breaking your rhythm or changing your alignment.

When you sight you will be taking a series of small mental snapshots and compiling them in your head into a bigger picture of what's ahead, not pausing to look around. By doing the little lifts you can adjust your course without having to make big adjustments to your swimming direction and stroke.

There are generally two approaches to sighting; the most popular is lifting your eyes just above the surface of the water (like a crocodile), but the alternative is to lift your whole head out of the water. Experiment with what feels most comfortable and natural to you. Sight on the pull part of the stroke, and work towards it not interrupting your breathing.

- CROC EYES: Some swimmers find that bringing just their eyes above the water level expends less energy and interferes less with the rhythm of their stroke.

  When you first catch the water, reaching forward with one hand push down on the hand to create stability and lift your eyes just above the water's surface to sight. The goal is to be able to sight without disrupting your stroke, and to breathe to the side as normal, repeating if necessary until you have sighted adequately.

- WHOLE-HEAD LIFT: Some swimmers prefer to lift their whole head out of the water and find this large movement easier to incorporate into their swim. It can give you a longer amount of time to see the surrounding area. Using the power from your pull, bring your whole head out of the water to sight and breathe at the same time. The push down on the water from your pull will help you to surge forward and up, giving you the time to be able to take in your surroundings as well as taking a breath.

Try not to lift your head further out of the water than necessary as this can waste time and energy. One weakness of this technique is that it is less weatherproof – you will not be able to combine breathing and sighting when swimming into a head-on wind or chop.

PEEING WHILE SWIMMING

Yup, peeing while swimming is a skill. If you are swimming a longer distance you will need to pee at some point; if you don't you could get serious stomach cramps. Some people 'take a moment' during a feed stop. Champion pee-ers don't even slow their swim stroke. It's a gift; just don't practise it in your local pool.

If you pee in your wetsuit, rinse it out before you exit the water by pulling out the neck so it takes a few gulps of whatever water you are in, which will then sluice down as you walk out.

WEATHERPROOF YOUR FRONT CRAWL FOR WIND, SWELL AND CHOP

High winds and exposed water bodies can make for 'exciting' conditions – tall waves coming straight at you, or up behind you, making it difficult to get hold of the water or into a rhythm. Like reframing 'cold', fans of rough water call it 'brutal and messy' with relish, and embrace swimming in the elements.

Weatherproofing your swimming means spending a lot of time in rougher weather, bouncing around and getting pummelled by waves, inhaling spray, being drummed on by rain, and trying to adjust your stroke, breathing and sighting to fit.

It's a psychological journey as well as a physical experiment: water looks more threatening without sun, and waves disperse and hide swimmers so you can soon feel like you're the only one out there. The mental detachment that often underpins swimming – the regularity of arm, arm, breath – is blown up, with random opportunities to breathe, and waves knocking our stroke about, so we catch air rather than water. Even temperatures start to wobble, with wind stirring up patchwork temperatures. With all this to unsettle you, one thing you can settle for yourself is acceptance of what is in front of you. So instead of 'oh no, it's windy', choose: 'wind, great: my conditions'.

Just as fell runners learn to lean into descents, and mountain bikers 'flow' over rough downhills, I try to 'slip through' through rough water, rather than fight it. Small waves will break over your head without you noticing. Trying to power through is pointless; however much energy you have, it has more.

Finding a stroke for rough water is a reactive thing, not a prescription. Swimmers may develop sufficient sensitivity that they can, for example, use their feet to anticipate following waves, timing their breath accordingly. Conditions are often caused by local winds and so will change throughout a swim – it may not be about finding a pattern, just about fluid reactions and keeping on.

TIPS FOR ROUGH CONDITIONS

- Bad weather can strain your neck, shoulders and arms; consciously staying as relaxed as possible will help counter that. On a long-distance swim waves can cause havoc to your shoulders if your hands are bashing waves on the recovery.
- Work out which side the wind and waves are coming from and breathe to the other side, which is more sheltered. You might need to rotate more to clear the rolling conditions.
- Wind moves the top layer of water, creating a current. If there is a side wind, consider sheltering to the left or right of another swimmer if the side current is fatiguing you.

• In swell, time your breathing to the crest (top) of a wave, not the trough.

• Also, in swell, sight from the crest of a wave, not the trough, and use bigger landmarks that are easier to see. If there aren't any, consider using the sun.

• In rough conditions, try widening your stroke entry to give you more stability.

• If a tailwind and swell are behind you, see if it works to lengthen your stroke and exaggerate the glide to benefit from the push of the waves. It does not always work to lengthen your stroke; too much of a tailwind can give you too much chop and slow down a swim, with waves lifting you up and pushing you forward to the point where you start to feel seasick. I once read about the great open water swimmer Tom Hecker abandoning a swim across the Maui Channel precisely because the tailwind was picking him up and throwing his feet over his head. If a tailwind is too intense, you can try a sideways tack across the waves. Also experiment with a water-polo stroke: a shorter, choppier, head-up front crawl with more aggressive kick.

• When swimming directly into the wind, expect your time to be slower than average, as you are swimming against a current. This is a great time to 'swim downhill': to keep your neck long and your head tucked down. It is not always harder than a tailwind: at least you can see the waves and adjust your stroke accordingly. When a the current or tide is against you, try speeding up your stroke rate.

POD SWIMMING

Pod swimming is when you swim front crawl together with one or more other swimmers, as a group or pod – swimming with them, rather than racing against them.

Pods work well when people train together as the most important thing for a pod is that you swim at the same pace. You can swim abreast, or as a group like a cycling peloton. I love pod swimming; with another swimmer by my side, I feel more visible to boats, my fears retreat, sighting and route-finding are better and my confidence is higher, all of which gives the experience more space to become vivid. There is great joy and love to be found swimming with someone: it can lead to deep friendships.

On swims that are a real challenge, staying together may compromise your ability to finish, as you all experience highs and lows, moments of strength and periods of cold and slackening off at different times. Here you may want to set up safety cover so that you can swim at your own pace throughout, increasing your chances of making it to the finish.

OTHER STROKES

Although front crawl is often considered the most reliable, it is always worth having a range of strokes available to you.

A GOOD SERVICEABLE BREASTSTROKE

There are two types of breaststroke: the social swimming and chatting version, when you are not really swimming in a purposeful way, and swimming breaststroke as your outdoor stroke of choice.

While not as fast as front crawl, breaststroke is a robust, seaworthy stroke that is great for sightseeing. Up until the 1960s, breaststroke was the go-to stroke in marathon swimming, with the popular view of front crawl as being something that could not be sustained for a long period of time. It is a stroke that is best enjoyed in togs – it is hard to do in a standard wetsuit, which provides too much buoyancy, leading to bobbing feet, torqued knees, a sore back and an inefficient kick. Natural buoyancy suits and suits designed specifically for breaststroke may get around this problem, however.

Like front crawl, physical and visual coaching are key to developing timing and streamlining. But some quick tips that may get a new journey started:

1. Have the sense of swimming downhill: contract your core to keep your hips and legs high. A strong core is key to the whole stroke; the kick also uses core strength. Your body follows your head, so don't lift it unnecessarily high to breathe otherwise your hips and legs will drop, creating drag. Think of charging forward, rather than moving up and down (or rising like a cobra about to strike).

2. Stretch yourself into a torpedo shape in every single stroke; fleetingly, everything should be tight and streamlined: hands and arms forward, legs squeezed together, toes pointed.

3. 'Reach long, kick strong'. A good strong kick is vital – around half the power of the stroke comes from the legs (according to research, sometimes more). A strong kick needs strong legs and buttocks.

4. Work on flexibility in your knees, hips and ankles – this will give you full range of motion in the kick. Heels should come to your bottom, and feet be flexed so toes come towards your shins.

5. You do not need to kick too wide – just over hip-width apart.

6. Recover quickly between the pull and the kick – whip back into position so momentum is constant.

SIDESTROKE

Sidestroke is a wonderful stroke to have in your armoury and used more often than you might think: Charles Sprawson used it to dampen his fear of sharks when swimming the Hellespont, and Al Mennie has described using it so he could hear in the dark. I find it a very soothing stroke when I'm in a wetsuit, all tired out and still not home: I like to rest my cheek on the surface of the water like a silk-cold pillow, stretch out and scissor-kick. It's a good stealth stroke; a variation (combat sidestroke) is used by Navy SEALS and the SAS for its low profile in the water and quiet non-splashiness. Outdoor swimmers can use it to quietly approach wildlife without causing alarm.

Breaststroke is hard when suited and booted, but sidestroke enables steady progress and long distances can be covered with it. It is a good stroke to do on both sides – when one side gets tired you can switch over while it recovers. It can be useful if you have injured one arm, or are struggling to put your face in very cold water, but want to get moving.

Sidestroke is used in lifesaving to tow people – variations of this include a cross-chest tow, where an arm is laid across the casualty with a hand just under an armpit, and an extended tow, where the hand is cupped under an unconscious casualty's chin and they are towed along that way.

Throughout the movements of the arms and legs, keep the body on one side. Contract your core for stability.

1. Swim as level as you can.

2. Move the arms in unison, the lower arm propelling you forward while the upper arm maintains balance.

3. Use a fluid scissor kick, with both legs bent slightly at the knees. The kick should be wide, to provide more thrust, and slow.

LONG-DISTANCE FLY

Swimming butterfly is something many swimmers dream of: mastering the natural undulations so that a wave moves down your body and your shoulders rise effortlessly out of the water and your dripping hands sweep forward... it's a metamorphosis, even if you only get it for a few strokes, for one day.

We have had fly swimmers do the Dart 10k and the Hurly Burly; long-distance fly has also crossed the Channel. So don't rule out learning it at any age. Adding different strokes to your repertoire adds interest, and strengthens the whole body – butterfly particularly works on the core muscles and back. Some tips:

1. The foundation of better fly is an underwater undulation, where with arms by your side or out in front of you like Superman you 'dolphin-kick' through the water. Dolphin kick (which is fun to do in training anyway, even if you're not working towards fly) is a continual up and down kick, with hips popping up to the surface on the down kick. If you're old enough to remember *The Man From Atlantis*: that's the movement.

2. Moving to fly – undulate close to the surface of the water. Let the kick propel your shoulders out of the water, and at this point lift your arm up and forward. It is a light movement, not a struggle through heavy water.

3. Keep your head down and chin tucked throughout the stroke – don't tilt your chin up to breathe; take a breath when your shoulders are raised out of the water.

DOGGY PADDLE

There is a current view of doggy paddle not being 'swimming properly', yet it is instinctive to children when they jump into outdoor water and start exploring, as it keeps their heads above water. Embrace it! Unhitch yourself from wanting to see what the swimming lessons paid for and 'allow' doggy paddle as a stroke that gives novice swimmers confidence, enabling them to move around and enjoy the experience.

There are many variations in leg movements: legs bicycling, doing a flutter kick or syncopated frog kick; anything goes.

Swim coaches also use it as a way of developing 'feel' for the water. Someone at my local pool does it, length after length, varying it with other strokes. It would not have been so unusual a century ago. 'A good mode of swimming, and a great relief when going a distance, is to emulate a dog's movements when in the water.' So wrote Montague A. Holbein, who had swum the Channel, in his book *Swimming*, first published in 1914.[1]

BACKSTROKE

Backstroke is not used often in open water because you almost always need to see where you are going and what is ahead, but it can be a great stroke to use in fitness training – it counteracts the forward rotation of the shoulders that happens at keyboards and in much of the rest of life, opens the chest, and adds variety. Double-arm backstroke – backstroke with either a flutter kick or breaststroke kick – can be a great shoulder and chest opener to finish a training set.

OTHER OPEN WATER SKILLS

Making yourself at home in open water can be about much more than just perfecting your stroke. Here are some other skills that may come in very handy. (In addition to those listed here see also Chapter 3, page 70, where we looked at duck-diving under waves.)

SWIMMING THROUGH AN EDDY LINE

In fast-flowing rivers or estuaries you may wish to enter an eddy to get out of a current and into calm water.

To get in one, anticipate it coming up and then swim hard, perpendicular to the flow of the water, at the first opportunity. Move decisively, quickly and with force. You will pop through the eddy line and then – after the rush of the fast section – all will be much calmer, perhaps even still, and water may be moving upstream.

You may also want to swim out of an eddy, if you have swum into one by accident – big rivers, estuaries and sea channels may all have eddies and we can wander into them and then, when sighting, realise we are no longer making forward progress. Be equally purposeful, and swim perpendicular to the eddy line, across the current.

FLOATING

Who says you can't 'go out for a swim' and then just lie back and float?

Floating is the start of all swimming: the human body is lighter than water, so we can all float; our lungs are like two balloons and if we relax and fill them up with air, they buoy us up. It is harder to float when muscles are tense, perhaps because our bodies contract and become asymmetric and lose surface area. It is easier to float when we are relaxed, confident and breathing deeply. The more body fat we have the easier it is. Men often find it harder, with legs being particularly prone to sinking. It is easier to float in the sea as salt water is denser than fresh.

Many teachers use floating as a building block to teaching people to swim, and as part of helping them overcome a learnt fear of the water. 'Even when one has become a good swimmer, floating is always a useful, enjoyable, and graceful pastime,' says Holbein. As an occupation, let's bring it back.

'BACK TO FLOAT'

If a swimmer becomes panicked, inhales water or starts to cough they will often stop swimming, put their head up to breathe, go from horizontal to vertical in the water, and at that point start to sink. Things can then get worse as they take on more water and panic further. The solution to this potentially fatal cycle is to learn how to move on to your back to float: in this position your face is out of the water and you can regulate breathing and maintain calm.

'Back to float' is an important reflex and lifesaving skill for all of us, including children, and should be practised in calm times so that it is familiar if ever needed (for example, if you've inhaled a wave or have atrocious cramp). It has given my children the confidence to start doing downstream swims; they know that if they ever run out of puff they can rotate on their backs and scull along like that, at ease, face out of the water, able to breathe, growing calmer.

To try floating on your back, go into shallow water and bend your knees until the water touches your chin. Lean your head back till there is water in your ears, extend your arms above your head, take a deep breath, take a step backwards and you will find your legs want to rise and you are floating on your back in the water.

- Tip your head back so your nose and mouth are out of the water. The head is heavy: let go of tension in the neck and shoulders so it can fall backwards, keeping your nostrils above water and yourself buoyant.

- Spread your arms out, either to your sides or – if you are to float for an extended period – spread out above your head.

- Breathe – getting air in will increase buoyancy.

- Push your stomach and hips up.

- Scull with your hands and, if necessary, kick lightly with your feet to keep them close to the surface of the water.

If helping someone else practise this skill, gently use the tips of your fingers to bob their legs up, for a reassuring supportive touch under their back, or to soothingly guide their head away from their shoulders so their neck is long and relaxed.

If in an emergency situation, stop thrashing around and move on to your back. Lean back, extend your arms and legs, and give yourself 60–90 seconds to become calm. Then, think about what you need to do next.

FRONT FLOAT

The front float is a drill that enables us to practise being horizontal and relaxed in the water. It is the foundation position for all strokes, reducing drag and increasing efficiency. If you want to practise this have someone next to you in the water, because you're going to look like you've drowned.

Start with knees bent in the water and feet on the bottom, put your hands over your head and push off lightly in a front float position. Let yourself drift across the surface of the water, like a relaxed torpedo, as your legs come up. Try to find your balance: what is tipping you, what enables you to become still? Experiment:

- How does filling your lungs alter buoyancy?
- Experience how relaxing and spreading out your body gives you buoyancy (and how holding tension drags you down).
- You are likely to feel that your legs are dragging you down – try tucking in your chin and elongating your neck to create a flatter profile and the sensation of swimming downhill.

LIFESAVING SKILLS

For UK swimmers, the RLSS Beach Lifeguard course is a great way to learn lifesaving skills and how to appreciate the sea, and the RLSS Open Water Lifeguard course is similar.[2]

Be aware that people who are drowning are usually silent – they don't holler and wave for help, they are trying to gulp air and can't shout. If you see someone in trouble, call the emergency services and find something buoyant you can throw to help keep them above the water: a life ring, tow float, a rescue line.

All lifesaving services say that you should not go into the water and attempt a rescue without a flotation device, training, experience and strong swimming ability. People in difficulty in the water will often try to climb up a rescuer, pushing them under and endangering both lives. Instead, shout instructions for the struggling person to move on to their back to float and take a few breaths. In the same way, lifeguards who go into the water carry a flotation device and stop a few metres away from the casualty, from where they issue instructions. They are also trained in defensive moves should the casualty try to grasp them.

WHEN YOU'RE NOT IN OPEN WATER: COPING WITH POOLS

It is not possible for most of us to maintain sufficient fitness for marathon or endurance events without using pools. Consistent regular swimming through winter and spring is the key to building up fitness for longer events and challenges, and if you want to be quicker you are also likely to need pool work: all the world's best 10k marathon swimmers do the bulk of their training in the pool.

What are we up against? The smell of chlorine that lingers on the skin for days. The monotony of counting lengths. The noise and garish lighting. And the people. Yes, the people. The swimmer who won't let you through at the end of the lane even though it's obvious you're swimming faster, and the pod doing intervals who tap at your feet one moment, then prevent you turning at the wall on the next.

So what do we do to make it more tolerable? Outdoor heated pools and 50-metre pools are easier for the outdoor swimmer to make peace with. Picking up a phrase used by US performance psychologist Michael Gervais to talk about American football, OSS coach in residence Mike Porteous suggests approaching each session as an opportunity to 'create a living masterpiece', with the pool being the canvas in which we work on our craft. Porteous recommends putting focus on:

- feel for the water: holding and pressing the water back.

- feel in the water: alert to which muscles are working and the effort you're making.

- feel at one in the water: the lovely sense of slicing through a narrow U-shaped pocket of water ahead, everything in sync and coming together, in rhythm and tune.

Porteous has taught me to arrive at pools flexible about the conditions that may greet me, in the same way as I try to arrive at a lake ready for weather. Rather than showing up with a specific workout in mind, I settle into a one-pace set, or technical drills, or interval work, depending on the space in the lane.

Most swimmers find 30–60 minutes of crawl to be their favourite swim time. Sixty-four lengths of a 25-metre pool is a mile, and takes most swimmers around thirty minutes. Most, but not all: in his book *Modern Long Distance Swimming* Gerald Forsberg shares how he can would rather do a five-mile swim than a five-mile walk anytime, an endeavour that took him around two and a half hours.

SNORKELLING AND AQUATIC STROLLS

Rather than focusing on distance, speed or technique, many swimmers just like going out for an 'aquatic stroll': a pleasant swim to see things, with focus both above and/or below the water. There is a whole subaquatic world down there to rival our terranean one. In 1972 Geoffrey Fraser Dutton published a book called *Swimming Free: One and Below the Surface of Lake, River and Sea*. He shared in passionate and poetic detail the endless harmonies he saw, of light and plant and fish and water. Yes we may see these things in tanks, books and rock pools. But 'once immersed,' he observed, 'you are included.'[3] It is a very different experience. Dutton loved being released from the tyranny of gravity, savouring the joys of weightlessness 'without infringing outer space'. In water, we sense and sway with the wildlife we watch.

Dutton floated far out on the sun-smacked waves around the Highlands of Scotland, lay among the trout in the peaty shadows of a Highland river, drifted home over kelp beds on an evening tide – all the time focused on what lay beneath. 'A stark glacial trench [is] as rewarding to the connoisseur of swimming as the most polychromatic tropical shelf,' he observed after a swim in grey Loch Quoich.[4] It's not just big things; if you are curious, time spent studying freshwater invertebrates can be fascinating. Ecologist Peter Hancock says that if you listen quietly enough you can hear lesser water boatman chirping.[5]

You can see most things just with goggles, but using snorkelling equipment is also an option. Here are some tips for successful aquatic strolls:

- Kit. Flippers make a big difference, allowing you to cover more ground and swim fast, and not use your hands. Other useful kit includes: things that make you highly visible – a snorkel and dive mask, or mask and nose clip. There are two ways to go on weight: some people add life jackets so they can bob about. Others use a weighted dive belt that makes it easier to duck-dive and stay underwater, exploring (the beginning of free diving). If you are in full neoprene it will be difficult to gain depth for any length of time without a dive belt. Be aware that they do make swimming a lot harder and so are best worn with flippers.

- Mask. You want a good seal, and a wide-angle view of the world. It is worth investing, and actively looking after your mask. Use diluted baby shampoo to keep it clear of fog. (This is a good tip for goggles generally.)

Many swimmers make a solution of baby shampoo in a small spray bottle and spray it onto their goggles or mask before getting in. Some do it the night before and put them on dry, while others then rinse them before the swim. Some swimmers do it before the swim, rinse and then put them on wet. All three methods leave a film behind on the lenses that keep them clear of fog.

• Look for periods of time, and seasons and weather, that are likely to give good visibility. A period of calm preceding your aquatic stroll may help. Spring can be a good time of year – after the winter storms, and before the plankton and algae blooms of summer.

• Choose a patch. In the sea a seagrass meadow, kelp forest, rocky outcrop, calm bay or sandy stretch are all likely to offer good viewing. Rivers and lakes depend very much on visibility.

Enjoy whatever you discover ...

AN
OUTDOOR
SWIMMER'S
DICTIONARY

Swimmers find themselves wanting more words. Words capable of pinning down what we are doing, where we are going, what we saw and how it all felt. Terms from geography, toponomy, physiology, pool swimming and surf slang have started to whirl together with words we made up ourselves, to make us a swimming vocabulary that enables us to see what we can name, name what we can see, and share it with anyone interested to listen.

So here's a dictionary deluge, a random glossary to rebuild or extend your vocabulary for the life ahead.

A

Aber – mouth of a river (Welsh). There are many places in Wales beginning with this word, sometimes followed by the name of the river (for example, the Aberteifi).

Acclimatisation – the phenomenon of adapting and becoming hardened to cold water.

Afon – river in Welsh.

Afterdrop – the conductive phenomenon of post-swim chilling, where you continue to cool down after getting out of the water.

Afterglow – the phenomenon of feeling relaxed, happy and 'better' after a swim.

Ait – river islands, especially in the Thames.

Algal bloom – rapid growth of algae and cyanobacteria, sometimes caused by high nutrient levels, warmth, sunshine and still conditions.

Alluvial – clay, silt, sand, topsoil and gravel deposited by rivers on floodplains, estuaries and wherever else a river slows (islands, the neck of a lake, the banks of meanders). From the Latin ***alluvius***, 'to wash against'.

Ammil – a Devon term for the icy sheaths that can form on grass (and leaves and twigs) when a freeze follows a partial thaw, making the land glitter in sunshine. From the old English *ammel*, which means 'enamel'. See also rime ice and hoar frost.

Aqueduct – a bridge that carries water (a river or canal).

Archipelago – group or chain of islands.

B

Backscatter – in underwater photography, the illumination of particles in the water (algae, plankton, sediment), creating a haze or veil between you and the image.

Backwash – when a wave breaks, water is washed up on to the beach (swash). When it flows back to the sea, this is the 'backwash'. The flow of water back to the sea can be strong.

Baltic – a description of water temperatures when the water is very cold.

Bathymetry – the measurement of depths of water in oceans and seas.

Bay – a body of water, generally at the coast, enclosed and often protected by a horseshoe of land. At some point bays become gulfs or sounds.

Beach break – a surfable wave that breaks over a sandbar. See also reef break and point break.

Beck – seen on maps when hunting for swims. Becks (and gills) are swiftly flowing streams on steep terrain, more commonly used in the north of England. Often has a stony bed. Other words for stream: brook, burn, creek, rill and runnel.

Billabong – Australian term for a backwater in a river or an oxbow lake.

Bioprene – swimmers' term for natural neoprene, i.e. an insulating layer of body fat.

Blash – liquid mud, a muddy splash perhaps.

Blowhole – blowholes aren't just for whales; you can also find them in rocks, with the sea surging up through a narrow vertical shaft from a cave below.

Bourn – southern English term for small stream, especially in chalk and limestone areas. See also winterbourne.

Brook – freshwater stream, smaller than a river.

Bumbel – the word we've been looking for: it means to flounder around in water (Shetland).

Burn – small stream or brook, used in Scotland and northern England.

C

Canyon – American term for a deep gorge with a river flowing along the bottom.

Catch – in swimming, the 'catch' is the moment in the stroke where you catch the water and start propelling yourself forward. A lot of work (in all four strokes) can go into feeling the water, the right water entry position for the hand, and initiating the catch. In front crawl, the propulsion involves both your hand and your forearm.

Cat's Paws – dark patches of tiny waves, observed on becalmed seas. They are caused by small gusts of wind.

Causeway – a raised path, road or railway across a wet area. Called a 'sarn' in Wales.

Cenote – subterranean groundwater lakes in Mexico.

Channel – (common swimmer use) the deepest part of a river, where the current is fastest.

Chop – bumpy windblown water, with chaotic rather than organised rolling waves, a result of local winds and currents.

Clart – the sticky mud that adheres to your boots and then to itself until you are hiking about in a heavy pair of platforms. A Scottish and northern English dialect word.

Close-out – when a wave breaks all at once.

Confluence – the point where two rivers meet and start to flow together.

Cove – small sheltered bay.

Cowbelly – sediment pillows that form at the edges of slow rivers that are soft and fine as a cow's belly when your feet sink into them.

Creek – a narrow sheltered waterway, such as an inlet for the sea (at e.g. Frenchman's Creek on the Helford River) or in a lake.

Crest – the highest point of a wave.

Current – movement of water in a river, or with the tide.

D

Dawn patrol – the act of getting up very early to go swimming and arrive before sunrise. Borrowed from surfers.

Dimpsey – Devon word for twilight or dusk.

Dook – to dip or plunge (Scottish).

Double capping – the practice of wearing two swim caps for warmth.

Drag – swimsuits, surf wetsuits and a bad body position in the water (one that is not horizontal) can all cause 'drag' in the water: resistance to moving forward that slows you down. Pro swimmers shave to reduce the drag of body hair.

Dryland training – what you do on land, to get yourself ready for the water.

Dub – an old word for a pool of water, with slightly different meanings in different locations. Can be a small river pool or a small pool of normally stagnant water.

Duck-diving – the technique of diving head first under the water – to see what's beneath, or go under a breaking wave. Momentarily, you may look like an upturned duck, bottom on the surface and head beneath.

Dumping waves – waves that break all in one go, rather than peeling left or right. Where they break on to the shore it is known as a 'shore break'.

E

Egress – the location where you get out or leave a river. A kayaking term that mostly refers to landowner access.

Epilimnion – the top layer of a lake that has stratified into different temperature bands.

Eyot – small island in a river of lake (see also ait).

F

Fetch – the distance over water that the wind blows in a single direction without obstruction. The wind will increase in speed, and waves in height, along the length of a lake.

Fizmer – an East Anglian term for the rustling noise produced in reed by petty agitations of the wind.

Flash flood – sudden local flood, generally after heavy rain.

Fleet – small inlet or creek, particularly in south-eastern Britain. Has various archaic and obsolete meanings such as to float or swim, to cause time to pass rapidly, and to glide rapidly along like a stream.

Flood – what happens when a river bursts its banks and spills onto the floodplain.

Floodplain – the low-lying ground next to a river that is prone to flooding during high rain.

Flotsam – floating debris of the sea, originally from wreckages. See also jetsam.

Flow – to move freely, as of a stream, effortless and continuous. A definition of water, but 'flow state' is now used to describe a mental state of absorption or immersion, where one is engrossed in a challenge and left feeling satisfied.

Flume – 'flu' comes from the Latin *fluxus*, where it means flow, giving us fluvial, fluid, flush, confluence and fluent. A flume is an artificial narrow channel conveying water, with a common modern use of carrying people (at water parks) and boats (in rides).

Fluvial – of or relating to or occurring in a river. See also pluvial (related to rain) and alluvial (related to soil).

Fogbow – white rainbows, sometimes formed by the interaction of sun with fog, mist or clouds.

Foss – A Viking word for waterfall, found in Iceland, Norway and the north of England, it means waterfall. Other words for waterfall include falls and force.

Fresh – positive term to describe water that feels a bit nippy.

Freshet – when a river floods after a spring thaw in North America, that's a freshet. Can also refer to heavy rain. As in: 'the river is subject to freshets' or 'the river is turbulent during spring freshets'.

Fwaw – sound you are likely to make on entering frigid water; good for simultaneously puffing out air and seemingly increasing determination and vigour. Best said at least twice (fwaw fwaw).

G

Gale – a strong wind. The meteorologically strict reserve the term for Beaufort Wind Force 7–9, where wind speeds are 50–88 km/h.

Gill or ghyll – an old Norse word, used to describe a ravine or a narrow stream or rivulet that flows through it. Romantic poet William Wordsworth is thought to have introduced the second spelling, ghyll.

Glassy – used to describe conditions when there is no wind to ripple the water's surface, and the water is so smooth it's like glass.

Glen – typically, a deep narrow mountain valley, especially in Scotland and Ireland.

Glide – the part of any stroke where you coast along.

Gloaming – you might find yourself wanting other words for 'twilight'. See also 'dimpsey', and 'wolf light'. For me, dimpsey fits when things start fading, blurring and greying, but the gloaming is a grander, more colourful, more epic experience: a rich and colourful kind of twilight, with the sky navy-purple, perhaps contrasting with a glowing horizon or moon.

Glumag – pool, usually in a river (Gaelic).

Gooseneck – American term for meanders that nearly double back on themselves (on their way to becoming an oxbow lake).

Gorge – a deep, narrow valley with steep sides, usually formed by a river or stream cutting through hard rock, and with a river still in it. Called a canyon in other countries.

Green room – surfing term for the space you may find inside a wave when it rolls over, creating a tunnel of air you can look down. Also called a tube or barrel.

Grimmer – an East Anglian term for a large, shallow, weed-infested pool. An easy one to adopt?

Gully – a small channel or narrow valley, often cut by heavy rainwater. A stream would be in the bottom of a gully, a river would be in the bottom of a gorge.

H

Halocline – when salt water meets fresh water they separate into layers. In a vertical water column, salt water will float, fresh water will sink, and the halocline is the zone where the two are mixed.

Hardening – the process of becoming tolerant of colder water.

Haze-fire – to quote Robert Macfarlane: 'luminous morning mist through which the sun is rising'.[1]

Headwater – tributary stream close to the source of a river.

Heapy – good word for a sea with big swell.

High tide/High water – the highest point of the tide.

Hoar frost – a feathery frost that forms when water vapour (dew) touches landscapes that are already below freezing. Hoar frost will cover reeds, trees, dead grasses, gates in iced white crystals. Occurs on clear nights. If the air temperature doesn't rise for days, hoar frost may layer, giving an increasingly spiky all-white world. See also rime ice and ammil.

I

Ice mile – under the rules of the International Ice Swimming Association, an ice mile is a one-mile swim in water temperature of 5 °C or less wearing only a standard costume, goggles and one swim hat.

Inshore – in the water but close to the shore. Inshore sea forecasts are the ones that swimmers most commonly want.

Intertidal – the zone between land and sea that is covered at high tide and uncovered at low tide.

J

Jabbly – agitated surface water.

Jetsam – washed-up debris of the sea. Jetsam originally referred to goods jettisoned into the water deliberately.

K

Keld – the still part of a river.

Kolks – like underwater tornadoes, kolks are a vortex of water that can create rock-cut basins, and (at size) move boulders and leave behind kolk lakes.

L

Lagan – goods lying on the seabed, perhaps attached to a buoy or other so it may be recovered. If you sink your wine or beer in a bag in a river or lake, attached to a tree by a string, it becomes lagan.

Lake – static or slow-moving basin of water. See also mere, loch, llyn and water.

Line – the route you take down a river or across a bay or lake.

Linne – Gaelic word for a pool in a river that is deeper than a glumag.

Littoral – the zone next to a shore, generally of the sea but also a lake. Some swimmers can only live in littoral spaces.

Llyn – Welsh term for a lake.

Loch – a Scottish word for lakes, and narrow arms of the sea that are surrounded by land in a similar way to lakes.

Lochan – small lake.

Loom – the slow and silent movement of water in a deep pool.

Low tide/Low water – the lowest point in a tide.

M

Meander – the loops of a winding river, which move slowly over time.

Meol – how are we not using this word? It describes dunes colonised by marram grass or other vegetation.[2] In use in Lincolnshire, from an Old Norse topographical name meaning 'sand-hills' or 'sand dunes'.

Mere – a regional word for lake. Meres are generally shallower than a lake, and broad in relation to depth, but bodies of water were named before geologists finished specifying definitions, so there are exceptions – Windermere, for example, is quite big and deep.

Messy – description of conditions where the water is chaotic, with waves, rebound waves, squalls, wind over tide, gusts and more.

Mire – an unpleasant situation from which to extract oneself, both figuratively and actually. Mires and quagmires are swampy bogs, full of sphagnum moss and saturated peat. Mires are anaerobic places with incompletely decomposed organic matter: blacker and more stinky than mud.

Misfit stream – one for the nonconformists among us. There are also misfit meanders: streams that are too small (or too large) for the valley they flow down. A misfit stream may have lost its headwater.

Moonglade – the path of light that flows between you and the moon over water. A glittering path that will always make its way across the water straight to you.

Mouth – the end of a river, where it empties into a lake, bigger river or sea.

N

Nant – stream (Celtic toponymy).

Neap tide – a smaller tide and smaller tidal range that happens in between moons, every two weeks.

Neoprene – an ultra-stretchy insulating synthetic rubber that traditionally uses non-renewable petroleum (manufacturers are increasingly moving to new natural rubber alternatives). Adds warmth and comes in different thickness: thicker is generally warmer, and more buoyant.

Noah's Woods – occasionally tree stumps rise up from estuarial or other mud: remains of a submerged forest called Noah's Woods on the east coast of England.

O

Offshore wind – wind that blows from the land to the sea or lake. Offshore winds are local and not reflected in weather forecasts.

Onshore wind – wind that blows from the sea or a large lake onto the shore. A local phenomenon not reflected in weather forecasts. At the coast, an onshore wind will blow waves over, evacuating surfers.

Ooze – ooze oozes through your toes when you stand on it. It's the soft deposit of mud and slime associated with estuarial mudflats and left behind at the bottom of a body of water.

Ottering – term coined in the Lake District. To otter, lie on your back, holding a tow float to your chest if you have one, and float downstream feet first – like an otter floating around feeding.

'Out the back' – where you may be headed if there is surf – beyond the breaking waves.

Overfall – a turbulent, rough area where water 'falls over' raised ground, such as an inshore reef, underwater ridge, ledge, rocks or a weir or dam, pushed by a current or tidal race.

Oxbow lake – a crescent-shaped lake left behind by a river. A meandering river may eventually form such deep S-bends that the river cuts through the narrow point to form a new, more direct channel, leaving behind this shape of lake, with silted-up ends.

P

Peninsula – land that juts out into water and is also completely surrounded by it (almost an island, but still connected to a larger land mass).

Period – the time it takes two wave crests (or troughs) to pass a fixed point. Useful to interpret surf forecasts; if a wave period is just a few seconds you may not have time to recover from one wave before the next is upon you.

Petrichor – the earthy smell that accompanies the first rain after a dry spell.

Photic zone – the sunlit surface waters of the sea.

Plunging wave – the crest of a plunging wave rises to a point then breaks, peeling left or right and creating a 'green room' or 'pipeline'. Occurs when swell meets a reef and a wave rises sharply, with the crest getting ahead of the wave and then breaking.

Pluvial – based on the Latin word for rain, *pluvia*; relating to rain, the action of rain, and particularly abundant rain.

Point break – a surfable wave where waves are created by a headland or point of land.

Pond – What is the difference between a pond and a lake? Ponds tend to be smaller, and not moving, and shallow enough to have plants growing at the bottom throughout. Lakes are too deep for light to penetrate and for plants to grow at the bottom.

Porpoising – technique used in open water competitions at surf beaches. To go underneath surf, swimmers dive for the bottom as a wave approaches, hold the sea floor, bring their knees to their chest and feet to the floor, then when the wave passes they 'explode' back out of the water, over the sea, taking a breath and going back down again, repeating this motion until it's deep and then starting front crawl.

Q

Quaking Bog – a wholly or partially floating peat bog that shudders and shakes when trodden upon.

Quicksand – unstable sand-and-water mix that it's possible to sink into, and hard to extricate yourself from.

R

Race – a strong or rapid current of water that flows through a narrow channel. See also tidal race.

Rapids – turbulent part of a river or stream where the current is moving faster than usual. Rapids have a gradient but not a sufficient drop to form a waterfall, and are characterised by the water surface being broken by obstructions such as rocks. On a continuum with a riffle.

Ravine – a deep narrow valley with steep sides (see also gill). A gully is small, a ravine is larger, and a gorge (or canyon in other countries) is bigger still.

Raw – popular description of winter swimming conditions, when the cold seems to strip your skin and leave it feeling raw.

Reef – a ridge of material on the ocean floor: can be made of coral, rock or by human hand.

Reef break – a surfable wave that breaks over a rock or coral reef. See also beach break and point break.

RIB – Rigid-hull Inflatable Boat: a small boat with outboard motor, with inflatable tubes.

Riffle – term for a rocky, shallow part of a river or stream where the water flows unevenly over rocks. Painful to walk on, impossible to swim in, but a good place for mayflies, stoneflies and caddis flies to live because a rocky sandy stream bed offers plenty of cobbly gravel to hide in.

Rip current/rip tide/rip – a localised surface current carrying water back out to sea. Looks identifiably different to surrounding water, like a calm patch among breaking surf, and flows a bit like a river.

Rill – either a small stream (smaller than a beck, more of a rivulet) or a fleeting one, that runs down a hill after rain.

Rime ice – occurs when dense and freezing fog comes into contact with materials already below freezing point. Different from hoar frost and ammil. Can evenly cover whole trees and landscapes, turning them white.

Rock basin – the round basin-shaped hollows in rocks that can look like bird baths or mini plunge pools. Naturally created by the erosive action of either water and wind or whirling rocks in currents, both make a small dip larger over time.

Roller/rolling wave – a wave that breaks in a rolling fashion.

Run-off – when there is more water than land can absorb it runs off hills and into rivers, lakes and seas, carrying pollutants such as cow manure, fertilisers and street dirt with it.

S

Sandbar – ridge of sand, partly submerged or fully submerged but created by waves.

Saltings – areas of land frequently covered by the sea, such as coastal marshes. May feature creeks, muddy marshes and small tufty islands.

Saturated – a state sought by swimmers: we don't want to be satiated (pleasantly full), we want to be saturated: brimful of water, landscape and experience. So full we couldn't, even if we wanted to, be any more part of it all.

'Scottish tan' – refers to the orange-purple-red colour skin can take on when burnt by wind or cold rather than sun.

Sea foam – also called 'spume', the froth or foam made in rough seas and storms, when the sea mashes up organic matter.

Seaglass – smooth pebbles of glass, tumbled by the sea. Once belonged to glass bottles.

Set – a group of waves. While science rejects the idea of them coming in sevens (with the seventh the largest), they do tend to arrive in groups.

Sgeir/skerry – a rock or rocky island in the sea called a 'sgeir' in Scotland and 'skerry' in England.

Shoaling – effect of waves increasing in height when they enter shallower water.

Shore break – a wave that breaks on to or very close to the shore. Happens on steep beaches and can be bone-crushing. A type of dumping wave.

Sill – when water tips over the edge of a weir, it can look like a thick sheet of molten glass.

Skim ice – first thin layer of ice on a water surface.

Skins – vernacular for swimming without a wetsuit.

Slack tide/slack water – the sea is generally either rising towards high tide or falling towards a low tide. Slack tide or slack water is the period of time either side of high and low tide when the water is 'slack' and the sea barely moves in or out.

Sound – a large inlet of water, bigger and wider than a fjord or a bay.

Source – the beginning of a river, or headwater.

Spate – a sudden flood in a river.

Spilling wave – gentle wave that rolls and breaks gently from the top, the crest of the wave appearing to spill down the face in bubbling white water. More of a wave collapse than a wave break. Approachable.

Spindrift – white frothy spray blown from the crests of waves by the wind. A sign of a Gale Force 8 wind, moving in the direction of the gale.

Spit – a narrow point of land jutting into the sea (thinner and smaller than a peninsula). See also tombolo.

Spring – a place where groundwater emerges from the earth.

Spring tides – the biggest tides of the month, with the largest high tides, and the lowest low tides (therefore the largest difference between high and low water). Occur on full moons and no moons, with the biggest springs of all on the seasonal equinoxes.

Spume – foam, froth or scum. Spume is whipped up by churning waters and organic matter such as plankton or seaweed, and appears as both sea foam (for example, being blown on to beaches during storms) and foam on rivers. Generally, not an environmental concern; caused by natural surfactants, not pollution.

Stack – a steep column of offshore rock, what's left behind when a headland has been eroded by wind and waves.

Steam fog – seen on cold clear mornings, when the water temperature is warmer than the air and you get a mist rising from the river. Also called sea smoke and frost smoke.

Strait – narrow passage of water between two bodies of water (e.g. the Bosphorus, or Strait of Istanbul, is the passage of water between the Sea of Marmara and the Black Sea).

Sunball – the white blob of the sun when seen or photographed from underwater (no rays).

Sunburst – diffused sun's rays in an image, either above or below water.

SUP – abbreviation of 'Stand Up Paddleboard'.

Surging wave – a wave that reaches the beach before it breaks. Occurs when big swell meets a steep beach. Tsunamis are an extreme example of surging waves; they have no face and generate extremely strong wash and backwash currents as they surge inland.

Swash – when a wave breaks, water is washed up the beach. This is called the swash. See also backwash.

Swell – an ocean's unbroken waves, caused by offshore storms.

Swell period/swell interval – the time it takes for two successive waves to pass the same point.

T

Tarn – high small body of water or lake. The term is used in the mountains in Cumbria and the north. From the old Norse *tjorn*, which means pool or pond.

Thalweg – the lowest point in a valley, which, if the valley holds a river, will also be the line of fastest flow or deepest water in a river and the channel you may wish to find to swim in.

Thermocline – the transition layer between bands of different-temperature water in a stratified lake. In summer, you can tell you have reached the thermocline when your feet (or head if you're duck-diving) go beyond the warm surface water into a much cooler layer of water below.

Tidal bore – a rare phenomenon in an incoming tide. Forms a tidal wave that travels up a river. From the Old Norse *bára* meaning wave or billow.

Tidal race – a place where a fast tide moves through a constriction, forming a fast current (a race), waves, eddies and even whirlpools. The constriction can be vertical (Portland Race) or horizontal (The Gulf of Corryvreckan, where the moving sea is squeezed between Jura and Scarba). The Gulf of Corryvreckan is a popular swim, only possible in brief pauses in the tidal race.

Tidal stream/Tidal current/Tidal flow – current caused by the movement of the tides, sea current. Mapped by the Admiralty to create tidal stream atlases, which show what currents flow and when (tidal stream alters with the time and size of tide).

Tidewrack – what the sea leaves behind when it's fly-tipping. Commonly a strip of detritus made of seaweed, driftwood, single shoes, plastic spades, jellyfish and fishing nets.

Tidal island – island attached to the mainland by a tombolo that is usually covered at high tide (for example, Burgh Island off the coast of Devon).

Tidal range – the height difference between high and low water.

Tied island – island attached to the mainland by a tombolo (see below) that remains above water even at high tide.

Tolmen – a hole in a riverside rock: where kolks keep spinning stones in rock-cut basins, a round hole in the rock may eventually appear.

Tombolo – formed when a spit connects the mainland to an island.

Tributary – a tributary is to a river what a capillary is to a vein.

Tripple/Threeple – gentle sound made by a quickly flowing stream. From Cumbria (with thanks to Macfarlane).[3]

Trough – the low point between two successive waves, the opposite of a crest.

U

Undertow – vague term often employed in media coverage and safety warnings to gesture at unknowable, unpredictable dangers of water. Ideally, remove from language and replace with known phenomena such as backwash and rip current instead.

W

Warp – the sediment carried by a river. The term covers sediment both in suspension and deposited on riverbanks after flooding. Warp lines on riverside branches mark a river or estuary's high-water mark.

Wash – wave of water kicked up by a

passing boat. The size of it is determined by many factors including boat speed, shape and size, which generally have a negative effect on both swimmers and life in the banks.

Water – another term for lake. As in Rydal Water and Derwentwater in the Lake District.

Water meadow – grassland that is sometimes flooded by a river or stream.

Wave height – the height of a wave, measured as the difference between a crest and neighbouring trough (lowest point).

Wave period – the time between two consecutive wave crests.

Wave train – a succession of similar waves at similar intervals.

Wavelength – the distance between two consecutive wave crests.

Weepy – a condition of the land, when it's so wet it's weepy, springing springs (with thanks to Macfarlane).[4]

Wellum – the radiating ripples set off by a surfacing fish.

Winterbourne – a stream that flows in water or after wet weather, a seasonal stream.

Witches' knickers – the ragged scraps of plastic bags seen snagged on barbed-wire fences and the branches of trees; as if a witch has taken off, without her flimsy knickers.

Wolf light – twilight, when the familiar becomes wild (See also dimpsey and gloaming. 'Wolf light' is when all the people have gone home, and it's just us and the animals.

Z

Zawn – a Cornish word for a narrow chasm or fissure in sea cliffs, like an overstretched yawn through which you can see the sea.

NOTES

1.Understanding Lakes

1. Elizabeth Haworth, George de Boer, Ian Evans, Henry Osmaton, Winifred Pennington, Alan Smith, Philip Storey, Brian Ware, *Tarns of the Central Lake District* (Brathay Exploration Group Trust Ltd, 2003).
2. W. Heaton Cooper, *The Tarns of Lakeland* (The Heaton Cooper Studio, 1970).
3. For more information about this mythical beast, see *A Book of Creatures* blog, 21 December 2020. Available at: https://abookofcreatures.com/2020/12/21/vatnaormur/
4. See Uwe Wollina, 'Peat: A Natural Source for Dermatocosmetics and Dermatotherapeutics' in *Journal of Cutaneous and Aesthetic Surgery*, January–June 2009, vol. 2(1): 17–20.
5. L. M. S. Seelen, S. Teurlincx, J. Bruinsma, et al., 'The value of novel ecosystems: disclosing the ecological quality of quarry lakes', *Science of the Total Environment* (January 2021). https://doi.org/10.1016/j.scitotenv.2020.144294
6. The Bill for this Act of the Scottish Parliament was passed by the Parliament on 23 January 2003 and received Royal Assent on 25 February 2003. See: www.legislation.gov.uk/asp/2003/2

2. Understanding Rivers

1. For more details, visit: www.strel-swimming.com/martin-strel-swimming-mississippi-river/
2. The Ordnance Survey website has guides to the Gaelic and Welsh origins of place names available at: https://getoutside.ordnancesurvey.co.uk/guides/the-welsh-origins-of-place-names-in-britain/
See also: https://getoutside.ordnancesurvey.co.uk/guides/the-gaelic-origins-of-place-names-in-britain/
For Gaelic place names, see also the 'Scottish White Water Guide' by Ron Camera (River Names and Pronunciation), available at: www.andyjacksonfund.org.uk/river-names-and-pronunciation/
And for Cumbrian place names, see: www.lakelanddialectsociety.co.uk/glossary and:
https://en.wikipedia.org/wiki/Cumbrian_toponymy

3. Understanding Seas

1. Quoted by Alan Hubbard in 'The world champion Channel hopper', *Independent*, 23 Sept. 2001. Available at: www.independent.co.uk/sport/general/the-world-champion-channel-hopper-9266342.html
2. British National Institute of Oceanography calculated this using a random process formula, suggesting that if you take the average height of waves in a wave train, then one wave in 23 will be twice that average height and one wave in 1,175 will be three times the average height. See: https://boattest.com/article/rogue-waves-part-one
3. Lynne Roper, 'Understanding Tides', The Outdoor Swimming Society website. Available at: www.outdoorswimmingsociety.com/tides/

Marine Field Guides

1. Lorna Siggins, 'Stinging Lion's mane jellyfish in Irish waters is larger this year', *Irish Times*, 26 June 2018. Available at: www.irishtimes.com/news/ireland/irish-news/stinging-lion-s-mane-jellyfish-in-irish-waters-is-larger-this-year-1.3543431

4. Understanding Estuaries

1. National Geographic Society Resource Library, available at: www.nationalgeographic.org/encyclopedia/estuary/
2. A. C. Moule, 'The Bore on the Ch'ien-t'ang River in China', *T'oung Pao*, vol. 22, no. 3 (Brill, 1923), pp.135–88. Available at: www.jstor.org/stable/4526695.https://www.jstor.org/stable/4526695
3. H. Chanson, H., 'The Rumble Sound Generated by a Tidal Bore Event in the Baie du Mont Saint Michel', *Journal of the Acoustical Society of America* (2009) 125 (6): 3561–68. Bibcode:2009ASAJ..125.3561C. doi:10.1121/1.3124781. PMID 19507938.

5. Weather

1. For more information, visit the Royal Meteorological Society website: www.rmets.org/metmatters/beaufort-scale
2. See: www.rmets.org/metmatters/beaufort-scale
3. Gerald Forsberg, *Modern Long Distance Swimming* (Routledge, Kegan and Paul, 1963), p.55.
4. See Lynne Cox, *Swimming to Antarctica* (Weidenfeld & Nicolson, 2005), pp.105–6.
5. Forsberg, p.55.

6. Understanding Cold

1. International Triathlon Union, *ITU Competition Rules*, 7 February 2011, p.13. Available at: www.communitymultisport.org/
2. Based on graphics created by the US Coast Guard: 'Addendum to the National Search and Rescue (SAR) Manual'. For an example, see *Coast Guard Rescue & Survival Systems Manual*, p.24.
3. Dr Heather Massey has kindly checked the references to her work in this chapter. For an accessible insight into her research see, for example, her article 'What Happens to the Body in Cold Water', Wild Swimming Cornwall website. Available at:
www.wildswimmingcornwall.co.uk/blog/what-happens-to-the-body-in-cold-water-with-dr-heather-massey.
4. F. S. Golden, G. R. Hervey, M. J. Tipton, 'Circum-rescue collapse: collapse, sometimes fatal, associated with

rescue of immersion victims', *Journal of the Royal Navy Medical Service* (1991), 77(3):139–49. PMID: 1815081.
5. Zaria Gorvett, 'Why pain feels good', BBC Future. Available at: www.bbc.com/future/article/20151001-why-pain-feels-good
6. M. J. Tipton, N. Collier, H. Massey, J. Corbett and M. Harper, 'Cold water immersion: kill or cure?', *Experimental Physiology*, 102.11 (2017), pp.1335–55. Available at: https://physoc.onlinelibrary.wiley.com/doi/pdf/10.1113/EP086283
7. Christoffer van Tulleken, et al. 'Open water swimming as a treatment for major depressive disorder.' *BMJ* case reports, vol. 2018 bcr2018225007. 21 Aug. 2018, doi:10.1136/bcr-2018-2250077.
8. See Hannah Denton and Kay Aranda, 'The wellbeing benefits of sea swimming. Is it time to revisit the sea cure?, *Qualitative Research in Sport, Exercise and Health* (2020), 12:5, 647–63, DOI:10.1080/2159676X.2019.1649714
9. Avijit Datta and Michael Tipton, 'Respiratory responses to cold water immersion: neural pathways, interactions, and clinical consequences awake and asleep', *Appl Physiol*, 100: 2057–64.
10. Ibid.
11. M. J. Tipton, N. Collier, H. Massey, J. Corbett and M. Harper, 'Cold water immersion: kill or cure?', Experimental Physiology, 102.11 (2017), pp.1335–1355. Available at: https://physoc.onlinelibrary.wiley.com/doi/pdf/10.1113/EP08628312.
12. See Giovanni Lombardi, Cristian Ricci and Giuseppe Banfi, 'Effect of winter swimming on haematological parameters', *Biochem Med* (Zagreb). 2011; 21(1):71–8.
13. Anna Lubkowska, Barbara Dołęgowska, Zbigniew Szyguła, Iwona Bryczkowska, Małgorzata Stańczyk-Dunaj, Daria Sałata, Marta Budkowska, 'Winter-swimming as a building-up body resistance factor inducing adaptive changes in the oxidant/antioxidant status', *Scand J Clin Lab Invest*. 2013; 73(4):315–25. doi: 0.3109/00365513.2013.773594. Epub 2013 Mar 20.
14. For more information, see: www.sruk.co.uk/raynauds/managing-raynauds/#:~:text=Exercise%2C%20within%20your%20own%20limits,exercise%20can%20trigger%20Raynaud's%20attacks.

7. Winter & Ice Swimming

1. For more on this traditions, see: www.themoscowtimes.com/2022/01/19/russians-brave-the-ice-in-annual-epiphany-swim-a76080

8. Night Swimming

1. Gerald Forsberg, p.177
2. For more on folk names for moons see, for example: Spanel Planetarium website, available at: www.wwu.edu/astro101/indianmoons.shtml; see also: 'The Naming of Moons', Eco Enchantments website, available at: www.ecoenchantments.co.uk/mynaming_of_moonspage.html

9. Planning a Swim

1. For a comprehensive introduction to the concept of flow, see Mihaly Csikszentmihalyi, *Flow* (Rider, 2002).
2. Described in more detail in his book *Beyond Adventure. Reflections from the Wilderness: An Inner Journey* (Cicerone Press, 2001). A helpful summary can be found at: www.arasite.org/mortlock.html
3. You can find the statement in full at the Outdoor Swimming Society website at: www.outdoorswimmingsociety.com/oss-swim-responsibility-statement
4. Scottish Outdoor Access Code, available at: www.outdooraccess-scotland.scot/
5. Countryside and Rights of Way Act 2000 (CRoW), available at: www.legislation.gov.uk/ukpga/2000/37/contents
6. For more details, see The Crown Estate website, which details includes annual reports. Available at: www.thecrownestate.co.uk
7. I am indebted to OSS lawyer Nathan Willmott for information here and later in this chapter concerning swimmers' rights to access waterways and issues concerning potential trespass.

10. Swim Better

1. Montague A. Holbein, *Swimming* (C Arthur Pearson Limited, 1914), p.46.
2. For more information about the RLSS Beach Lifeguard and RLSS Open Water Lifeguard courses, visit: www.rlss.org.uk/national-vocational-beach-lifeguard-qualification and www.rlss.org.uk/open-water-lifeguard-qualifications
3. Geoffrey Fraser Dutton, *Swimming Free: One and Below the Surface of Lake*, River and Sea (St Martin's Press, 1972).
4. Ibid.
5. Peter Hancock, private correspondence.

11. An Outdoor Swimmer's Dictionary

1. Robert Macfarlane, *Landmarks* (Penguin, 2016), p.40. (The Outdoor Swimmer's Dictionary was heavily inspired by both Macfarlane's book *Landmarks* and Tyler's book *Uncommon Ground*.)
2. Described by Dominick Tyler in *Uncommon Ground: A word-lover's guide to the British landscape* (Guardian Faber Publishing, 2015), p.226.
3. Macfarlane, p.123.
4. Macfarlane, p.30.

ACKNOWLEDGEMENTS

A glide of swimmers, friends and family assisted with both the knowledge and making of this book. With huge thanks to Kari Furre, Morgan Jones, Nathan Willmott, Colin Hill, Paul Smith, Al Mennie, Heather Massey, Peter Hancock, Katie Maggs, Susan Elderkin, Ash Ranpura and Al Humphries for their particular oversight and insight into the text. Thanks to all the OSS team past and present for their part in creating this movement and sustaining a community where this knowledge could form, rise and circulate, including all the current team: Oliver Pitt, Anna Morell, Ali Couch, Beth Pearson, Calum Maclean, Imogen Radford, Owen Hayman, Lance Sagar, Mike Porteous, Susie Wheway, Robert Macfarlane, Simon Kerslake, Jo Snow, Mark Harper, Lou Barber, Rob Aspey, Chris Dalton, Dave Pye, Sus Davy, Liz Vancura and Gilly Waddell. Two leading lights of the early days, Jonathon Joyce and Lynne Roper, are no longer with us but our memories are still with them and the positive changes they brought to others.

Thank you to all the wonderful community photographers out there who have changed people's perception of what it is to be in water and what an everyday adventure looks like, with particular tribute to the work of Niall Meehan, Dominick Tyler and Alex Voyer.

Thanks to my editor Bianca Bexton for never faltering in our drive to make this book what it wanted to be, and to my brilliant sea-loving agent Patrick Walsh who always picks up the phone and waited thirteen years for this.

Finally, thanks to my family. Thanks to Tim Bridges, our boys Jack and Eddie, my step dad Tony, my mother-in-law Jean who has made my professional life possible this last decade – I couldn't have done it without you – and in memory of my mum who had a real way with words. I am sure most of us spend whole lifetimes recreating the fun we had when we were children, so finally thank you Mum, Dad, Alex and Lisa for the river and all the joy we had running carefree and feral.

TEXT PERMISSIONS

PHOTOGRAPHY CREDITS

INDEX